TIME CAPSULE/1927

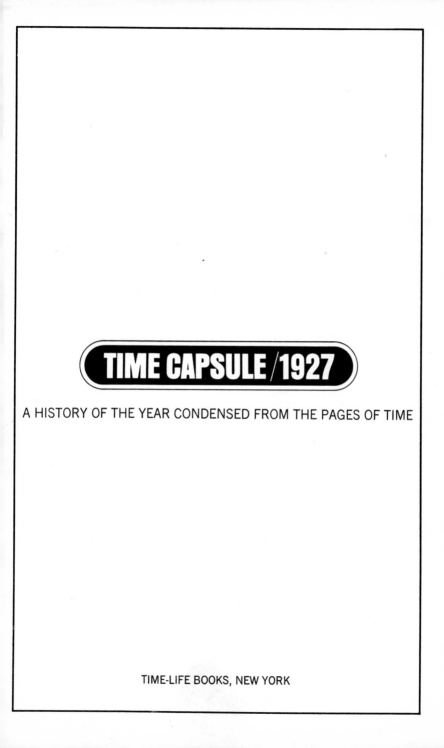

TIME CAPSULE /1927

A HISTORY OF THE YEAR CONDENSED FROM THE PAGES OF TIME

TIME-LIFE BOOKS, NEW YORK

TIME / **1927**

EDITORS *Briton Hadden and Henry R. Luce*
ASSOCIATES *Arnold Bernhard, Laird S. Goldsborough,*
John S. Martin, Wells Root, Myron Weiss
WEEKLY CONTRIBUTORS *Elizabeth Armstrong,*
Willard T. Ingalls, Peter Mathews,
Newton Hockaday, Noel F. Busch, John Farrar,
S. J. Woolf

EDITOR *Maitland A. Edey*
EXECUTIVE EDITOR *Jerry Korn*
TEXT DIRECTOR *Martin Mann*
ART DIRECTOR *Sheldon Cotler*
CHIEF OF RESEARCH *Beatrice T. Dobie*

SERIES EDITOR *John Dille*
ASSISTANT EDITOR *Carl Solberg*
RESEARCHERS *Jill Adams, Louise Samuels*
ASSISTANT ART DIRECTOR *Arnold Holeywell*
ASSISTANT DESIGNER *John Woods*
COPYREADER *Rosemarie Conefrey*

PUBLISHER *Rhett Austell*

COVER ILLUSTRATION *Lou Lomonaco*

EVENTS OF THE YEAR

Editors' Note

The year 1927 was full of momentous events both in the U.S. and abroad. But not even Babe Ruth's 60th home run or the firing of Leon Trotsky by Joseph Stalin would have the same dramatic effect on history that was created by a young airmail pilot named Charles Lindbergh who flew alone across the Atlantic to Paris. Lindbergh's feat electrified the entire world, and brought the U.S. almost immediately into the air age. Flying clubs sprang up across the country, the construction and sale of aircraft zoomed, and once-hesitant passengers, both reassured and enthralled by Lindbergh's safe journey, began lining up for tickets. TIME Magazine first noticed the young pilot one week before his epic flight, as he made his way eastward from San Diego to try his luck. In succeeding issues it kept close track of him. The story starts on page 32.

■

TIME CAPSULE/1927 is one of a series of volumes, each adapted and condensed from a year's contents of TIME, the Weekly Newsmagazine. The words, except for a few connecting passages, are those of the magazine itself, and therefore reflect the flavor, the attitudes and the state of knowledge of the day—sometimes innocent, sometimes opinionated, sometimes prescient. The book is divided, like the magazine, into departments, and is organized so that each department forms a chronological chapter for the entire year. The dates in the margin are the issue dates of the magazine.

NATIONAL AFFAIRS

The Presidency

Born in Vermont and descended from a long line of New England farmers, Calvin Coolidge settled in Massachusetts at the age of 24 to study and practice law. He rose from a career in local politics to become governor of the state for two terms and gained national attention for his part in breaking the Boston Police strike of 1919. Elected Vice President of the United States the following year, Coolidge succeeded to the Presidency in 1923 at the death of Harding. A popular President, Coolidge was re-elected on his own in 1924. His terms were characterized by a devotion to economy and thrift in government, the reduction of taxes and the maintenance of a climate highly favorable to business.

JAN. 3 **CHRISTMAS:** On Christmas Day, President Coolidge was astir before 7 a.m. Going out on the rear grounds of the White House, he greeted his pet raccoon, who wore his gift, a gleaming collar bearing the legend: "Rebecca Raccoon of the White House." Returning indoors, the President gazed reflectively at the three Christmas trees in the Blue Room, decorated by Mrs. Coolidge and their son, John. This was the first time that there have been Christmas trees in the White House since the death of Calvin Coolidge Jr. [who had died in 1924, as a result of a foot infection].

Later the Presidential family gathered upstairs to open their presents. Among the gifts received by the President were innumerable turkeys; more than a dozen canes, which the President does not use; cigars by the hundreds, some of which he will smoke; cigar holders, intended to displace the paper holders which he uses.

TALK: Comment on the Presidential campaign of 1928 has begun early, chiefly because of the possibility of a third term for President Coolidge. Last week, Frank R. Kent, whose able pen pleases the Democratic readers of the Baltimore *Sun*, plunged into the enigma of the man in the White House. Said Kent: "As to Mr. Coolidge wanting another term, that is too obvious to argue. No President ever liked the White House better than he. No President ever wanted to hold on to it more, but he doesn't want to fight for it—and he won't. In the whole of his political career there is no record of a fight.

"To sum up the other Coolidge liabilities, there is the inherent feebleness of the man himself, the admitted fact that he is largely a combination of machine support, party propaganda and accident. There is the further fact that Old Guard leaders cordially dislike him personally and resent the accident that projected him into the White House. But for the death of Mr. Harding no one would ever have seriously suggested Mr. Coolidge for the Presidency. The fact is he was so negligible a quantity that he might easily have failed for renomination as Vice President. He was in 1922 a political joke."

OPEN HOUSE: On New Year's Day any inhabitant of the world can grasp the hand of the President of the U.S. He must go to the White House between 1 and 3 p.m. He will stand in line, enter at the front door, notice the mistletoe hung from the chandelier, proceed to the Blue Room, extend his right hand to the President and Mrs. Coolidge, take leave with dignity. On Jan. 1, 1927, 3,185 people did these things.

JAN. 10

MORAL PRECEPTOR: According to the Constitution, it is the duty of the President to administer and enforce the laws of the land, to advise the Congress on the state of the Union, etc. The Constitution does not require the President to be the great moral preceptor of the people. President Coolidge has taken unto himself this extra-legal duty, as has many another President. In his speech on the 150th anniversary of the Battle of Trenton last week, President Coolidge confined himself to revolutionary history and morality. Excerpts:

"We are placing a great deal of emphasis on prosperity. Our people ought to desire to be prosperous, but it ought not to be their main desire. There are other things that they ought to want more. Prosperity is not a cause; it is a result. It is all summed up in a single word. It is character.

"Under our institutions the only way to perfect our government is to perfect the individual citizen. It is necessary to reach the mind and the soul of the individual. I know of no way that this can be done save through the influences of religion and education."

JAN. 24 **DIET:** From the White House came news that the President's physicians had prescribed ham and eggs for breakfast instead of New England sausages. Sausages are fattening. Two days later, Senator Watson of Indiana told his friends how, at a White House breakfast, Rob Roy, Presidential white collie, had stolen half a sausage from his plate.

FEB. 7 **FIRST LADY:** Mrs. Coolidge received the graduating class of Public School No. 47 of New York City. They were deaf. She talked to them in sign-language which she had learned when she taught in a school for deaf-mutes at Northampton, Mass.

FEB. 21 **WALKS:** President Coolidge has decided to resume his daily walks—three times around the ellipse on the south grounds of the White House, a total of two miles. This is his daily minimum.

Ever since the Washington Disarmament Conference of 1922, which stipulated that the U.S., Britain and Japan would limit their tonnage of battleships and aircraft carriers to a ratio of 5:5:3, respectively, the idea of naval disarmament had been a popular one in the U.S. President Coolidge stressed the theme repeatedly in 1927.

NAVAL DISARMAMENT: Next to economy, prosperity, morality and Divine Providence, President Coolidge's favorite speech-making topic is naval disarmament. Last week he did not make a speech, but he dispatched to Congress and to Great Britain, Japan, France and Italy a plan of naval disarmament. It was received as the most statesmanly document of his administration.

BUT, what are the reactions of the other nations?

Great Britain welcomed the proposal of separating land

and naval armaments. It must be remembered, however, that the Washington conference of 1922 attained partial success chiefly because the U.S. was the biggest "giver" in capital ships. At the proposed Geneva conference Great Britain will have to be the biggest "giver" in cruisers. Her future attitude, particularly concerning submarines, will depend on France and Italy.

Japan was enthusiastic and its government prepared to draw up an acceptance of President Coolidge's plan.

France is essentially interested in land armaments, will brook no naval disarmament unless land disarmament is considered at the same time.

In Italy, Premier Mussolini was silent; the Pope looked with favor upon the plan. Italy, whose need for submarines is great, will certainly be loath to indulge in any wholesale scrapping of them.

MOUNTAINS: Vermonters, unable to find any single moun- FEB. 28 tain upon which to bestow the name of their distinguished native son, have decided to christen four mountains "Coolidge Range." The bill to accomplish this, now pending in the Vermont legislature, originally included Killington [4,241 feet], Pico [3,967 feet] and Shrewsbury [3,737 feet] Mountains. Last week Salt Ash Mountain [3,278 feet] was added to "Coolidge Range."

CREDENTIALS: Through the Blue Room and into the Red Room of the White House stepped briskly last week the British Ambassador Sir Esme W. Howard, escorting into the presence of President Coolidge the Hon. Vincent Massey, first Canadian Minister ever accredited to the U.S. [and brother of actor Raymond Massey].

Minister Massey: "I consider myself highly fortunate, sir, to have the privilege of being the first envoy from my country to be accredited to the Government of your great republic. I have the great honor of placing in your hands the letters of credence by which his Britannic Majesty accredits me as his Envoy Extraordinary and Minister Plenipotentiary to represent the Dominion of Canada in the United States."

It having been established that Canada is a "country"—

whatever that may mean—President Coolidge was at liberty to read the King Emperor's letter:

George, by the grace of God of the United Kingdom of Great Britain and Ireland and of the British Dominions beyond the seas, King, Defender of the Faith, Emperor of India, etc., to the President of the United States of America sendeth greeting:

Our good friend: We have judged it expedient to confer the rank of Envoy Extraordinary and Minister Plenipotentiary upon our trusty and well-beloved the Hon. Charles Vincent Massey, member of our Privy Council in Canada, with the especial object of representing in the United States of America the interests of our Dominion of Canada.

We request that you will give credence to all that Mr. Massey may represent to you in our name, especially when he shall assure you of our esteem and regard, and of our hearty wishes for the welfare and prosperity of the United States of America. And so we commend you to the protection of the Almighty.

Given at our Court of St. James's, Dec. 7, 1926, in the seventeenth year of our reign.

Your good friend,
GEORGE REX IMPERATOR

MARCH 14 **NEW HOME:** At No. 15 Dupont Circle where the President will reside while the White House is being refurbished, President Coolidge stood late one afternoon last week with his white collie, Rob Roy, followed the dog over the threshhold. Through the huge foyer he walked, past the costly Gobelin tapestry at his left, up the marble stairway lined with heads of mountain goats, lions, elk and caribou. Into the large room next to the library that is to be his workshop he stepped, paused, smiled at friendly objects: his desk, his favorite chair, many of his books, all brought carefully from the White House.

MARCH 21 **PRESIDENTIAL ZOO:** Not content without her, the President brought Rebecca, famed raccoon, from the back yard (south grounds) of the White House to the back yard of No. 15 Dupont Circle. Rebecca rode with the President in his limousine.

Wilson Jackson, Negro porter and keeper of the Presidential

zoo of raccoons, bees, dogs, cats, owls, etc., quivered last week when President Coolidge told him that two lion cubs were on the way from Johannesburg, South Africa—the gift of the mayor of that city. Keeper Jackson said he would be glad to care for the lions "if they are young enough and not too ornery." The President explained that they are supposed to be especially playful, even though one of them had bitten off a man's foot just before being shipped to the U.S.

TEAPOT DOME: Back to the Navy Department the President APRIL 11 gave the naval oil reserves, revoking the Executive order issued by President Harding under which Secretary of the Interior Fall negotiated the illegal leases with Mr. Doheny and Mr. Sinclair. Only the Teapot Dome reserve remains to be returned.

WONDERFUL FEET: The President took off his shoes, extended APRIL 18 first his right foot, then his left. "Wonderful feet . . . size 8 . . . almost perfect for walking purposes . . . indicative of a cool, steady life," said Dr. Peter Kahler, Manhattan orthopedist, who measured the presidential feet and took orders for presidential footwear. Flappers, he added, might well be proud of feet like Mrs. Coolidge's, also "almost perfect," size 4½. Dr. Kahler's grandfather made size 14 shoes for President Lincoln.

VETO: "I therefore return the bill without my approval."— Calvin Coolidge.

The bill had been passed by the Philippine legislature and repassed by a two-thirds majority over Governor General Leonard Wood's veto. It proposed to hold a plebiscite among the islanders on the question: "Do you desire the immediate, absolute and complete independence of the Philippine Islands?"

Important words from President Coolidge's document:

"American defense is a corollate of American sovereignty, not of foreign sovereignty. Where there is no sovereignty there is no obligation of protection. The best security to the Philippines is the protection of and by the United States."

PREDICTION: Among the gentlemen who called on the Presi- APRIL 25 dent last week were: Clarence W. Barron, financial publisher, who reported that hard-times cycles are rapidly becoming impossible in the U.S.

IRONY: Rubbernecks and idlers were offered rusty nails at $1 apiece, from the White House roof, now being repaired, before the police stopped the workman who was selling them.

"HISTORIC INCIDENT": The presidential nominating conventions are more than a year distant; the election is more than a year and a half distant—but conspicuous now, throughout the land, are booms, prophecies. The forest of presidential timber is thickening with oaks and acorns, with green wood and dead wood. Each party has an oak which towers higher than any of the rest. In the Republican party the oak is Calvin Coolidge and the feeling is that if he wants the 1928 nomination, he can have it. In the Democratic party the oak is Alfred Emanuel Smith and the feeling is that he is the one substantial hope of victory in 1928.

Last week, more than ever, the Governor of New York held the centre of the presidential forest. He attempted to scotch for all the time the talk that his Roman Catholic religion would interfere with his upholding the U.S. Constitution in any office to which he might be elected. In a letter published in the *Atlantic Monthly* and addressed to a Manhattan lawyer who had asked him certain questions, Governor Smith set forth his creed "straight-forwardly, bravely, with the clear ring of candor."

Significant excerpts from Governor Smith's letter:

"Taking your letter as a whole and reducing it to commonplace English, you imply that there is conflict between religious loyalty to the Catholic faith and patriotic loyalty to the United States. Everything that has actually happened to me during my long public career leads me to know that no such thing as that is true. . . .

"I summarize my creed as an American Catholic," Governor Smith wrote. "I believe in the worship of God according to the faith and practice of the Roman Catholic Church. I recognize no power in the institutions of my Church to interfere with the operations of the Constitution of the United States or the enforcement of the law of the land. I believe in absolute freedom of conscience for all men and in equality of all churches, all sects, and all beliefs, before the law as a matter of right and not as a matter of favor. I believe in the absolute separation of Church and State. And I believe in the common brotherhood of man under the common fatherhood of God.

"In this spirit I join with fellow Americans of all creeds in a fervent prayer that never again in this land will any public servant be challenged because of the faith in which he has tried to walk humbly with his God."

Said the *Atlantic Monthly*: "This is an historic incident, historic for the country and for the Church."

BEST DRESSED: Speaking in Philadelphia last fortnight, Sir MAY 2 Charles Higham, British tea man, told the Poor Richard Club that President Coolidge is the best dressed man in the U.S., one of the few U.S. men who have their shoes shined. Later, Robert Barry, New York *World* correspondent, unearthed the following details concerning the President's attire:

His suits are of a type for which from $125 to $140 is standard price. He likes to wear double-breasted coats. His trousers have no cuffs. He shuns soft collars, prefers black foot-gear to brown, high to low. He wears no jewelry save a ring (left third finger). No fop, the President disturbed the White House valet by putting three cigars in the pocket of his formal evening clothes. The valet maintained that more than two cigars made a bulge in the pocket. The President answered that less than three cigars would not carry him through a long dinner.

BOOMS: In 1924, Franklin D. Roosevelt, on crutches as a re- MAY 23 sult of an attack of infantile paralysis, pleaded for party unity to warring factions of the Democratic party in convention assembled at Madison Square Garden.

Last week Mr. Roosevelt, who still walked with the aid of a cane, discussed a six months' tour of the South, undertaken, he said in the interests of "party unity." But Mr. Roosevelt, who was the Democratic candidate for Vice President in 1920, is generally regarded as the unofficial manager of Governor Smith's unofficial campaign for the presidential nomination. Said Mr. Roosevelt:

"I found among them (Southern Democratic leaders) a growing conviction that Governor Smith was the man with

President Coolidge. He joins Sitting Bull as a chief of the Sioux. Page 20.   *Franklin Roosevelt. He booms Democrat Al Smith for the Presidency.*

the best chance of winning. While the leaders haven't come out for him for the nomination, they will support him, in my opinion, once he is nominated."

JUNE 6 **VACATION SPOT:** President Coolidge let it be known last week that Custer Park, S.D. had been chosen for his summer vacation. At once observers began to drape his choice with political significances.

Politically speaking, indeed, President Coolidge will be traveling "Out Where the Blues Begin." Most South Dakotans are farmers, most farmers are disgruntled, most disgruntled among farmers are the farmers of South Dakota. It also happens that South Dakota holds its presidential primaries earlier than any of its sister states.

JUNE 20 **CHEESE:** The Swiss can make Swiss cheese cheaper than U.S. cheese-makers can make Swiss cheese. To keep Swiss Swiss cheese-makers from underselling U.S. Swiss cheese-makers President Coolidge increased the duty on Swiss Swiss cheese from 5¢ to 7$\frac{1}{2}$¢ per pound.

MORE ROOM: Mrs. Coolidge was playing with her dogs. Said she, laughingly, to a visitor: "Isn't it nice that Calvin is President? You know we really never had room before for a dog."

VACATION: An eight-car special train was ready. Into it stepped President and Mrs. Coolidge; the White House office staff and household employes; newspaper men and photographers. Into it also, strapped in harness, went Rob Roy and Prudence Prim, Presidential collies. Then the engine chugged, the wheels revolved, the first lap of the 1,900-mile journey to the Black Hills began.

CHEERING SECTION: As the vacation-bound presidential spe- JUNE 27
cial crossed South Dakota, the state turned into a 400-mile-long cheering section. Farmers stood in fields of young, ankle-high corn, forgot mortgages and vetoes, cheered. Townspeople gathered at railroad stations; in their hands were hats and flowers; in their hearts were peace and goodwill.

Though making frequent car-end appearances at various brief stops, the President said hardly a word, left greeting-acknowledgments largely to Mrs. Coolidge. Dispatches reported that one farmer nudged his wife, observed to her: "He don't talk; she does the talking."

Fishermen everywhere were shocked to learn that President Coolidge, on his first fishing expedition in Squaw Creek, had used worm-bait in catching five trout. Flies, they said, were the only proper trout-bait, but the President specifically stated that he had used worms and showed a coffee-can full of wrigglers to prove it.

Prudence Prim, younger of the two collies (the senior is Rob Roy) taken on the trip, was indisposed on the morning following her arrival. Having taken a walk and sat in the sun with Mrs. Coolidge, she was reported as greatly improved. Rebecca Raccoon, confined in a hayloft, eyed speculatively the eggs of a neighboring hen. The five canaries first reported as accompanying the presidential party were later found to have been left at home, though Mrs. Coolidge said that she felt lost without them.

ADOPTION: Sioux Indians, planning to adopt President Coo- JULY 4
lidge into their tribe when he visits Deadwood in August, have been debating an Indian name for him. It was reported that *Still Waters* was the name most favored, but that no final decision had yet been reached.

REBECCA AGAIN: Rebecca Raccoon got out of her stable again, climbed a high tree. The White House staff formed a posse, located Rebecca, could not induce her to come down. Mrs. Coolidge coaxed, President Coolidge whistled, Rebecca remained insurgent. Dispatches added that another raccoon had been prowling about the State Lodge since Rebecca's arrival, added sex appeal to Rebecca's escapade.

ACCIDENT: Fishing, Mrs. Coolidge caught a fish hook in her finger. The hook was cut out, and by evening Mrs. Coolidge was reported again in her usual good spirits.

JULY 25 **PRUDENCE PASSES:** Prudence Prim, pet white collie of Mrs. Coolidge, died at Fort Meade, S. Dak. Cause: Distemper with complications.

AUG. 1 **NEW TITLE:** President Coolidge last week received an additional Presidency, though of the honorary variety. He accepted the position of Honorary President of the South Dakota division of the Izaak Walton League of America. Onetime Judge J. M. Dickinson, national president of the League, approved the South Dakota action, despite the regrettable worm-bait tendency of President Coolidge. He said the League was more concerned with having fishermen throw small fish back into the water than with the type of bait they used.

NEW DOG: A successor to Prudence Prim, deceased White House Pet, was offered to Mrs. Coolidge and accepted by her. The new arrival is one Diana of Wildwood, a four-month old white Scotch collie.

AUG. 8 **AIR-MINDED:** Establishment of municipal airports in large U.S. cities was advocated by the President. Long enthusiastic about the development of aviation, the President's vacation has made him even more interested in the plane's future. He has seen the efficiency of the air mail. The pet dog recently presented to him made the trip from Detroit by airplane. There is a plane at Custer State Park, S. Dak., ready to rush the President to Washington in any emergency. So, remote from centres of population, the President has more than ever realized the airplane as a factor in decreasing distance.

SURPRISE DECISION: "I do not choose to run for President in 1928." These were not spoken words. They were typewritten on slips of paper by Edwin Geiser, the President's stenographer.

Promptly at noon, Aug. 2, newspapermen, at the President's behest, entered his schoolroom office. Everett Sanders, his secretary, closed the door, stood guard-like. The President was smoking a cigar held in an ivory holder. He did not smile as usual, but solemnly inquired: "Is everyone here now?" and directed his professional visitors to file past him. As they did so, he handed each one a slip on which, a few minutes previously, Typist Geiser had imprinted the ten words "I do not choose to run for President in 1928."

More the President would not say. Who will succeed him? Most commentators were left to exclaim with U.S. Senator Hiram Johnson: "I am astounded. The Republican race will be a free-for-all."

BIG CHIEF: The President was made White Chief and Protector of the Sioux Indians. Chief Henry Standing Bear administered the oath of fealty, said: "Mr. President, it is a great honor to us that you have come among us and into our camp. Our fathers and our chiefs, Sitting Bull, Spotted Tail and Red Cloud, may have made mistakes, but their hearts were brave and strong, their purposes were honest and noble. They have long gone to their Happy Hunting Ground, and we call upon you, as our new High Chief, to take up their leadership to protect and help the weak." AUG. 15

To cap the ceremony, Rosebud Robe (soon to appear in vaudeville as "the most beautiful Indian maiden in the world") placed upon White Chief Coolidge's brow a war bonnet of 200 feathers. Nineteen of the warriors who had helped kill General Custer's men on June 25, 1876, cheered vigorously.

SHOCK: The country, and especially its Republican politicians, spent the week recovering from what Pat McKenna, White House doorman since before Calvin Coolidge was even married, described as the greatest shock in all the 24 years of his official life. The shock had come to Mr. McKenna just as the President answered, "None," to a news correspondent who asked if he would add anything to the sentence, "I do not choose to run for President in nineteen twenty-eight."

Later, to a caller, the President was said to have said, "There are plenty of other men in the country for the job. This is not a one-man country. Ten years is a long time to be President."

Mrs. Coolidge has been more than hoping that her husband would not subject himself to the physical strain of another four years as chief executive. President Coolidge has himself remarked that only one onetime President—William Howard Taft—is still alive.

AUG. 22 **21-TREE SALUTE:** It was the first time that the eyes of public cameras had seen President Coolidge on the back of a horse. Dressed in complete cowboy costume down to Mexican spurs, the President rode three miles up the side of Mount Rushmore in the Black Hills, accompanied by his riding instructor, "Dakota Clyde" Jones, and others. Following a presidential salute of 21 blasts, President Coolidge dedicated the national memorial which Gutzon Borglum began to carve on the granite face of Mount Rushmore. "We have come home to dedicate a cornerstone that was laid by the hand of the Almighty," said the President. The salute was jerky because it consisted of the blasting of 21 trees instead of the firing of guns. Since the trees had to be blasted, this salute was cited by Republican newspapers as an example of Coolidge economy.

AUG. 29 **AFTERMATH:** The Rapid City police learned that a wrecked flivver had been found near their town with these words scrawled on the windshield: "I do not·choose to run in 1928."

SEPT. 19 **FAREWELL:** Miss Ruth Wells, choir leader of the Hermosa Church, paid tribute to Mrs. Coolidge: "We shall lose the best singer in our congregation when Mrs. Coolidge goes. Mrs. Coolidge knows the words of every hymn without looking at the book. She has joined us in singing every Sunday; in fact, almost leads the congregation with her strong, clear soprano. She seemed to enjoy it."

The ladies of the Rapid City Fortnightly Club were in a state. "Who speaks first?" sputtered one fluttering matron.

"You don't think we ought to call her 'your Grace' do you?"
"Nonsense, my dear, she'd think you were using her first
name." Into the midst of the furor walked Mrs. Coolidge.
One lady, Mrs. M. W. Pangburn, immediately fainted, because, as she explained later, "the prospect of meeting the
wife of a President" had caused her to lose consciousness.
This was the first Black Hills social function that Mrs. Coolidge had attended. That she chose to make her debut at a
meeting of the Fortnightly Club was due, not to her favorit-
ism, but to the fact that the members of this club had been
the first courageous enough to invite her.

The day before the President's departure for Washington,
Rapid City editors addressed to him their farewells. The
Democratic *Gate City Guide* said: "In your own quiet way
you have shown us still another winning of the West." The
next day bands played and the people cheered, waved, called
"Good-by . . . Good-by Grace! . . . Good-by Cal. . . ."

RETURN: President Coolidge, Mrs. Coolidge, John Coolidge,
two white collies, two chows, Rebecca Raccoon arrived in
Washington. At the station to meet the Presidential party
were Cabinet Members Mellon, Kellogg, Jardine and Sargent.
After handshakes and animal pattings, the Coolidges and
their companions got into several limousines and swept
rapidly through the Capital. Rob Roy, veteran collie, disturbed the ride with bounds, plunges, whines; shedding his
white hair on formal apparel, then, he pressed his cold nose
against the glass, to get a first glimpse of the White House.
Arriving, he bolted down the corridor, into the elevator;
jumped on the seat, and gazed upward, eager to rise. Mrs.
Coolidge, good housewife, was enthusiastic over the im-
provements; insisted on touring the house before permitting
the President to go to bed.

BOOM: Senator Borah of Idaho called on Secretary of Com- SEPT. 26
merce Herbert Hoover in Washington and invited him to go
to his state next month and hunt wild animals. Senator
Borah promised "cougar, elk, moose, mountain goats, deer,
bears or eight delegates. It is really a wonderful country."
Mr. Hoover declared he would gladly hunt in Idaho.

Senator George H. Moses of New Hampshire had not such

variety of wild animals to offer and did not invite Mr. Hoover to go hunting. But New Hampshire has eleven delegates at the national nominating convention and these Senator Moses promised to Mr. Hoover. In doing so, he advised the G.O.P. at large to choose its man, not for 1928 alone, but for re-election in 1932 as well, for party solidarity.

For this purpose a young man is needed. In Senator Moses's opinion, Mr. Hoover is the only outstanding man young enough.

Senator Borah invites Herbert Hoover to hunt animals in Idaho.   *The Secretary of Commerce may also hunt delegates in New Hampshire.*

OCT. 24 **AIR EGG:** In Nebraska, a hen which had laid 165 eggs in 165 days laid another egg on the 166th day. This egg was fitted into a jewel case, sent by air mail to President Coolidge.

NOV. 7 **"WE HAVE PROSPERED":** "Under the guidance and watchful care of a divine and beneficent Providence this country has been carried safely through another year. Almighty God has continued to bestow upon us the light of His countenance, and we have prospered.

"Now that these twelve months are drawing to a close, it is fitting that we should humbly pray that we may be worthy of a continuation of divine favor. . . ."

Thus and therefore did President Coolidge make his fifth Thanksgiving Day Proclamation. This year it comes Nov. 24.

SOCIAL: It seemed like "Ladies' Week" at the White House, NOV. 21 socially. Actress Billie Burke (Mrs. Florenz Ziegfeld) called informally after the opening night of her show, *The Marquise*, which President Coolidge had attended. Gertrude ("Trudy") Ederle called and President Coolidge said: "I am amazed that a girl of your small stature could swim the English Channel!" Mrs. Ruth Elder Womack came for luncheon— together with Colonel Charles Augustus Lindbergh, Clarence D. Chamberlin, Commander Richard Evelyn Byrd, Bernt Balchen. That evening all the air notables stood by while President Coolidge pinned the National Geographic Society Hubbard medal on Colonel Lindbergh [who just five months earlier had electrified the world with his solo flight to Paris. See page 32].

A HAPPY MAN: President Coolidge was lighthearted. As he DEC. 19 popped his dress shirt-studs into position and adjusted his crisp white bow-tie and the wings of his collar, he was a happy man.

That afternoon he had repeated his withdrawal from the 1928 presidential race in such terms that the Republican National Committee would not again ply him with insistent questions—at least, not for some time. Meantime he was still the President, and would continue so for 15 months to come.

The President's light-heartedness was nowhere more evident than at his press conferences. Not that he sat back in his chair and made jokes. But his voice ran along more freely.

At one press conference the President said he had had "something of importance" to tell, but that he had forgotten what it was. Instead of becoming annoyed with himself, he laughed and took Rob Roy out for a walk.

PLANNED THAT WAY: Some one noticed that a bedspread, DEC. 26 knitted nearly a year ago by Mrs. Coolidge and intended to be left in the White House, bore a prophecy. On one side was knitted "Lincoln 1861-1865." On the other side: "Calvin Coolidge—1923-1929."

Long before President Coolidge announced his "choice," Mrs. Coolidge said, to a friend who exclaimed at her bedspread, "I know what I'm doing."

The Cabinet

JAN. 10 **NICARAGUA:** Seven weeks ago, Secretary of State Kellogg was pleased to hear that Señor Adolfo Diáz had been elected President of Nicaragua by that republic's congress in joint session. With startling speed he sent U.S. recognition to President Diáz, a Conservative, an oldtime friend of the U.S. Department of State, who was recently employed by a U.S. mining company for a few dollars per week.

Headline readers in the U.S. said: "Isn't it nice that those Nicaraguans are fixed up at last?" But shrewder observers in Washington and all of Central America knew that President Diáz's soup was not without sediment. The chief trouble was and still is that Nicaragua has another "legal" President —Dr. Juan Sacasa, Liberal, the Vice President who came into power when President Solorzano resigned a year ago.

It was inevitable that these two "legal" Presidents and their backers should do battle. Nicaraguan squabbles are no great cataclysms, since the peacetime strength of their army is 2,500 men. Mexico complicated matters by selling arms to President Sacasa's Liberals, who were doing well in a military way until Rear Admiral Julian L. Latimer landed U.S. Marines a fortnight ago. Acting on instructions from the Department of State, Rear Admiral Latimer set about to maintain a neutral zone, ordered armed forces of both factions not to enter therein, reported that he had the situation well in hand.

The Mexico City *Excelsior* howled: "The Colossus of the North, enriched by the World War, swollen with imperialistic pride, continues shamefully to trample down the rights of little nations."

La Liberté of Paris said: "The Monroe Doctrine, which forbids Europeans to stick their noses in American affairs is a very convenient fence behind which countries like Colombia and Haiti have been already strangled."

Intermittently since 1909, Nicaraguan affairs have been much as they are today. Marines were stationed in Nicaragua during most of the Taft and Wilson Administrations; they have landed three times within the last year. President Coolidge and Secretary Kellogg certainly cannot be accused of changing the tradition.

PAPER-CUTTING: Easterners in (say) Santa Fe, N. Mex., put- JUNE 6
ting down a five-dollar bill for a pack of cigarets, are likely
to receive four large round silver dollars in their change. No
animus is intended—Southwesterners are used to the silver
dollars—solid, tangible, clanking evidence of wealth. But
Easterners and the U.S. public in general have not taken
kindly to the silver dollars which are deemed cumbersome,
given with apology, received with reluctance.

Even less popular than the silver dollar has been the two-
dollar bill. Probably the prejudice against it results from the
ease with which it may be mistaken for and handed out as
a one.

With the failure of the silver dollar and the two-dollar bill
to win universal favor, the Treasury Department found itself
printing (in 1926) 227,566,949 sheets of currency, a large pro-
portion of which was in the form of one-dollar bills. It is the
one-dollar bill that has been the great staple of U.S. currency.
Even the most modestly salaried individual can "flash a roll"
of ones. Homely, democratic, sanctified by custom, the one-
dollar bill has been taken to the U.S. bosom, lovingly christened "bean," "buck," "berry," "simoleon," "iron man,"
"smacker," "plunk," "rock," "kelp" (always in the plural
which employs no "s"; e.g. "14 kelp"). Meanwhile the Treasury has found itself faced with a printing bill of millions of
dollars yearly. It was costing money to make money.

But last week Secretary of the Treasury Andrew W. Mellon
found a way of lessening expense without changing national
customs. He announced that the dollar bills of the future
will be considerably reduced in size. The new bill will measure
$6\frac{1}{8}$ inches by $2\frac{5}{8}$ inches, therefore will be about an inch
and one-half shorter and half an inch narrower. It will last
longer because it will not have to be folded so much.

COMMERCE REPORT: Are the "good times" so good? Can DEC. 12
they continue?

Business men who ask these questions had waited to hear
what the Secretary of Commerce would say this year. Secretary Hoover published his report for fiscal 1927 last week. The
gist of his generalizations was that never in the world's history had a nation worked and lived so well as did the U.S.
last year; never was prosperity so solidly founded.

The Congress

JAN. 3 **THE LEGISLATIVE WEEK:** The Senate passed the Rivers and Harbors Bill authorizing an expenditure of $70,000,000, after Senator Norris of Nebraska had broken the solemnity of debate by falling out of the clerk's chair. (Bill went to conference.)

JAN. 17 **REVOLT:** ". . . For this reason I gladly join the gentleman from Connecticut in revolt against the President of the United States."

It was not an unusual remark for Representative Garrett of Tennessee, the Democratic floor leader. But who was the "gentleman from Connecticut?" As everyone knows, there are no Democratic Congressmen from Connecticut. The gentleman referred to was Representative John Quillin Tilson, duly elected leader of Republican forces on the floor of the House. Next to him sat Speaker Nicholas Longworth, who had just added his emphatic voice to the revolt against President Coolidge. Not since 1917, when Champ Clark fought the draft, had a Speaker of the House taken part in debate from the floor.

The occasion for this slashing of precedent and snapping of party lines was Mr. Tilson's amendment to the Navy appropriation bill, which asked for $450,000 to begin construction of three cruisers. President Coolidge had said in his budget message and many times since that he would brook no immediate appropriations for cruiser building. "Big Navy" men in the House were confident of defying him; potent and regular Republican leaders were backing them. The vote was taken last week; Mr. Tilson's amendment was rejected, 183 to 161.

So, there will be no cruisers unless the Senate votes for them and bullies some of the 183 Representatives into changing their opinions.

FEB. 28 **WIND & FOG:** Last week the Senate heard some four hours of prolific bile from Senator James Thomas Heflin of Alabama on his stale subject of Roman Catholic conspiracy to control U.S. politics. Said Mr. Heflin: "A Catholic bullet brought Roosevelt down. [In 1912 a saloon keeper named John

Nepomuk Schrank, who had been reared a Catholic but had abandoned the faith, made an unsuccessful attempt to assassinate former President Theodore Roosevelt in Milwaukee.] If I am murdered, many Catholic priests will pay the penalty. But I have suggested a course to carry on. I am anxious to see how much notice the press will give me."

Senator Ashurst interjected: "The press ought to say that it saw a Senator who was both windy and foggy at the same time."

FISTIBUSTER: In the House Office Building ladies were present; so were preachermen. A "blue law" bill was under discussion by the House Committee on the District of Columbia. Chunky Representative Sol Bloom of New York politely insinuated that square-jawed Representative Thomas L. Blanton of Texas was a liar. Mr. Blanton, who wants to close the cinema theatres on Sundays, leaped at Mr. Bloom, who wants them open; put his Texan arm around Mr. Bloom's neck. They grappled, heaved, fell across the committee table.

One L. B. Schloss joined the fray, was knocked to the floor, kicked. The Rev. Harry L. Bowlby, secretary of the Lord's Day Alliance, was reported as having picked out the smallest man in the room (a stenographer), knocked off his glasses, punched him. Somebody called the police, but they did not arrive until after Hattie Pitts of the McKendree Methodist Church lifted her hands and her voice in prayer, shrieked: "O Lord, O Jesus, have mercy on these men."

This, the third recent fistibuster in Congress, caused Representative Gallivan of Massachusetts to pass around among his friends a resolution providing that all future bouts be conducted in Statuary Hall "under the paternal eyes of the Fathers of the Republic," with Dry Representative Upshaw as referee. "I think these bouts are due to Prohibition," said Mr. Gallivan.

THE 69th: The 69th Congress entered its last session like a MARCH 7 mild, limping lamb and exited like a wild, snorting lion. In December, many a critic predicted a do-nothing session. "It will be lucky," said some, "if it passes the appropriation bills." As March 4 approached, it appeared that this session, unfamed, unsung, had accomplished more than any short session of Congress since Woodrow Wilson's first administration and seldom missed an opportunity to defy, vex, prod the Calvin Coolidge Administration. Important doings:

¶ Farm Relief. The McNary-Haugen bill [see page 46], for three years a thorn in the side of Congress, was put through both houses by a defiant farm bloc which crushed the Administration cohorts.

¶ Banking. The McFadden-Pepper branch banking bill was approved. Last week the President signed it. It enables national banks to compete more effectively with state banks in branch banking activities.

¶ Naval Armaments. Appropriation to begin construction of three 10,000 ton cruisers, an item of small importance, became the bone of contention between the "Big Navy" men in Congress and the President. The House agreed with the Senate against the President.

¶ World Court. The Senate refused to discuss the World Court, but rejoiced when it heard that Great Britain would not accept the U.S. reservations. The result: the World Court is for the present a dead issue in the U.S.

A major piece of legislation before the Congress was a bill authorizing government funds for the building of a huge dam —known as the Boulder Canyon Project—on the Colorado River to provide for flood control, irrigation and power. The bill was being sponsored in the Senate by California's Hiram Johnson. It was strenuously opposed by the state of Arizona, which felt that it had proprietary rights on the water flowing through the state, that California would benefit at Arizona's expense and that the dam should be built by private industry— which then could be taxed by the state. The issue came to a head in February and set off a historic filibuster in the U.S. Senate which the New York Times described as one of the greatest displays of "sectional feeling since the Civil War." As a result, the bill did not pass until the following year.

NO SLEEP, NO DAM: One night last week at 2:30 a.m., Mrs. Hiram Johnson, a weary spectator of the filibuster against her husband's Boulder Dam bill, looked down from the Senate gallery on 29 Senators. Some were sprawled out on the lounges, asleep; Floor Leader Curtis and some others were said to have been rolling dice.

An order was adopted, authorizing Sergeant-at-Arms David S. Barry to arrest absentees. Mr. Barry and five assistants scurried to telephones, told Senators to hurry to work. An hour later, he made the following report to the Senate: "Mr. Bayard could not come because he is getting ready to go out of town to attend a funeral. . . . Mr. Caraway's telephone, it is said, has been disconnected. . . . Mr. Heflin is reported as being ill. . . ." Eight other Senators said they were sick. Twelve could not be reached.

Senator Heflin claims Catholics try to control U.S. politics. Page 27.
Senator Johnson of California fights a filibuster on Boulder Dam.

Soon Senators began to straggle in—some in evening clothes, some with their morning ties askew, some unshaven, many vexed. Senator Hawes of Missouri said that his taxicab had caught on fire, that he had to call a fire engine. Senator Reed of Missouri rushed down the aisle, shouted: "This is an inexcusable outrage."

At last, a quorum was present. But the filibusterers kept the floor, allowed no one to move a vote on the Boulder Dam bill. At 4:30 p.m., after 28½ hours of talk, they achieved their victory. The Senate had previously agreed to take up other business at that hour. The result: the Boulder Dam project is likely to be doomed this session. The question asked by many: what is the Boulder Dam?

The Colorado River, which men have called "devilfish" and "Destiny," drains the Southwest without replenishing. Gnawing at the Rocky spine of Wyoming and Colorado it writhes to the Gulf of California through flame-tinted canyons and dun gulches, forever arid. Its annual flood would cover 16 million acres a foot deep. Its 14,000-ft. fall would generate six million horsepower. Men have spent $2,000,000 figuring how and where to rein and tap it.

Six of the seven states the Colorado drains have agreed to a $125,000,000 Federal project calling for the world's tallest dam and a huge power plant; calling also for an "All American" canal further south to irrigate the Imperial Valley.

Arizona has bitterly fought the Boulder Dam project charging:

1) That the Colorado is Arizona's great resource.

2) That the seven-state project is a California manipulation.

NOV. 28 **COMPOSITION:** The 70th Congress assembles on Dec. 5. Its component parts began filtering into Washington last week.

The House membership:

Republican 237
Democrats 195
Farmer Labor 2
Socialist 1

The Senate stands:

Republicans 48
Democrats 47
Farmer Labor 1

DEC. 19 **BILLS, BILLS, BILLS:** The numbers on the bills filed in the House passed well beyond 6,700 before the first week of the 70th Congress was out. *Congressional Record* was flooded with entries like the following:

"Also, a bill (H.R. 3,589) granting an increase of pension to Sarah Bottle."

"By Mr. Tucker: A bill (H.R. 5,340) granting permission to Lieut. Col. Harry N. Cootes, United States Army, to accept certain decorations tendered him."

Still another bill has been proposed by Mr. Blanton of Texas, himself a booming and persistent orator, to punish persons who proclaim or "cry out" disturbingly in the District of Columbia.

Heroes

In 1926 a New York hotel man named Raymond Orteig offered a $25,000 prize to the first aviator to fly nonstop between New York and "the shores of France." By 1927 a number of flyers, both European and American, had entered the competition. TIME reported most of this news in its Aeronautics section (page 177). But when the prize was finally won by Charles A. Lindbergh, the story transcended the subject of aeronautics and TIME shifted it to the section that follows.

"FLYIN' FOOL": Two weeks ago, the name of Captain MAY 23
Charles A. Lindbergh meant nothing to the average U.S. inhabitant. Last week, he became a sudden, romantic national hero with a collection of nicknames: "Lone Wolf" Lindbergh, "Lucky" Lindbergh, "Flyin' Fool" Lindbergh, etc.

Having farmed in Little Falls, Minn., and frightened old ladies with reckless motorcycle exploits, he learned to fly at the age of 20. In accordance with his father's dying wishes, he took his father's ashes aloft in a plane and scattered them over the old homestead. Then he went into the air mail service, gained a creditable record.

Last week, single-handed he piloted the Ryan monoplane, *Spirit of St. Louis,* from San Diego to Curtiss Field, L.I., stopping only at St. Louis. His flying time—21 hr., 20 min.—was the fastest ever made from coast to coast. Grinning like a schoolboy emerging from a showerbath, he told inquisitive reporters that all he needed before hopping across the Atlantic was a little sleep, good weather, a couple of sandwiches and a bottle of water.

Romantic speculators placed bets that Lone Pilot Lindbergh, 25 and tousled-haired, would be the first to reach Paris.

FLIGHT: The Atlantic in its immense indifference was not MAY 30
aware that man-made cables on its slimy bottom and the silent heavens above pulsed with news—news that would cause housewives to run out into backyards and shout to their children: *"Lindbergh is in Paris!"*

Late one evening last week Capt. Charles A. Lindbergh studied weather reports and decided that the elements were propitious for a flight from New York to Paris. He took a two-hour sleep, then busied himself with final preparations at Roosevelt Field, L.I. Four sandwiches, two canteens of water and emergency army rations, along with 451 gallons of gasoline were put into his monoplane, *Spirit of St. Louis.* "When I enter the cockpit," said he, "it's like going into the death chamber. When I step out at Paris it will be like getting a pardon from the governor."

Charles A. Lindbergh shows his grin to Paris, four sandwiches, two canteens and 451 gallons after his takeoff in the "Spirit of St. Louis."

He entered the cockpit. At 7:52 a.m. he was roaring down the runway, his plane lurching on the soft spots of the wet ground. Out of the safety zone, he hit a bump, bounced into the air, quickly returned to earth. Disaster seemed imminent; a tractor and a gully were ahead. Then his plane took the air, cleared the tractor, the gully; cleared some telephone wires. Five hundred onlookers believed they had witnessed a miracle. It was a miracle of skill.

Captain Lindbergh took the shortest route to Paris—the great circle—cutting across Long Island Sound, Cape Cod, Nova Scotia, skirting the coast of Newfoundland. He later told some of his sky adventures to the aeronautically alert New York *Times* for syndication:

"Shortly after leaving Newfoundland, I began to see icebergs. . . . Within an hour it became dark. Then I struck clouds and decided to try to get over them. For a while I succeeded at a height of 10,000 feet. I flew at this height until early morning. The engine was working beautifully and I was not sleepy at all. I felt just as if I was driving a motor car over a smooth road, only it was easier. Then it began to get light and the clouds got higher. . . . Sleet began to cling to the plane. That worried me a great deal and I debated whether I should keep on or go back. I decided I must not think any more about going back. . . .

"Fairly early in the afternoon I saw a fleet of fishing boats. On one of them I saw some men and flew down almost touching the craft and yelled at them, asking if I was on the right road to Ireland. They just stared. Maybe they didn't hear me. Maybe I didn't hear them. Or maybe they thought I was just a crazy fool.

"An hour later I saw land. I flew quite low enough over Ireland to be seen, but apparently no great attention was paid to me."

Captain Lindbergh then told how he crossed southwestern England and the Channel, followed the Seine to Paris, where he circled the city before recognizing the flying field at Le Bourget. Said he: "I appreciated the reception which had been prepared for me and had intended taxiing up to the front of the hangars. But no sooner had my plane touched the ground than a human sea swept toward it. I saw there was danger of killing people with my propeller and I quickly came to a stop."

He had completed his 3,600-mile conquest of the Atlantic in 33 hours, 29 minutes, at an average speed of 107½ miles per hour.

He did not collapse in his cockpit immediately after landing, as some early dispatches stated. His first words were, "Well, here we are. I am very happy."

Some of the crowd of 25,000 attempted to strip souvenirs from the *Spirit of St. Louis,* while the majority escorted Captain Lindbergh, on somebody's shoulders, to a nearby clubhouse. Then, there were congratulations from U.S. Ambassador Myron Timothy Herrick and French officials, a massage and some coffee (he had refused to take coffee on the flight), a motor trip through dense traffic to Paris and ten hours' sleep in the U.S. Embassy.

Next day, he talked with his mother over radiophone, related his flight to newspapermen, glanced at hundreds of cablegrams.

Some say he had "a boyishly stern squint"; others proclaim him a practical joker and tell how he once answered his roommate's desire for a drink of water with a glass of kerosene. He is 25, more than six feet tall, rangy, handsome, blond. He knows flying as the barnstormer with a $250 plane and as the chief pilot for the St. Louis-Chicago air mail route. He is a prominent member of the Caterpillar Club, having four times become a butterfly and descended to earth in a parachute.

His father, the late Congressman Charles A. Lindbergh of Minnesota, was born in Stockholm, the son of a member of the Swedish Parliament. Congressman Lindbergh was progressively a Republican, a "Bull Moose," a Farmer-Laborite.

Mrs. Evangeline Lodge Lindbergh continued her duties as chemistry teacher, at the Cass Technical High School in Detroit, while her son was somewhere in the atmosphere between New York and Paris. Said she: "I am proud to be the mother of such a boy."

A 27-year-old engineer, Donald Hall, designed the Ryan monoplane, *Spirit of St. Louis*. It was built in 60 days at San Diego, Calif. It was christened in St. Louis while Captain Lindbergh was pausing in his flight across the continent. The fact that it is equipped with a 200-horsepower Wright whirlwind motor, caused Wright Aeronautical Corp. stock, usually inactive, to jump from $29\frac{3}{4}$ to $34\frac{3}{8}$, with the news of Captain Lindbergh's progress.

Over and over again "Lucky" had repeated that his "luck" had consisted chiefly in a faultless motor, a periscope by which he watched ahead without exposure, and in an earth induction compass by which alone he steered to a point within three miles of his theoretic arrival point in Ireland.

Not only did Captain Lindbergh win the $25,000 prize offered by Raymond Orteig, Manhattan hotelman, for the first New York-Paris non-stop flight, but he established for himself the immemorial right of extracting dollars from the hero-gaping U.S. public by appearing on the vaudeville stage, in the cinema, etc. A money-minded New York *Herald Tribune* writer figured out that Captain Lindbergh, as a professional hero, could (if he chose) earn $1,000,000 in one year in the following manner:

Cinema	$200,000
Vaudeville	400,000
Radio	50,000
Book	50,000
C.C. Pyle spectacle	150,000
Articles for the press	50,000
Advertising concessions	75,000
Orteig prize	25,000

[Lindbergh did accept the Orteig prize and wrote his book, *We*, and a few articles, but he refused all other offers.]

MODEST & LOVABLE: It may be true that heroes are made, JUNE 6 not born. But it is a fact that many a hero has unmade himself.

Inhabitants of France, Belgium, England and the U.S., heaping glory, poetry and publicity upon 25-year-old Captain Charles Augustus Lindbergh, found him so natural and so tactful that they predicted he would never unmake his fame.

It was a modest, a natural, a lovable, a well-prepared man, whom Europe honored last week, while the U.S. swelled with pride and prepared a homecoming. Unquestionably, Captain Lindbergh is a stimulating hero. He conquered alone—with only his monoplane.

At Paris, President Gaston Doumergue pinned the cross of the Legion of Honor upon Captain Lindbergh and the French Chamber of Deputies cheered with gusto. On the day when Marshal Ferdinand Foch said to him: "Come right next to me and stand very straight, so that the whole world can see that you are bigger than I am," Captain Lindbergh blushed, crouched.

He climbed into a French fighting plane, a 300-horsepower Nieuport; did loop-the-loops, head-spins, side-drifts, grapevines, fluttering-leaves over Paris. He told French senators: "My flight has not done anything to advance the cause of civilization. Yet I am not unaware that it marks a date."

He arose at 6:30 a.m., worked on his own plane *Spirit of*

St. Louis, at Le Bourget airport. Then he left the soil of France, circled the Eiffel Tower twice, flew low over the Arc de Triomphe, dropped a farewell message on the Place de la Concorde. It read: "Good-bye, dear Paris. Ten thousand thanks for your kindness to me."

Having arrived at Brussels promptly and greeted Albert, King of the Belgians, with: "I have heard much of the famous soldier-king of the Belgians," Captain Lindbergh was decorated by his Majesty with the order of Chevalier of the Royal Order of Leopold. Next day, he flew to London.

There, more than 100,000 people were waiting for Captain Lindbergh at the Croydon Aerodrome. They broke down police barriers, swarmed on the landing-field as soon as his plane was sighted. He swooped down looking for barren ground, saw none, returned skyward. On the second attempt, his plane touched ground, but was forced to rise again because hero-worshipers insisted on dogging his path. His third attempt was rewarded with a clear field. Before he could climb out of his plane, the sea of the mob surrounded him —bowling over women, leaving the official reception committee stranded in the distance. Finally, the police succeeded in roping off the *Spirit of St. Louis,* and Captain Lindbergh was carried by automobile to U.S. Ambassador Houghton and Sir Samuel Hoare, British Secretary for Air.

When Captain Lindbergh arrives in the U.S., he will find Barnum-scale welcomes wherever he goes. He will see his picture on U.S. Army recruiting billboards. He will discover that the New York *Daily News* (tabloid) has distributed sepia photographs of him, "ready for framing," to its gum-chewing readers. He will see shopgirls wearing his features on their handbags, his monoplane models on their hats.

Inhabitants of the U.S. have not been slow to outline Captain Lindbergh's future for him. James Joseph [Gene] Tunney, fighter, suggests that he make a fortune in cinema or vaudeville, while the making is good. Will Rogers, funnyman and newspaper philosopher, suggests that the U.S. Government give him a life pension and a high position in the aviation service. Others believe that he should glorify the U.S. by new exploits, flights to Australia, to the South Pole, around the world.

Meanwhile, Captain Lindbergh is saying little, waiting

until he returns to the U.S. to make his plans. Said Benjamin F. Mahoney, president of the Ryan company which built his monoplane: "Lindbergh flies, but he keeps his feet on the ground."

TO WASHINGTON: At dawn the U.S. cruiser *Memphis* was JUNE 20 steaming up the Potomac River. Soon people in Washington began to stir—in the temporary White House, President and Mrs. Coolidge, and Mrs. Evangeline Lodge Lindbergh were arising. As the sun grew brighter and hotter, the tempo of the capital approached *allegro.* One hundred Army and Navy airplanes darted above and below and around the dirigible *Los Angeles,* like sharks baiting a whale. The guns of the presidential yacht *Mayflower* boomed a salute. Factory whistles shrieked. Nautical tunes bounded over the waters of the Potomac. The *Memphis* docked at the Navy Yard. Mrs. Lindbergh went aboard to embrace the son who had quickened the tempo of the world's chronicle since she last saw him.

Then mother and son were driven up Pennsylvania Ave., as 150,000 people became hoarse. President Coolidge and another 150,000 were waiting in the vicinity of the Washington Monument. Radio Announcer Graham McNamee was telling the rest of the land: "Here comes the guard of honor ahead of Lindbergh's car. . . . The cavalrymen with drawn sabres make a dashing picture. . . . Here's the boy. . . . He comes forward unassuming, quiet, a little stoop in his shoulders. . . . Now I will turn the microphone to the reviewing stand, where President Coolidge and the boy Lindbergh stand quietly together."

President Coolidge, warming up more than usual, called the boy "our ambassador without portfolio"; pinned on his coat lapel the Distinguished Flying Cross; gave him his commission of Colonel in the Officers' Reserve Corps. The boy replied with seven short sentences, keeping his promise to Europe by delivering a message of friendship to the U.S.

That night, Col. Charles Augustus Lindbergh slept in the temporary White House at Dupont Circle.

Next day, he went to church with his mother and President and Mrs. Coolidge, placed a wreath on the tomb of the Unknown Soldier at Arlington; visited disabled War veterans at the Walter Reed hospital, made plans for flying to New York early the following morning.

Because his *Spirit of St. Louis* had a sticky valve, Colonel Lindbergh hopped from Washington to Long Island in an Army pursuit plane, transferred (at Mitchel Field) to an amphibian plane, alighted on New York Harbor. Long before the hero touched foot on the island of Manhattan, the air was full of shrieks, confetti and shredded ticker tape. Twelve thousand police carried no clubs; but linked arms, used hands, charged on horseback to keep the crowds from absorbing the parade on narrow Broadway.

At the City Hall, Mayor James J. Walker presented Colonel Lindbergh with the city Medal of Valor, said to him: "We are familiar with the editorial 'we' but not until your arrival in Paris did we learn of the aeronautical 'we.'" At Central Park the struggling grasses were brow-beaten while 250,000 humans watched Governor Alfred Emanuel Smith pin upon Colonel Lindbergh the state Medal of Honor.

Such were the outstanding spectacles last week in the welcome of Colonel Lindbergh. To these were added many a side-show:

¶ Shrewd underlings of the Western Union Telegraph Co. and the Postal Telegraph-Cable Co. fattened the purses of their employers by evolving a set of 20 stereotyped messages of congratulations to Colonel Lindbergh. Examples: No. 2: "Glad you're back, Captain. When you fly out this way drop in and see us." No. 6: "Back seats for George and Albert. We're prouder than kings. Welcome home." No. 11: "The flight was wonderful, the reception marvelous, but we are proudest of your modesty and eternal sense of the fitness of things. Welcome home."

These messages were advertised on handbills bearing the caption: *"Your Choice for 36 Cents"*—the price varying in different cities. Western Union and Postal Telegraph could well afford to give these reduced rates, because the messages were dispatched in bulk during slack hours, using a simple formula of numbers and names of senders. Whatever the methods, 75,000 telegrams were delivered to Colonel Lindbergh in Washington.

¶ Three U.S. mail trucks, displaying large signs which read: "The People of the United States by Air Mail Congratulate

Lindy," carried 500,000 letters to Colonel Lindbergh when he disembarked from the *Memphis* at the Washington Navy Yard. How much mail he received via regular railroad services is unknown.

¶ Before hopping across the Atlantic, Colonel Lindbergh made a contract with a Manhattan clipping bureau to watch for any newspaper stories concerning his flight. Faithful, the bureau collected two freight cars full of clippings.

FADEOUT: As one title on a cinema screen slowly fades out JUNE 27 and another title slowly takes its place, so with the beginning of this week the name *Lindbergh* was gradually vanishing from the black, multi-column newspaper headlines. Street-sweepers were clearing away the petals of the roses that were thrown at him in St. Louis. Newspapers, ranged in rows on newsstands, no longer looked like photograph galleries of a single face.

Probably Colonel Lindbergh himself was glad when the last cheer was cheered and the last speech was spoken. "Never have I seen anything as hopelessly tired as that boy," said Historian Hendrik Willem Van Loon. Toward the end of his receptions, indeed, Colonel Lindbergh appeared tired, gloomy, haggard. Asked how he felt one morning, he replied: "I don't know. I haven't read the newspapers yet." He has received a gold, diamond-studded pass, entitling him to life-time admission to all Shubert theatres. What he most needed was rest, sleep.

"What will Colonel Lindbergh do now?" is the universal question, universally unanswered. The Ryan Aircraft Corp. has already received orders for 20 similar ships. With such stimulation of increase in aviation, it was thought that Colonel Lindbergh might head a commercial-and-passenger aviation company, financed by his flight backers.

For the first time, the gospel of aviation was preached by a national hero to whose words the country was ready to listen. Since the Colonel's return, aviation recruiting centers have been swamped by applicants for the flying service.

Through it all, the hero of the occasion has been, appropriately, the most heroic aspect of it. Never has his tongue or his balance slipped, always has he been what kindly old ladies might call "a real nice boy."

DEC. 26 **AMBASSADOR:**

MEXICO CITY

COLONEL CHARLES A LINDBERGH
WASHINGTON D C

IT HAVING REACHED MY KNOWLEDGE THAT YOU INTEND A FLIGHT FROM NEW YORK TO HAVANA IN THE ANTILLES I INVITE YOU TO DO SO VIA MEXICO WHERE YOU MAY REST ASSURED OF THE WARMEST WELCOME

PLUTARCO ELIAS CALLES
PRESIDENT OF THE REPUBLIC

WASHINGTON D C

PRESIDENT CALLES
MEXICO CITY

AFTER THE WISHES OF COLONEL LINDBERGH I HAVE THE HONOR TO INFORM YOU WITH PLEASURE THAT TODAY AT 12:26 HE STARTED ON HIS DIRECT FLIGHT TO MEXICO

MANUEL TELLEZ
AMBASSADOR

TALLULAH LA

TO U S NEWSPAPERS

AN AIRPLANE BELIEVED TO BE COL LINDBERGHS WAS SIGHTED AS IT PASSED OVER TALLULAH BY FRANK HULE A TRAIN DIS-PATCHER AT 11:10 CENTRAL TIME TONIGHT

ASSOCIATED PRESS

HOUSTON TEXAS

TO U S NEWSPAPERS

AN AIRPLANE BELIEVED TO BE THAT OF COL LINDBERGH PASSED OVER HOUSTON AT 2:20 OCLOCK THIS MORNING

ASSOCIATED PRESS

MEXICO CITY

TO MANY U S NEWSPAPERS

THOUSANDS OF MEXICANS WERE AT THE VALBUENA FLYING FIELD AT DAWN THIS MORNING EAGER TO GREET COL LINDBERGH AT 8:40 PRESIDENT CALLES ARRIVED ACCOMPANIED BY HIS ENTIRE CABINET WITH REPORTS AT 10:30 THAT COL LINDBERGH WAS HALF WAY BETWEEN TAMPICO AND MEXICO CITY NINE MEXICAN ARMY AIRPLANES HOPPED OFF TO MEET HIM RETURN-

ING SCOUT PLANES LANDED AT 11:42 WITHOUT HAVING SIGHTED
COL LINDBERGH SILENCE ALMOST APPROACHING GLOOM PRE-
VAILED OVER THE GREAT CROWD AS THE 25TH HOUR PASSED
WITH LINDBERGHS WHEREABOUTS UNKNOWN THE AUTHORITIES
SET FIRE TO DRY GRASS WHICH COVERS THE FIELD TO MAKE A
SMOKE SIGNAL   BOTH PRESIDENT CALLES AND AMBASSADOR
MORROW WERE UNABLE TO CONCEAL GRAVE EMOTIONS

THE ASSOCIATED PRESS

MEXICO CITY

NEW YORK HERALD TRIBUNE
NEW YORK CITY
   THE INTREPID AMERICAN FLYER BROUGHT HIS SPIRIT OF ST
LOUIS DOWN ON VALBUENA FIELD AT 2:39 FROM THE CROWD
DELIRIOUS SHOUTS OF JOY

JACK STARR-HUNT

MEXICO CITY

PRESIDENT CALVIN COOLIDGE
WASHINGTON D C
   IT PLEASES ME PROFOUNDLY TO SEND YOUR EXCELLENCY MY
MOST CORDIAL FELICITATIONS AT THIS TIME WHEN COLONEL
LINDBERGH HAS ARRIVED AT MEXICO CITY AFTER HIS NOTABLE
FLIGHT ACCOMPLISHED WITH GREAT SUCCESS

PLUTARCO ELIAS CALLES
PRESIDENT OF MEXICO

WASHINGTON D C

COLONEL CHARLES A LINDBERGH
MEXICO CITY
   THE PEOPLE OF THE UNITED STATES ARE PROUD TO APPLAUD
THE SUCCESSFUL CULMINATION OF ANOTHER OF YOUR COURA-
GEOUS VENTURES I WISH TO ADD MY HEARTIEST CONGRATU-
LATIONS TO YOU IN BEING THE FIRST TO FLY WITHOUT A STOP
BETWEEN THE CAPITALS OF THE TWO NEIGHBOR REPUBLICS

CALVIN COOLIDGE

MEXICO CITY

NEW YORK TIMES
NEW YORK CITY
   PRESIDENT CALLES ISSUED A STATEMENT TONIGHT "THE

LATTER PORTION OF COL LINDBERGH'S FLIGHT OVER TERRITORY ABSOLUTELY UNKNOWN TO HIM OVER ZONES OF A PARTICU- LARLY DIFFICULT AND DANGEROUS NATURE BECAUSE OF A LACK OF MEANS OF COMMUNICATION AND THE DEVIATION FROM HIS ORIGINAL ROUTE PUT TO THE PROOF HIS GREAT SKILL FOR NAVIGATING ALOFT HIS MARVELOUS RESOLUTION AND ENERGY ALONE PREVENTED HIM FROM COMING DOWN MAINTAINED HIM IN HIS FIRM INTENTION TO REACH MEXICO WITHOUT A STOP."

DETROIT

NEW YORK TIMES
NEW YORK CITY

"THAT'S ALL THAT MATTERS," SAID MRS. LINDBERGH, TOLD OF HER SON'S SAFE LANDING IN MEXICO CITY "HE HAS ALWAYS TALKED OF SEEING MEXICO"

MEXICO CITY

NEW YORK TIMES
NEW YORK CITY

THIS HAS BEEN IN SOME WAYS THE MOST INTERESTING FLIGHT I HAVE EVER MADE I MANAGED TO GET COMPLETELY LOST IN THE FOG OVER MEXICO SOMETHING WENT WRONG I GUESS IT WAS ME I AM SORRY THAT THOSE WAITING FOR ME HAD SUCH A LONG TIME UNDER THE HOT SUN BUT I WAS JUST AS ANXIOUS TO COME DOWN AS THEY WERE TO HAVE ME IT WAS FAR FROM PLEASANT FLYING UNABLE TO GET BENEATH THE FOG I WENT UP AGAIN AND SET A COMPASS COURSE FOR MEXICO CITY WHEN I DIVED DOWN OUT OF THE CLOUDS TWO AND ONE HALF HOURS LATER THERE WAS NOT A SIGN OF MEXICO CITY I GOT COM- PLETELY LOST I KNEW I WAS IN A BAD COUNTRY TO PLAY AROUND IN I TRIED TO PUZZLE IT OUT BY THE WATERSHEDS BUT IT WAS NOT UNTIL I SAW A SIGN OF THE HOTEL TOLUCA THAT I REALLY MANAGED TO GET LOCATED AND THEN SET MY COURSE AGAIN FOR MEXICO CITY I SAW THE PLANES OF THE MEXICAN ARMY COMING TO GREET ME OF THE RECEPTION I CAN ONLY SAY THAT IT WAS EQUAL, IN ALL ITS SINCERITY, WITH THAT WHICH I RECEIVED IN FRANCE AND ENGLAND MEXICO HAS SOME SPLENDID PILOTS I AM GRATEFUL TO PRES- IDENT ELIAS CALLES

CHARLES A LINDBERGH

Women

WORTH A MILLION: Miss Vera Bloom, daughter of Con- MAY 16
gressman Sol Bloom, Democrat of New York, spoke at the
second world welfare conference of the Women's Universal
Alliance. Miss Bloom said: "Mrs. Coolidge is worth $1,000,-
000 a year to the Republican Party. Her grace and charm are
real assets in the White House and contribute much to the
prestige of the Administration."

INCOHERENT: That feminine volubility depends upon a lim- JUNE 6
ited and domestic audience was last week maintained by Mrs.
Arthur L. Livermore, honorary president of the Women's
National Republican Club of New York. Speaking at the
Hannah Penn House, Philadelphia, to a conference of Republican women from eight states, Mrs. Livermore said: "Wom-
en become incoherent on the public platform. They are so
accustomed to talking to husbands and brothers that they
can't seem to get used to talking to anyone else."

"NOT PERSONALLY": Among the questions answered by JULY 11
persons filling out applications for U.S. citizenship is Question No. 22, asking whether the applicant, if admitted to
citizenship, would bear arms for the U.S. In reply to this
question Mme. Rosika Schwimmer, organizer of the Henry
Ford "peace ship" in 1915, wrote: "Not personally. I understood that women are not required to bear arms in the
United States."

In view of Mme. Schwimmer's prominence among pacifists, this answer may well have been considered pert by
naturalization authorities. At any rate, she was last week
refused on grounds that she was "lacking in nationalistic
feeling" and also because she had announced herself as an
atheist. The American Civil Liberties Union and other liberals
have interested themselves in what threatens to become "the
Schwimmer Case."

Mme. Schwimmer, a Hungarian, has an international repu-
tation as author, lecturer, pacifist, has frequently accused the
U.S. of "militarism." Her eloquence helped in persuading
Henry Ford that he could take an ocean trip and stop the
World War—a proceeding which was generally felt to have

Mrs. Livermore: "Women become incoherent on the platform."   *Rosika Schwimmer: "I would not kill a man, even if he tried to kill me."*

added much to the existent European impression of the U.S. as a country richly peopled with moneyed madmen.

OCT. 24 **PETITION DENIED:** Mme. Rosika Schwimmer, 54, beetle-browed Hungarian Jewess, indefatigable publicist, onetime Hungarian Minister to Switzerland, has been trying for some time to become a U.S. citizen. Last week the Schwimmer Case was heard in the U.S. District Court by Judge George A. Carpenter, who asked Mme. Schwimmer a question.

"If you were a nurse," mused the Judge, "caring for a wounded American soldier, and observed an armed enemy approaching, would you take up a pistol and shoot the enemy?"

"No," stoutly answered Madame Schwimmer, "but I would warn the soldier. I would not kill a man, even if he tried to kill me." She added that she might fling herself upon the enemy and try to disarm him.

"That's all," said Judge Carpenter. "Petition denied."

Then the Judge rose from his seat. He pointed at the U.S. flag over his courtroom door and sternly said to Mme. Schwimmer: "You cannot be a halfway citizen under that flag. . . . We have a great deal to give when we confer citizenship upon an alien. It is like admitting a new stockholder, and he or she should be willing to do what the other stockholders have obligated themselves to do." [In 1946 the Supreme Court ruled that new citizens were not required to take an oath that they would fight for the U.S. Rosika Schwimmer, who did not take advantage of this ruling, died in 1948.]

Farmers

RELIEF?: For five years the farm-threat has hung dagger-like FEB. 14 above the Republican party. For three and one-half years, President Coolidge has unequivocally opposed every farm bill which the farm bloc desired. He has confined himself to advising farmers to co-operate on their own initiative. Hitherto, the President has avoided vetoing a farm bloc bill by using his influence to kill the bill in Congress. Last week it became clear that he could no longer avoid the issue.

Consideration of the U.S. farmer involves thousands of facts, hundreds of theories, dozens of nostrums, bushels of sentiment and clouds of politics. Some of the facts:

¶ U.S. farms produce more than U.S. people eat, wear, or otherwise use or waste.

¶ There is therefore a farm surplus available for sale in competition with foreign-produced comestibles. Hence its price-value (which like water seeks a level) is in part determined by foreign price-values, and foreign price-values are relatively low.

¶ The U.S. protects most of its manufactured products by tariff. Protection means keeping prices and wages up. Thus farmers must buy their clothes, building materials, labor, cosmetics, etc., in a protected market, although they must sell in an unprotected market.

¶ Many a U.S. farmer makes money and wants no government aid.

The McNary-Haugen bill is the most famed remedy for the farmer's ills. Its most easily comprehended elements are:

1) There shall be a Farm Board—a great government brokerage corporation.

2) To it will be turned over $250,000,000 of government money.

3) When it sees fit to do so, it will declare that more of a certain crop has been produced than the U.S. can consume.

4) It will determine how great the surplus is, and will proceed to dispose of the surplus either by:

    a) buying the surplus and holding it against a lean year, or

    b) buying the surplus and selling it abroad at whatever price it can get.

The Senator joint-author of the McNary-Haugen bill is Charles Linza McNary who did not stay down on the Oregon farm where he was born. A lawyer and gentleman, he became Dean of an Oregon law school, whence he was elevated to the bench.

The Congressman-author is Gilbert Nelson Haugen, a sincere, likable old politician, who was reared in Wisconsin and rose in Iowa. He never had much education. He has never permitted insidious urban barbers to run away with his rural idea of a proper tonsure.

Senator McNary, former law dean, sponsors a controversial farm bill.

Rep. Haugen has little education, but knows what farmers want.

FEB. 28 **TO THE PRESIDENT:** Having been informed that both houses of Congress had passed the McNary-Haugen bill, President Coolidge called for his Cabinet, found that it unanimously disapproved of the bill. Secretary of the Treasury Mellon had already made public his attitude that the bill is unsound, unworkable and highly costly. Secretary of Agriculture Jardine, who would have to direct the farm experiment if the President makes it law, abhors it. If the President signs the bill, Secretaries Mellon and Jardine would have good reason to resign.

To veto the bill is President Coolidge's expected and logical course. The farm bloc cannot muster the necessary two-thirds majority in either house to pass the bill over his veto, but it can embarrass him by holding up other legislation.

VETO: "I am therefore obliged to return Senate bill 4808 MARCH 7 without my approval."

The Senate received last week a document (nearly 11,000 words) concluding with these words and signed with the big C-flourish of the signature: Calvin Coolidge.

Said the Baltimore *Sun* (Democratic): "Mr. Coolidge did not merely refuse to sign the measure. He kicked it out of the White House with as strong denunciation of its provisions in sum and in detail as has been heard in or out of Washington during the months of its consideration. That is what the country wanted him to do."

Some of the President's sentences:

"It runs counter to the principle of conservatism, which would require us to produce only what can be done at a profit, not to waste our soil and resources producing what is to be sold at a loss to us for the benefit of the foreign consumer. . . . Many other reasons exist why it ought not to be approved, but it is impossible to state them all without writing a book."

Radicals

SACCO & VANZETTI: The World War lasted four years and APRIL 18 was duly chronicled as an international episode. The case of Sacco & Vanzetti is seven years old and is still an international episode. It is a tale filled with blood and tears, with Reds and bigwigs, with bombs and laws.

April 15, 1920. A paymaster and a guard were shot to death on the streets of South Braintree, Mass., and robbed of a payroll of $15,000 by two men who "looked like Italians."

May 5, 1920. Two Italians who lived near South Braintree —Nicola Sacco, shoemaker, and Bartolomeo Vanzetti, fish peddler—were arrested as suspicious characters. The U.S. was then on a rabid radical hunt. Messrs. Sacco and Vanzetti were on the Red lists.

Nicola Sacco (right) and Bartolomeo Vanzetti. After seven years in prison they are executed for a crime that some witnesses say they did not commit.

July 14, 1921. A jury found Messrs. Sacco and Vanzetti guilty of the South Braintree murders on the following evidence: Factory-window witnesses, who had previously identified other Italians as participants in the crime, swore that Messrs. Sacco and Vanzetti were the killers. But, 20 Italians said they had purchased eels from Mr. Vanzetti at the hour of the crime, and the Italian consul in Boston swore that Mr. Sacco had been in his presence at that time. However, the police who arrested them swore that they had drawn guns. This was interpreted as "evidence of guilt." The jury was asked to do its duty as "did our boys in France"—an effective plea, considering the fact that Messrs. Sacco and Vanzetti were pacifists as well as radicals.

1921-1927. Motions for a new trial were repeatedly turned down, while radicals flung bombs at many a U.S. embassy, while liberals such as Anatole France, Fritz Kreisler, Albert Einstein protested against the injustice being done to the fish peddler and the shoemaker. Mr. Sacco went on a month's hunger strike. Mrs. Louis Dembitz Brandeis, wife of the U.S. Supreme Court Justice, turned over her Dedham home to Mrs. Sacco so that she could be near her husband and cook for him while he was in jail.

Last week in a Dedham courtroom, there was a scene, wherein seven years of emotion simmered and boiled over. The Supreme Court of Massachusetts had finally and flatly rejected evidence for a new trial on the grounds that there had not been a "failure of justice." Judge Webster Thayer, clad in black robes, with a face as still and as pallid as an ancient cameo, entered the courtroom to sentence Messrs. Sacco and Vanzetti to the electric chair. Bluecoats fingered sawed-off shotguns. Secret service agents with crimson rosettes in their lapels posed as Reds. Women sobbed. The clerk droned: "Nicola Sacco, have you anything to say why sentence of death should not be passed upon you?"

In the prisoners' box, a clean-shaven Italian, with a high forehead and a son named Dante, stood up. "Yes, sir, I, I am not an orator," said Nicola Sacco. "It is not very familiar with me, the English language. I never know, never heard, even read in history anything so cruel as this court."

The clerk droned again: "Bartolomeo Vanzetti, have you anything to say. . . ?"

The fish peddler was an orator: "Yes, what I say is that I am innocent. . . . I have never stole, never killed, never spilled blood . . . but I have struggled all my life, since I began to reason, to eliminate crime from the earth. . . . I am suffering because I am a radical; I have suffered because I was an Italian, and indeed I am an Italian . . . but I am so convinced to be right that you could execute me two times, and if I could be re-born two other time, I would live again to do what I have done already. I have finished; thank you."

Forthwith Judge Thayer sentenced Messrs. Sacco and Vanzetti to die by "the passage of a current of electricity" through their bodies during the week of July 10, 1927. The court adjourned.

Governor Alvan T. Fuller of Massachusetts was flooded with telegrams and petitions urging a pardon for Messrs. Sacco and Vanzetti, or at least an impartial investigation of their case. Twenty-two members of the British Parliament demanded immediate freedom for them. Bread-makers and taxi-drivers in Buenos Aires, Argentina, and laborers in many another land went on protest strikes.

APRIL 25 **PARDON?** In the hands of "the richest man in Massachusetts" lie the lives of two Radicals. For only Alvan Tufts Fuller, Governor of Massachusetts, can by the exercise of his right of pardon save Nicola Sacco and Bartolomeo Vanzetti.

Like many another far-sighted man who was young when the automobile industry was an infant, Alvan Fuller hitched his wagon to the horseless-carriage. He went to Detroit, came back with a contract giving him the New England territory for the Packard car. As the Packard car prospered, as more and more motorists began to "Ask the Man Who Owns One," Alvan Tufts Fuller prospered also. Today he is rumored to be worth 40 million dollars. None of the Governor's fortune, however, has resulted from his career in public life. As a member of the Massachusetts State Legislature, of the U.S. House of Representatives, as Lieutenant Governor of Massachusetts, and as Governor of Massachusetts, he has returned, uncashed, all salary checks.

Last week in London, in Paris, in The Hague, police guarded U.S. embassies and consulates, fearing that European radicals will let bombs express their disapproval of Massachusetts justice. Girls of Wellesley and Barnard colleges have petitioned the Governor to intervene. And a long list of liberal intelligentsia, including Jane Addams of Hull House, Felix Frankfurter of the Harvard Law School faculty, have enrolled themselves with the Sacco-Vanzetti sympathizers.

The outcome now rests solely with Governor Fuller. The Governor may 1) appoint a committee to review the entire proceedings, with the possible result of giving the condemned a new trial; 2) of his own responsibility, grant pardons to Mr. Sacco, to Mr. Vanzetti; 3) may let the law take its course. When, in his office beneath the Golden Dome of the State House at Boston, he sits down to consider his decision, what arguments are there that might lead him to decide in favor of the shoemaker and the fish peddler? What is the case for Nicola Sacco and Bartolomeo Vanzetti?

That case rests partly upon the contention that Messrs.

Sacco and Vanzetti, because of their avowed Communistic principles, did not receive a fair trial owing to prejudice against their political beliefs, partly upon the contention that since their conviction, important new evidence has developed sufficient to justify a re-trial.

Were Messrs. Sacco and Vanzetti, ask their adherents, convicted not of murder but of radicalism? As an illustration of prejudice, Liberals also put forward a remark alleged to have been made, before the trial, by Jury Foreman Ripley, who is said to have informed a friend that he was going to serve on the jury in the trial of the two "ginneys" (vulgar term for Italians) and, upon his friend's opining that they were innocent, replied, "Damn them, they ought to hang anyway."

In addition to attacking the trial itself, friends of Mr. Sacco and Mr. Vanzetti also have collected new evidence to answer the question: If Messrs. Sacco and Vanzetti are innocent, who is guilty? For in November 1925, a convict, confined in the same prison with Mr. Sacco, made a written confession of having taken part in the payroll robbery and stated that Messrs. Sacco and Vanzetti were not in the bandit-gang.

As against the allegations discussed above, Governor Fuller will doubtless consider the facts that Mr. Sacco and Mr. Vanzetti, tried by a jury of their peers, were found guilty; that Trial Judge Webster Thayer, before whom have come repeated petitions for a new trial has steadfastly refused to consider any of the matter contained in these petitions as important enough to justify re-opening the case.

THAYER FLAYED: Did Webster Thayer, trial judge in the case MAY 16 of Nicola Sacco and Bartolomeo Vanzetti, refer during the trial to Messrs. Sacco and Vanzetti as "those bastards"? Did he say "a bunch of parlor radicals are trying to get those guys off," but that he "would get those guys hanged"?

According to an affidavit of Robert C. Benchley, dramatic editor of *Life*, Judge Thayer said all these things to Mr. Loring Coes, of the Coes Wrench Co., Worcester, Mass. at the Worcester Golf Club. But Mr. Coes last week "flatly denied" the truth of Mr. Benchley's affidavit.

Mr. Benchley's affidavit formed, with four other affidavits, part of a petition sent last week to Governor Fuller of Massachusetts by Mr. Vanzetti. Frank P. Sibley, Boston reporter, said that during the trial Judge Thayer repeatedly discussed the case with reporters, that Judge Thayer said: "I'll show them that no long-haired anarchist from California can run this court." The "long-haired anarchist" was Fred H. Moore, defense attorney, who had a reputation for defending radicals. Mr. Sibley added that Judge Thayer often called defense attorneys "those damn fools."

Judge Webster Thayer. Did he vow to "get those guys hanged"?

Robert Benchley. His affidavit claims the judge used prejudicial language.

MAY 23 **DYNAMITE:** Sorting mail at the Burlington Ave. Station, Boston, last week, Postoffice Clerk Frank W. Steele came upon a suspicious-looking package, five inches long, four inches wide. Wired to the parcel was an envelope, with the address "Mr. Governor of Massachusetts" written in an illiterate hand.

Next morning the package, after having stood all night in a bucket of water, was opened. It contained about a pound of powdered dynamite. Meanwhile in the envelope had been found the following letter:

"Governor of Massachusetts:

"I have succeeded in getting a quarter of a ton of this. If Sacco and Vanzetti are going to be murder, I am going to get more and use it."

The package contained no detonating mechanism.

COMMITTEE: Last week sympathizers with Nicola Sacco and JUNE 13 Bartolomeo Vanzetti thought they saw a rescue party starting out for an eleventh hour salvation of the two men who are scheduled to occupy the electric chair during the week of July 10.

Governor Alvan Tufts Fuller of Massachusetts, who last fortnight had somewhat curtly replied to a request that he appoint a committee of investigation with the statement that the matter was his responsibility to be investigated as he saw fit, last week, suddenly, surprisingly, did appoint exactly the kind of committee which he had been asked to name.

Consisting of Judge Robert Grant (lawyer and novelist), President Abbott Lawrence Lowell of Harvard University and President Samuel W. Stratton of the Massachusetts Institute of Technology, the advisory committee will make an investigation independent of the Governor's own inquiry and report to him.

RESPITE: Two cells in the "death house" at the Charlestown JULY 11 (Mass.) State Prison last week failed to receive two occupants who were scheduled to move into them. For Nicola Sacco and Bartolomeo Vanzetti, sentenced to be electrocuted during the week of July 10, were given a one-month respite by Governor Alvan Tufts Fuller of Massachusetts to permit further investigation of their case.

SACCO-VANZETTI HEARINGS: To the State House in Boston JULY 25 last week came a six-year-old child, Inez Sacco, accompanied by her mother, Mrs. Nicola Sacco. While Mrs. Sacco talked to Governor Alvan Tufts Fuller of Massachusetts and to his Advisory Committee, Inez chatted with newspapermen. An unconscious witness to the law's delay was Inez, born while her father was in jail, growing up with her father under a death sentence.

Yet last week, at least, Massachusetts legal machinery moved with an accelerated rate. Many witnesses told their stories of the Sacco-Vanzetti case. Among those interviewed were the Misses Minnie E. Kennedy and Louise Kelley, who were employes of the Slater & Morrill Shoe Co. at the time of the South Braintree murder of which Messrs. Sacco & Vanzetti were found guilty.

The Misses Kennedy and Kelley were new witnesses, both of whom claimed to have been eyewitnesses of the Braintree payroll robbery and who maintained that Mr. Vanzetti was not an occupant of the "murder car." Neither of these women had been called as a witness in the original trial.

AUG. 1 **"WOE IS ME":** To his six-year-old daughter Inez, last week wrote Nicola Sacco, condemned to die during the week of August 10. To the child whom he has seen only on her visits to his cell, he said:

"It was the greatest treasure and sweetness in my struggling life that I could have lived with you and your brother, Dante, and your mother on a neat little farm and learn all your sincere words and tender affection. But it was not so and the nightmare of the lower classes has saddened very badly your father's soul. The men of this dying old society, they brutally pulled me away from the embrace of your brother and your poor mother. But, in spite of all, the free spirit of a father's faith still survives, and I have lived for it and for the dream that some day I would have come back to life, among our friends and comrades again, but woe is me."

Despondent, indeed, was the outlook for both Mr. Sacco and Mr. Vanzetti. The pendulum that has for seven years swung between life and death last week swung toward death again.

Both Nicola Sacco and Bartolomeo Vanzetti spent the week virtually without food, having begun a hunger strike. The strike is a protest against the secrecy of the investigations and began after a visit from Mrs. Sacco, whose account of her interview with Governor Fuller apparently indicated that the Governor was not disposed to interfere with the due operation of Massachusetts law.

Governor Fuller last week spent 15 minutes with Mr. Sacco and an hour with Mr. Vanzetti. Both men walked unassisted to the prison warden's office, through they had at that time been fasting for six days. No report of the interview was given out, but reports agreed that Mr. Vanzetti, who entered the Governor's presence with every appearance of confidence, came out dejected, dull-eyed, head-hanging.

AUG. 8 **NO ENCOURAGEMENT:** Last week was made public a letter written by one Van Valkenburgh of Manhattan to Nicola

Sacco. Mr. Van Valkenburgh told Mr. Sacco not to despair, assured him that his "long-suffering" would soon "end in freedom." Said Mr. Sacco, in his reply:

"Only an international clamor—a protest—can free us. And yet, while we are so near the tomb, your letter amazes me with its unwarranted optimism. How you are deluded! This is not even common sense, coming from you. I would say nothing if such talk came from a man in the moon, but from you this is too much. Do you not know the ends to which the defenders of this decrepit old society will go? Are you waiting to see them kill us first so that you can build us a monument? I am not writing this out of prison irritation, nor yet because of their cruelty in bringing us back to this stifling place to torture us some more before they burn us, but I want the comrades to know what kind of creatures they are dealing with."

THE NEWS: In their cells in the death house of the Massachu- AUG. 15 setts State Prison, Messrs. Sacco & Vanzetti heard last week that they were to die. Mrs. Sacco and two advisers brought the news. For an hour and a half, they talked together, while prison guards listened and looked. Mr. Sacco (then on the 19th day of a hunger strike) mumbled over and over: "I told you so, I told you so," as if in rhythm with his throbbing, withered arteries. Said Mr. Vanzetti: "I don't believe it."

In that hour and a half, Messrs. Sacco & Vanzetti each found time to write a letter to friends. Mr. Vanzetti's: "Governor Alvan T. Fuller is a murderer. We die for anarchy. Long life to anarchy." Mr. Sacco's: "We are not surprised by this news, because we know the capitalist class is hard, without any mercy to the good soldiers of the revolution. With warm fraternal regards to all."

Last week, Governor Fuller announced that the committee had unanimously agreed with him that Messrs. Sacco & Vanzetti were guilty of murder and had been given a fair trial. Hence, he would not intervene to prevent the passage of electricity through their bodies.

On the important question of radicalism, Governor Fuller said: "Complaint has been made that the defendants were prosecuted and convicted because they were anarchists. As a matter of fact, the issue of anarchy was brought in by them as an explanation of their suspicious conduct."

The Chicago *Tribune* said: "The nation has reason to be grateful that the most elaborately organized movement to defeat justice in the history of our courts has not prevailed and that a cruel, sordid and atrocious crime will be punished. This is a victory for justice, for order and for humanity."

Novelists & Columnists who lifted their voices last week, were nearly unanimous in proclaiming Messrs. Sacco & Vanzetti the victims of injustice. In England, John Galsworthy, H. G. Wells and Arnold Bennett implored Massachusetts not to stain her name. Referring to the Lowell committee, Heywood Broun, a Harvard man, wrote in his syndicated column: "It is not every prisoner who has a President of Harvard throw the switch for him."

AUG. 22 **RESPITE:** It was 36 minutes before midnight. Straps of the electric chair in the Massachusetts state prison had been oiled, adjusted, inspected by the executioner. Machine guns had been placed along the prison walls to prevent violence. In adjoining death cells Nicola Sacco and Bartolomeo Vanzetti were waiting for a man to slit their trouser legs, make them ready for metal strips through which would pass a current of electricity.

That man did not appear. Instead came Warden William Hendry with the words: "Well, boys, it's all off. Buck up. Be men and start eating." Warden Hendry then informed the prisoners that Governor Fuller of Massachusetts had granted them a 12-day respite from death to allow the courts to consider petitions for a new trial.

Mr. Sacco was too weak and too gloomy to say anything. He continued his hunger strike which had then reached its 24th day. Mr. Vanzetti said: "Well, I'm damned glad. I'd like to see my sister before I die." (His sister sailed last week for the U.S. on the *Aquitania* from Cherbourg.) Soon Mr. Vanzetti began to swallow liquids and, later, salads.

John Dos Passos, author of *Manhattan Transfer*, and Dorothy Parker, humorous poet, were part of a little parade carrying Sacco & Vanzetti placards in front of the State House, where an officer informed them: "Loitering and sauntering is against the law. You have seven minutes in which to disperse. Move on." The little parade continued and soon two patrol wagons arrived. Mr. Dos Passos began to sprint from the scene, awkwardly, at his top speed; bumped into a policeman. On being collared Mr. Dos Passos insisted that he was hurrying to his newspaper office not running away from patrol wagons. He and his friends were fined $5 apiece.

Later when Mr. Sacco was on the 30th day of his hunger strike he was ordered to go into the prison barber shop where he found Dr. Joseph I. McLaughlin, Warden William Hendry, Mr. Vanzetti, Mrs. Sacco and others. Dr. McLaughlin spoke first: "The time has come, Sacco, when you must eat."

"I don't want to eat," said Mr. Sacco.

Dr. McLaughlin pointed to a rubber bag, tube and funnel; held Mr. Sacco's nose; said firmly: "You know I can use these on you if I want to."

Soon Mr. Sacco drank a quart of hot beef tea slowly, morosely, without the aid of a funnel.

EXECUTION: After seven years of premeditation, blood was AUG. 29 shed beside a so-called cradle of American liberty, Boston. The shedding of blood caused restlessness. The restlessness caused by this particular bloodshed was exceptionally widespread, gloomy and violent because, in seven years, a seed of doubt can grow into a harvest of sincere conviction; and because their particular harvest of conviction had been fertilized by the animus of two irreconcilable philosophies of life, SOCIALISM and CAPITALISM.

Guilty or not, justly or not, Nicola Sacco, clean-shaven factory worker and Bartolomeo Vanzetti, mustachioed fish peddler, were informed last Monday evening that they must die that midnight for the murders—which to the end they denied committing.

Prisoners Sacco and Vanzetti refused last rites from the prison priest. They would die as they had lived, they said. Faith in a communistic order of mankind was enough for them.

Five guards took their posts in the death house, two to adjust electrodes, one at the blue lethal door, two to call at the cells.

Prisoners Sacco and Vanzetti died in the order that their names had long been coupled, seven minutes apart.

Something of the horrid dismay their clients must have felt was reflected in the renewed efforts of Lawyer Arthur D. Hill and associates last week. They went to the highest Massachusetts court, pleading error and prejudice at the original trial. The highest Massachusetts court replied, in five typed pages, that it could not act.

They docketed the case for review by the highest court in the country hoping a) to give Governor Fuller of Massachusetts grounds for a further reprieve since the case was still, technically, before a court; and b) to give any one of the nine Justices of the U.S. Supreme Court opportunity to request a review of the case, which request would have given Governor Fuller broader grounds for a reprieve.

They telephoned Chief Justice William Howard Taft of the U.S. Supreme Court. Mr. Taft was in Canada. The wire connection was faint. He asked them to telegraph. They telegraphed and Chief Justice Taft telegraphed back explaining that he could not act, being out of the U.S., could not reach the U.S. in time. He referred them to three Associate Justices of the U.S. Supreme Court then in the northeastern part of the U.S.

They went to Associate Justice Oliver Wendell Holmes, at Beverly Farms, Mass. He said he felt unauthorized to meddle with a state case.

They went to Associate Justice Louis Dembitz Brandeis at Chatham, Mass. He said he must decline to act because of his personal relations with people (his wife included) actively interested in the case.

They went to Associate Justice Harlan Fiske Stone at Isle au Haut, off the Maine coast. He echoed the reply of his colleague, Justice Holmes, "as to the merits of the application and the action of counsel in presenting it."

They waited on U.S. Attorney General Sargent at Ludlow, Vt. Mr. Sargent listened attentively for three hours to their account of the relation of the U.S. Department of Justice to the case. He said it was the first time he had ever understood this relation, but later announced that he would not act, that Department of Justice affairs were for the time being in the hands of his subordinates in Washington, D.C.

They went to Acting Attorney General George E. Farnum in Washington, D.C. He said that Department of Justice confidential records would be furnished for inspection to no one save at the request of Governor Fuller or the latter's advisory committee headed by President A. Lawrence Lowell of Harvard University. Neither Governor Fuller nor President Lowell would make the request.

They asked the Massachusetts Superior Court again; were refused. They asked the Federal District Court again; were refused.

They returned to Justice Holmes for a writ of *Habeas Corpus*. He wrote no writ.

Governor Fuller of Massachusetts. Execution day was "beautiful."   *Edna St. Vincent Millay wrote a poem, picketed, went to jail.*

They asked Governor Fuller again, in six petitions. He did not reply. On the execution Monday he showed himself not to have been unnerved by his trying position and said to newsgatherers in front of his office, "Good morning, gentlemen. It is a beautiful morning, isn't it?" Governor Fuller received insistent callers up to two hours before the execution. He could not change his mind.

They wired President Coolidge. Silence answered.

Edna St. Vincent Millay wrote a poem beginning, "Let us abandon then our gardens and go home." She also picketed, was jailed.

Boston Common, for the first time in history, was closed to public orators.

Machine guns, searchlights and fire-hoses were added to the defenses at Charlestown Prison, which none might approach closer than 1,000 feet. Relatives of the prisoners, however, were admitted to the death house. To reach the death cells they had to pass the electric chair. Prisoner Vanzetti was allowed to leave his cell and embrace his sister, Luigia, whom he had not seen for 19 years. Prisoner Sacco saw his wife and 14-year-old son, Dante, to whom he later wrote a farewell letter telling him to comfort his mother, fight the rich, help the weak.

In Union Square, Manhattan, 10,000 people stood shoulder to shoulder before a bulletin of the *Daily Worker*. Toward midnight they read:

SACCO & VANZETTI CALMLY AND HEROICALLY AWAIT END
WITNESSES OF EXECUTION BEGIN TO ARRIVE
THEY ENTER THE DEATH CHAMBER
ONLY WORKERS' COURTS CAN GIVE JUSTICE TO WORKERS (Perfunctory cheers)
STRENGTHEN YOUR UNIONS TO PROTECT OUR FUTURE CHAMPION (Louder cheers)
MORE NEWS TO FOLLOW

The bulletin: SACCO MURDERED! (Loud but orderly cries of indignation, boos, catcalls. But no fiercer than the noise that a 10,000 baseball-crowd makes when a favorite disappoints. Flares and the *Internationale,* which soon died.)

The bulletin: DON'T FORGET OUR MARTYRED COMRADES. KEEP ON FIGHTING. (Moderate cheers)

JOIN THE WORKERS PARTY AND FIGHT ON
VANZETTI MURDERED!

Voices in the crowd: "Take your hats off! Hats off, there!" There was no violence.

The crowd dispersed.

SEPT. 5 **SACCO AFTERMATH:** A state law required that the bodies be burned or buried before sunset the Friday following Execution Tuesday. Boston health officials extended the time to Sunday.

When the brains and hearts of the corpses had been removed for examination by Harvard medicos, Massachusetts returned what remained of its prisoners to their friends, who straightway sought a public hall for a public wake. But Boston hall owners refused to lease their property. Owners of the building in which the Defense Committee had offices caused a stout joist to be nailed in the building's doorway so that no coffin might be carried in. The Defense Committee had to be content with a small mortuary chapel in the Italian section of Boston.

The mortician, an artist in his way, wanted to dress the bodies in dinner jackets, but the Defense Committee said no, let them lie in their plain laboring-men's Sunday best—black cloth suits, black four-in-hand ties, uncomfortable black shoes. Let the coffins be of plain mahogany draped with Red, banked with odorous Red flowers. So it was, and their neighbors saw them as they had often seen them.

In the cemetery, a fire blazed, its smoke trailing thin and mournful from the crematorium's high smokestack. The limousines were parked there, one with its shades drawn to hide the prostration of Miss Luigia Vanzetti, Mrs. Sacco and her son Dante. On the rim of the surrounding natural amphitheatre, the crowd watched the wisp of smoke until nightfall.

Crime

RUIN: "Shady Rest" was a funny kind of roadhouse. It had JAN. 17 dynamite in the cellar, machine guns in the windows. Men sat around, spat on the floor, fingered the triggers of their rifles. One day, last November, an airplane flew over and dropped some bombs which missed the house. Nobody was killed; it was only a minor disturbance. Last week "Shady Rest" trembled, burned, collapsed. It became a ruin overnight. And what is more, it contained four bodies, charred beyond recognition, full of ugly bullet holes.

There had been another gangster battle, and of all the places for a good machine-gun-spattering, bomb-throwing fight there was none better than the late "Shady Rest." Not far from Herrin, Ill., it was the citadel of Charles Birger, bootlegger, gunman, gang chieftain. Carl Shelton, whose profession is the same as Mr. Birger's, had set out to get Mr.

Birger. The ruins and the four dead bodies were the result. But Messrs. Birger (who was away) and Shelton are still alive and plotting. Perhaps, they will really get one another some day. Their attempts in the last five months have resulted in the killing of 13 people.

FEB. 21 **PEACE?:** On the night of Dec. 12, 1926, two men rang the doorbell at the home of Joseph Adams, 300-pound mayor of West City, Ill. The mayor, incautious, unsuspecting, opened the door. His callers took hasty shots at the 300-pound target, ran for their machines, left Mayor Adams dying across his threshold. Now the State of Illinois holds Charles Birger, gunman, gangster, as accessory to the murder.

With the imprisonment of Charles Birger, the two gangs which have for ten months terrorized the district in and around Williamson County, Ill. are leaderless.

As in all wars, each party has its victories to boast. The Shelton adherents slapped thighs, exchanged felicitations over the destruction of "Shady Rest," an old roadhouse fortified as Birger headquarters. Less than a month later, Birger more than evened the score. For it was his evidence that convicted the Shelton Brothers of robbery. Allied with the law for the duration of the Shelton trial, Charles Birger, sleek, suave, smartly-tailored, stepped into the witness' box, said, "Howdy, Sheltons!" spent 20 minutes swearing away 25 years of three men's lives. Beneath his well-cut coat he wore a steel vest, bullet proof.

With Sheltons disposed of, with Birger awaiting trial, optimists hope for peace in "Bloody Williamson." [Birger was hanged for the murder of Mayor Adams. Carl, Earl and Bernie Shelton were released on the robbery charge after a new trial and continued to operate in Williamson County until they moved to East St. Louis in the 30s. Carl and Bernie were later shot to death in gang feuds.]

APRIL 4 **LAUNDRYMEN'S WAR:** Tong! The magic word. City editors rolled it in their mouths. A sweet morsel.

When, in the ordinary course of events, several Chinese are murdered during a short space of time, a tong war automatically comes into being, under the auspices of news-hungry editors.

There are two fighting tongs in the U.S. They are the On Leongs and the Hip Sings.

The On Leongs are the wealthier organization and are numerically stronger than their rivals the Hip Sings.

The Hip Sings, on the other side, are made up largely of small merchants, laundrymen and waiters, at whose head is a small group of leaders, unscrupulous as weasels.

In Brooklyn last week, at midnight, Li Poy, 45, dishwasher, Hip Sing, was stooping over his sink in King's Tea Garden. In and out pattered the waiters. Then a strange Chinaman swung through the door. He fired two shots into Li Poy's bent back. Poy pitched forward and his face sank like a yellow teacup into the brown dishwater. A scream drowned in the water.

In Pittsburgh two On Leong laundrymen crumpled up dead on the sidewalk with blood bubbling from wet bullet holes. The assassin faded smoothly back into the blue.

In Chicago three humble Hip Sings and two obscure On Leongs disappeared from society.

In Cleveland, Jim Yee, of the On Leongs, was riddled with gunfire as he slept in his laundry basement.

In Newark a Hip Sing yellowman made the error of invading a Chinese quarter settled almost entirely by On Leong Tongmen. There were 26 bullets in his body when the police found it in the gutter.

Police authorities in the above named cities herded droves of the inscrutable Orientals into local station-house bull pens for questioning. All declared they knew nothing, their leaders asking in reply, "What tong war? There is no war!" Disgusted lieutenants turned the droves loose. Flags with Chinese characters, denoting peace, were seen flying over all Chinese headquarters buildings. The war, if any, ended.

The previous war that ended two years ago claimed over 50 lives and was stopped only after Federal promise of deportation to all Chinamen unless their nasty practices were stopped. By way of emphasis, 59 were shipped back to the land of dragons and lilies.

CALIFORNIA CONVICTS: California sends her "repeater" DEC. 5 convicts to Folsom Prison, a stronghold whose ashen walls command a desolate stretch of the American River valley laid waste by goldseekers. Prisons are gruesome places at best but

Folsom ranks with the worst as a focus of human distemper and desperation. Last week, Folsom was the scene of the greatest prison revolt in California history.

The 1,200 pallid inmates of one of the cellhouses were assembled for a Thanksgiving Day cinema. The silence was broken by a shuffling of feet and hoarse muttering. Seven or eight convicts had slipped from their places and surrounded Assistant Turnkey Ray Singleton. They were dragging him toward a door from the cellhouse into the adjacent hospital. They were telling him to get the master key. Turnkey Singleton was answering that the master key, which would open the main door of the cellhouse, had been taken away from its usual place. Weapons began to flicker in the half-light of the prison—daggers and stilettoes wrought out of files, kitchen utensils, shovels, razor blades. One man had an automatic pistol. As Turnkey Singleton stammered his answers, some one shoved a knife in his back. Someone else struck him deep in the stomach.

The furious convicts turned their attention to Guard Charles Gorhanson, who was trying to drag out the dying Singleton. Pricking his back with their knives, they made Gorhanson buzz to the switchboard the signal for opening the cellhouse. Guard Gorhanson buzzed long and angrily. The switchboard man guessed something was wrong and slammed the door shut.

Prodding Gorhanson afresh, the convicts marched him to the prison ballfield. They captured Guard Walter Neil on the way. At the ballyard door, Guard Neil was sent out first, then Guard Gorhanson. Before the convicts could follow, Guard Neil flung his weight against the door to lock them in. Tony Brown, San Francisco thug, the convict with the "roscoe" (pistol), tried to shoot Neil's foot out of the way, but the lock clicked. The cursing convicts retired to secure the rest of their guards as hostages and hold a council of war.

When the alarm reached the prison gate, aged Gatekeeper Charles Gilles died of heart failure. The 1,800 inmates of another Folsom cellhouse were locked in their cells before they knew what had happened. In the rioters' building, yells and commotion arose as the messhall and library were barricaded against siege.

Warden Court Smith was beleaguered in his office. To

reach the prison wall, he would have to cross a bald court-yard under whatever fire the convicts might loose. He tele-phoned to Governor Clement Calhoun Young in Sacramen-to, 25 miles away, to send over soldiers, bombs, artillery. He ordered all available riflemen to the prison wall.

Close-fitted bars over the cellhouse windows screened out the tear-gas bombs hurled by police and militia, but screams and uproar told what effect the barrage of rifle-fire was hav-ing. The convicts returned the fire with their one gun, injuring only one attacker. Seeing that they needed heavier weapons to batter in the cellhouse doors, police and militia withdrew to await the arrival of tanks, airplanes. Warden Smith, who safely left and returned to his office, warned the prisoners that he could flood the cellhouse and drown them. He offered to let them march out in peaceable surrender. They refused.

The sniping continued. Floodlights were arranged to pre-vent a night sortie. The convicts asked for a doctor. The Prison Physician went in to them and he found a whole night's work. Nine men, including Turnkey Singleton, lay dead. Four more were dying. Thirty-one convicts were wounded, one of whom died while the doctor was amputat-ing his leg.

From Governor Young came word to cease firing, except on any fugitives trying to scale the walls or swim the river. At midnight, having meantime ordered the guard doubled at California's other big "pen," San Quentin, Governor Young reached Folsom in person. A mass attack by 700 troopers, preceded by tanks, was planned for the next morning.

At dawn, Warden Smith's telephone rang. "The men want to come out," said a voice. "If we surrender will you guar-antee to punish only the leaders and that none of us will be beaten, abused or starved?"

Warden Smith promised.

"We will not be abused?"

"You will be put in solitary confinement and you will get one square meal a day."

Surrender followed. In ominous silence, the guards lined up their charges and took the roll. Six haggard men—Tony Brown and two burglars, a murderer, a forger, a robber—went to dark cells to await trial for murder. Governor Young re-turned to Sacramento and Folsom Prison to bitter routine.

DEC. 19 **GLUM GORILLA:** Chicago newsgatherers hurried out one day last week to interview Alphonse ("Scarface Al") Capone, gunman. They found him arrayed in hunting clothes at his hotel.

Mr. Capone had not been hunting humans, though that is his reputation. He had just returned from a pleasure trip in the "north woods" where he had been shooting bears, deer, rabbits. He was holding a press reception to announce that he was going South for the winter.

The Capone interview commanded large headlines. Mr. Capone's fame rests upon the fact that whenever—as so often happens—a Chicago thoroughfare is raked & riddled with machine-gun fire, Chicagoans take it for granted that Mr. Capone or his men have driven in again from their suburban headquarters at Cicero, Ill., to shoot down some rival gangster who has overstepped one of the underworld boundary lines which divide all Chicago into four parts.

"Scarface Al" is proud of his record, but not of all his reputation. That was why he was plaintive, even glum, at his press reception last week. That was why he said:

"I'm going to St. Petersburg, Fla., tomorrow. Let the worthy citizens of Chicago get their liquor the best they can. I'm sick of the job—it's a thankless one and full of grief. I don't know when I'll get back, if ever.

"I've been spending the best years of my life as a public benefactor. I've given people the light pleasures, shown them a good time. And all I get is abuse.

"Well, tell the folks I'm going away now. I guess murder will stop. There won't be any more booze. You won't be able to find a crap game, let alone a roulette wheel or a faro game.

"Public service is my motto. But I'm not appreciated. My wife and my mother hear so much about what a terrible criminal I am. It's getting too much for them and I'm just sick of it all myself. Today I got a letter from a woman in England. Even over there I'm known as a gorilla. She offered to pay my passage if I'd kill some neighbors she's been having a quarrel with.

"I wish all my friends and enemies a Merry Christmas and a Happy New Year. That's all they'll get from me this year. I hope I don't spoil anybody's Christmas by not sticking around."

Army & Navy

POOR RATIONS: Last week Major General Charles Pelot JAN. 24
Summerall, Chief of Staff, told the House Military Affairs
Committee that the Army food rations were lower than those
of convicts in Federal prisons. The soldier gets only one good
meal a day, he said. Secretary of War Dwight Filley Davis
added that President Coolidge and the Budget Bureau were
responsible for the Army's meagre diet. Hearing these words
and many others, the House Military Affairs Committee set
about to expand the War Department appropriation bill. It
increased the daily food ration from 35¢ per day to 40¢
(a total recommendation of $2,167,187). Skeptics wondered
whether the extra five cents a day would mean beefsteaks or
merely better hash.

YELLOW FEVER: One night in a tent pitched about a mile MARCH 28
from Quemados, Cuba, thirsty mosquitoes sang their monotonous whining song; on a cot, Private John R. Kissinger
lay awake. It was hot and sticky; he did not slap the stinging
pests away. He had volunteered to Dr. Walter Reed, head of
the U.S. Yellow Fever Commission, to subject himself to the
bites of mosquitoes that had sucked the blood of men ill with
the fever; in this way the Commission hoped to find whether
the mosquito carried the deadly germ. He made the offer
knowing that his chances for life were less than one in 20, if
he became infected.

The night was nearly 27 years ago. Last week scientists and
doctors opened a campaign to raise money to help onetime
Private Kissinger. Not long ago friends had found him nearly
destitute, broken in body and mind from the illnesses that
followed the yellow fever he caught that night near Quemados. For nearly 20 years, he has lain in a wheel-chair suffering from spinal myelitis. His wife has nursed him and supported him. But the U.S. has not been overgenerous with its
rewards to the men who helped stamp out yellow fever.

For Mr. Kissinger, his country has done little. When he
left the army in 1901, he refused a reward for his sacrifice; in
1907 the Government awarded him a pitiful pension of $12 a
month; in 1922 they increased it to $100. Now his wife lies
seriously ill, too; the pension is not enough to keep them alive.

Yet Mr. Kissinger has lived to learn that his sacrifices have been worth while even if unrewarded. In 1900, yellow fever was the scourge of the American tropics; last year in the whole of North and South America, only two cases of yellow fever were reported. [Kissinger later received a house and a larger pension. He died in 1946 at the age of 68.]

General Summerall says soldiers get worse food than convicts.

Colonel William Mitchell: "The Navy lives principally on hot air."

JUNE 27   **AGAIN, MITCHELL:** "Today the Navy lives principally on hot air, manufactured and spread by their Washington lobby."

This acrimonious accusation last week marked the return to the public ear of onetime Col. William Mitchell, deposed in 1925 as Assistant Chief of the Army Air Service. It has long been Mr. Mitchell's conviction that airplane development has made battleships obsolete, that Navy men have retarded aviation progress lest the fleets of the future should be exclusively fleets of the air.

Last week, the failure of Col. Charles A. Lindbergh's *Spirit of St. Louis* to function properly when the aviator attempted to fly in it from Washington to Manhattan, prompted Mr. Mitchell to further criticisms. After maintaining that the *Spirit of St. Louis* suffered exposure to corrosive salt air while being transported home on the U.S. cruiser *Memphis* ("there was no excuse for not keeping this plane safe and dry"), Mr. Mitchell added that the plane was under naval care at Washington. Calling the plane's inability to take Colonel Lindbergh to New York the "one failure in the *Spirit of St. Louis*'s performance," Mr. Mitchell added: "and it was caused by the organization in this country which has always impeded and held up aviation—the Navy."

CAVALRY MANEUVERS: Not since the Civil War had U.S. OCT. 10 cavalry engaged in maneuvers on the scale of those conducted last week on 120 square miles of terrain in and about Marfa, Tex. Some 280 officers, 4,000 men, 3,200 horses and 1,500 mules were deployed over gulches, hillocks and sagebrush plains. Tanks, cannon, airplanes, Red Cross ambulances and every appurtenance of real war, right down to hot weather, secrecy and red tape, accompanied the show.

Following the maneuvers, horses, mules and men assembled for a review and a horse show. Troopers were paid off and sent back to their stations while officers continued to argue about which "army" had "won." Among other stratagems weighed for merit was that of dyeing white horses brown to camouflage them from aerial observation. Other modern cavalry camouflage: dull metal mountings on harness; dun netting to dull the flash of shiny saddle seats.

MITCHELL AGAIN: Shouted William Mitchell, onetime Colo- NOV. 7 nel and Assistant Chief of the Army Air Service: "President Coolidge is the worst public official in office. He has made an industry of office-holding and is trying to rule the country, not govern it!"

Prohibition

In 1927, Prohibition had been in effect in the U.S. for seven years. It had seven years to go before it would be repealed.

"SMART YOUNG MEN": Two big sedans roared through the MARCH 21 night in Chicago's southwest side last week. The second car drew up alongside the first, poured into it a stream of machine-gun, shotgun and revolver fire. Brakes shrieked; the first sedan careened toward the curb. Like rats leaving a doomed ship, two men jumped out. One sprinted 100 yards, fell on his face on the pavement—dead, full of little holes. The other floundered across a vacant lot, died with seven bullets in his flesh. They, Frank Koncil and Charles Hrubek, were members of "Polack Joe" Saltis' bootlegging gang. Rival thugs had killed them.

This was only another episode in Chicago's intra-mural liquor war, which has killed more than 100 gangsters, an assistant district attorney, a lawyer and a few policemen in the last two years. It ends the treaty of peace, signed last October by greasy chieftains in a Loop hotel, while a captain of the police held their guns. More killings may soon be expected. The Saltis gang is eager for revenge; its rivals are eager to get Gangster Saltis.

One would think that Chicago with its $100,000,000 annual liquor business, with its $30,000,000 paid for protection, would have enough profits for all the hoodlums. But each gang has its eye on a monopoly. They encroach upon one another's territory, raid one another's warehouses, capture one another's beer trucks, slaughter one another's men.

There are four major gangs: one on the north side (with a onetime assistant state's attorney as its adviser); two on the south side (one of which is led by "Polack Joe" Saltis); one on the far west side with headquarters in Cicero where famed "Scarface Al" Capone is king.

As King Capone once said:

"It (the Prohibition law) looked like a good opening for a lot of smart young men."

APRIL 4 **DECISIONS:** Last week in Chicago, Judges George T. Page and Albert B. Anderson of the U.S. Circuit Court of Appeals ruled that "nose evidence" is good evidence, that the mere smell of liquor in a restaurant is enough to cause that restaurant to be padlocked for a year. Law-abiding restaurant-keepers must now employ detective-waiters to search customers for hip-flasks and hidden bottles before they serve them with cracked ice or ginger ale. Prohibition agents need no longer search and buy; they may sit at tables and sniff; a good smell will convict.

On June 1 the Province of Ontario, Canada, went Wet, giving U.S. tourists from the neighboring states the prospect of an easy source of liquor. However, the hopes of parched Midwesterners fell when Ontario put into effect regulations specifying that liquor could be sold only in government stores and only by special permit.

OLD CROW: Last fortnight Chairman D. H. Hanna of the JUNE 13 Ontario Liquor Commission saddened thirsty U.S. citizens by stating that tourist permits to buy liquor would not be granted to "excursionists," that "American visitors" expecting "big blowouts" in Ontario would be "disappointed."

When the Ontario liquor stores actually opened, however, it quickly became obvious that an "excursionist," unless roped, hog-tied and branded as such, could not possibly be distinguished from a "tourist." Any U.S. citizen who found himself in Ontario and considered himself to be a tourist could secure a tourist permit and quaff beer, wine, ale, whiskey, champagne, gin in any legal "residence," including his hotel room.

"Opening Day" in Ontario found no riots, no tremendous exodus from the U.S., no Detroit invasion of Windsor. It did find, however, interminable queues of applicants lined up before the liquor-store doors. The first U.S. citizen to make a purchase was one Fayette Bristol of Highland Park (Detroit suburb). Mr. Bristol toted away an undetermined quantity of Old Crow whiskey.

Political Notes

BLACK JACK: Along a strip of frosty marshland at Red Deer JAN. 17 Ranch, Cherry County, Neb., Gen. John Joseph Pershing prowled with a gun. Two companions crouched beside him. On a nearby pool they espied a flock of wild ducks cutting the water zig-zag. General Pershing approached.

A voice, menacing, came from the woods behind him. General Pershing turned, heard gruff phrases from the lips of a distraught plainsman, obviously the owner of the land on which he, General Pershing, hunted.

Spoke one of the General's companions: "We just wanted a couple. This is General Pershing with us."

Excitedly the figure in the rawhide boots advanced: "You mean Black Jack Pershing? Well, shake hands with your old private that used to peel potatoes for you. Yes, Sir, General —in the Sioux Indian campaign, buck private in Seventh Cavalry at Fort Niobrara. Black Jack himself! Yes, sir, all the ducks you want. I'll be danged."

FEB. 7 **FLOGGING O.K.:** In Raleigh, the North Carolina Supreme Court last week determined that flogging of convicts in the Tar Heel State is legal.

FEB. 21 **MUD-SLINGER:** A more-than-six-foot 200-pounder stood upon the stage of the Four Cohans' Theatre in Chicago last week. His paunch heaved like a vexed hippo's, his ham of a hand smote the air, his flabby face howled. Technically, he was no vaudeville actor; he was William Hale Thompson, candidate for Mayor of Chicago. Yelled he: "I wanta make the King of England keep his blasted snoot out of America. This is the issue of the campaign (he draped the Stars and Stripes over his arm). What was good enough for Washington is good enough for me. In the face of an issue such as this, the only issue for a true American, do you folks wanta re-elect your present Mayor (popular, able William E. Dever, Democrat). Do yuh? Do yuh? If you don't look out all history books are going to be full of things belittling George Washington. They're teaching un-Americanism. And if you elect me I'll fire out the whole blasted caboodle, including King George of England. That's what Big Bill will do."

APRIL 18 **IN CHICAGO:** Chicagoans awoke one morning last week to find that 512,740 of their number had elected William Hale Thompson as Mayor.

Said the liberal New York *World:* "The majority which voted for Thompson are not intelligent, free, self-governing citizens of a republic. They are suckers. They are not the only suckers in the land, but at the moment they are the most conspicuous ones."

CATFISH?: Senator William E. Borah of Idaho, as piscator, JUNE 27 scoffed at President Coolidge catching trout with angleworms in South Dakota: "They must have been imbecile trout. My interpretation is that the President must have caught not trout, but catfish. I never heard of catching a trout with a worm."

Senator James A. Reed of Missouri, as piscator, said of President Coolidge's method of catching trout with angleworms in South Dakota: "Any trout that would bite on a worm is degenerate."

ENGINEER: According to correspondent Clinton W. Gilbert OCT. 24 of the New York *Evening Post,* one objection to the presidential candidacy of Herbert Clark Hoover has been voiced as follows: "We have never had an engineer in the Presidency and I doubt whether we ought to have an engineer in the Presidency. An engineer is experimental. An engineer always wants to do something."

Judiciary

LINDSEY OUT: "The Juvenile Court in Denver is known JULY 11 throughout the civilized world."—*H. G. Wells*

Upon Judge Benjamin Barr Lindsey of the Denver Juvenile Court was last week served a court order officially ousting him from his position. The order was the result of the Colorado Supreme Court's decision last winter that Judge Lindsey's election in 1924 had been illegal.

Said Judge Lindsey: "The ouster writ is the temporary triumph of bigotry and intolerance, of dishonesty and injustice. I have not been given the rights of a yellow dog."

In his 28 years of service with the Denver boys and girls who came before him, Judge Lindsey made the Juvenile Court of Denver internationally famed. Its work has been studied by sociologists everywhere; has exerted a strong influence on the nation's Juvenile Court system as it stands today.

Yet many a U.S. citizen doubtless cheered Judge Lindsey's ousting, rejoiced at his "downfall." For within the past year he has become to many thousands of his countrymen a radi-

General Pershing. A private lets him shoot all the ducks he wants. Page 73. *Judge Ben Lindsey. The famed authority on juveniles is ousted.*

cal, a lunatic, an attacker of the sanctity of the home, an advocate of free love and of birth control. By his advocacy of what he terms "companionate marriage," he has made many warm admirers but countless bitter enemies.

What is this Companionate Marriage idea which has made Judge Lindsey almost a symbol of evil in many U.S. minds? Briefly, it is based on the fact that some marriages are entered into with the expectation of the wife's bearing children, that other marriages are entered into with no such expectation. Why not, urges Judge Lindsey, recognize the childless marriage as a different but legal form of union? Let a boy and a girl who wish to marry, but who cannot well afford to have children, marry and, with the aid of widespread birth-control knowledge, take care that they have no children. Then, if they do not get along with each other and wish to separate, let them be granted a divorce on grounds of mutual consent and take up single life again. If they do get along with each other and if they decide that they wish to have children, let them enter the regular Family Marriage state as it is at present constituted.

Opposition to this idea has, of course, been based on its advocacy of birth control and of free divorce. Bishop William T. Manning of the New York Episcopal Diocese called it "wicked . . . damnable," said that it was legalized fornication. Vivid pictures have been drawn of girls and boys leaping from one "companion" to another; of the "licentiousness" which would result from widespread and legalized use of contraceptive measures.

Meanwhile Judge Lindsey has maintained that most of the Companionate Marriages would lead into Family Marriages, that there would be fewer illicit sex unions, that venereal disease would be less prevalent and that a great deal of "hypocrisy" would be taken out of the national domestic life.

SECRETS: A slender, partly bald little man with a bristling SEPT. 26 mustache last week carried a mass of official-looking documents to a vacant lot in Denver, tore the papers to tatters, heaped them high, squirted them with kerosene, touched off a match and cried out over the flames: "Do you think I want homes in Denver ruined? All you poor girls, you troubled women, who have given me your confidence that I might help you, rest now in peace. Your secrets are safe."

The burning papers were intimate confessions of some 5,000 women who had come before the little man, whose name was Benjamin Barr Lindsey, during the 27 years that he was judge of Denver's famed Juvenile Court.

Catastrophe

WATER, WIND: Last week residents of Memphis, Tenn. saw APRIL 25 somebody's house bobbing down the Mississippi, headed toward the Gulf of Mexico. Soon other houses followed, plus bodies of drowned cattle, plus debris of every description. For the Mississippi, rain-swollen, high-rising, was aflood from Cairo, Ill. to the Gulf of Mexico. Many a levee "went out," thousands of lowland acres turned into lakes, 24,000 refugees appealed to the Red Cross for aid, eleven lives were lost.

Southern Illinois, Kentucky, Tennessee, Missouri and Arkansas were the worst flood sufferers. One estimate placed 2,000,000 Arkansas acres under water. Levees at Memphis, Tenn., were populous with slimy, writhing snakes, flooded out of their swampy homes.

MAY 2 **DELUGE:** Levees crumbled in the night. State militia went into action, forcing stubborn and panicky people to leave their homes. Secretary of Commerce Hoover established an executive base at Memphis. All around raged tragedy.

"Better leave!" neighbors warned three families living on the Flynn plantation, twelve miles east of Little Rock, Ark. "Think we'll stay—river won't get near us," they answered. Late that night, dwellers on higher ground saw lights, heard screams on the Flynn plantation. Soon the lights went out, the screams were silenced. In the morning there was deep water where three houses had stood.

Of all menaces, the greatest was pestilence. Typhoid broke out. Measles, scarlet fever and dysentery threatened. Weakened by their drenching, the refugees succumbed easily. The flooded zone is all rich cotton land. Most of the victims were small farmers—owners of several acres, a few pigs, chickens, cows, a mule.

MAY 9 **STILL ROLLING:** Crawling southward at the rate of a mile an hour, the crest of the Mississippi flood last week spread through Arkansas and Louisiana the desolation that last fortnight it had brought to Kentucky and Tennessee. More than 6,000,000 acres were inundated, more than 300,000 were homeless and figures were being daily revised upward. Secretary of Commerce Herbert C. Hoover traveled tirelessly up and down the river. Once his boat was fired at from the shore —probably as a hint to keep midstream lest the wash endanger a levee.

At New Orleans, fishermen came in with news that the Gulf Stream had been darkened by the Continent's prodigious discharge of silt; that great fishes were schooling seaward to escape suffocation.

MAY 23 **TORNADOES, TOO:** Sweeping last week through Texas, Arkansas, Kansas, Missouri, Illinois, tornadoes killed 255, injured more than 1,000. Hardest hit was Poplar Bluff, Mo., with 103 dead.

MAY 30 **"NOTHING IN ITS CLASS":** Observers united in terming the flood the greatest of peacetime national catastrophes of all time. Said Frank R. Kent, of the Baltimore *Sun*: "The San

Francisco earthquake and fire does not compare with this as a national calamity. Nothing else since the Civil War is in its class."

Meanwhile President Coolidge steadfastly refused to call a special flood session of Congress. Hostile Administration critics maintained that:

1) The last session of Congress left the Government without sufficient funds for normal activities—let alone flood relief. Assuming that there are 500,000 refugees and that there is $10,000,000 (the Red Cross relief fund) to spend on them, money available for flood relief would be only $20 per victim. By calling a special session, the Government could get both the money for relief work and the authority to spend it.

2) President Coolidge has refused to make a personal visit to the flooded section. The flood has not caught the imagination of the country because it has not caught the imagination of the country's chief executive. Were Roosevelt President for instance, he doubtless would long since have been personally piling sandbags on threatened levees.

RECEDING: With the Mississippi River steadily falling, with JUNE 6 New Orleans generally considered safe from disaster, it last week became possible to estimate with some degree of accuracy the extent of what Flood Relief Director Herbert C. Hoover has called the "greatest peace-time calamity" in U.S. history.

Loss of Life. According to official Red Cross figures, 114 lives have been lost in the flood.

Red Cross relief has been given to some 560,000:

166,781 victims in Arkansas
210,481 victims in Mississippi
145,231 victims in Louisiana
20,823 victims in Missouri
13,105 victims in Tennessee
7,401 victims in Kentucky
4,200 victims in Illinois

"HIGH GROUND": Herbert C. Hoover appeared generally AUG. 8 regarded as the "hero" of the flood. Inhabitants of one flooded region arranged a Hoover celebration, presented him with a loving cup. On the cup was inscribed:

Presented to
HON. HERBERT HOOVER
In token of appreciation and gratitude
for his wonderful work and sympathy
during
Flood of 1927
BY THE COLORED PEOPLE OF
ARKANSAS

One of the Negroes was quoted as having said: "Sho' would have had a hard time didn't Mr. Hoover come to fetch us to de high ground. Sho' would make a noble President." And a white man was said to have remarked: "We think Hoover is the most useful American of his day. Why, he'd make a fine President."

Races

FEB. 14 **BLACK BODIES:** Crawford Allen, Mississippi Negro, lay sick abed in his shanty just across the Louisiana line. It was night and his wife Anna slept deeply beside him. Nearby slept his three children, Teelie, Lewis, Myra. None of the Allens had any clothes on; it was August, hot. . . .

Two white men came in, flashed lights, grinned, shouted. At the point of a gun they shuffled the Allens into an automobile with only a towel more or less to cover their nakedness. Before dawn, white faces and black bodies were in Louisiana. White faces talked with a farmer. White hands took $20 and left black bodies with the farmer.

For several months last year the black bodies did what the farmer told them to, and were fed.

The tale of the selling of the Allens into slavery was set forth last week in a Federal grand jury indictment charging one John D. Alford and one Webb Bellue with violation of the Peonage Act. Both black-slavers were in hiding.

JUNE 6 **BRAGGADOCIO:** Citizens of a Missouri town called Braggadocio hammered and sawed industriously in their town square. Idlers eyed the workmen judiciously and offered suggestions. The workmen were building a scaffold.

The night before, Mrs. Ella Henderson, a Braggadocio widow of 31 with two children, had called the constable and told him that she had been attacked. From her emotional description the constable made out that Mrs. Henderson's assailant was Will Sherod, 30, a Negro, whom he forthwith lodged in Pemiscot County jail, 15 miles from Braggadocio.

Now the Braggadocians had taken Mr. Sherod from jail and brought him home. Now the scaffold was finished. Now they tied Mr. Sherod's hands and suspended him thereby from the scaffold. Now the Braggadocian guns were loaded, Braggadocian epithets flew, Braggadocian powder burned. Mr. Sherod died by writhes and jerks after a dozen bullets had passed through his dangling body. The Braggadocians smiled grimly at one another and went home to bed.

APOLOGY TO JEWS: Henry Ford, having permitted his week- JULY 18 ly magazine, the *Dearborn Independent,* generally to vitu-perate Jews since 1920 and so stir up an anti-Semitism strange to the U.S., last week recanted everything that that weekly had printed against Jews. His confession of error:

"To my great regret I have learned that Jews generally, and particularly those of this country, not only resent these publications as promoting anti-Semitism, but regard me as their enemy. Trusted friends have assured me that the charac-ter of the charges and insinuations made against the Jews justifies the righteous indignation entertained by Jews every-where toward me because of the mental anguish occasioned by the unprovoked reflections made upon them.

"This has led me to ascertain the exact nature of these articles. As a result of this survey I confess that I am deeply mortified that this journal has been made the medium for resurrection of exploded fictions, for giving currency to the so-called protocols of the 'Wise Men of Zion,' which have been demonstrated, as I learn, to be gross forgeries, and for contending that the Jews have been engaged in a conspiracy to control the capital and the industries of the world.

"Had I appreciated even the general nature, to say nothing of the details, of these utterances I would have forbidden their circulation without a moment's hesitation, because I am fully aware of the virtues of the Jewish people as a whole, of what they and their ancestors have done for civilization and for mankind toward the development of commerce and industry, of their sobriety and diligence, their benevolence and their unselfish interest in the public welfare.

"I deem it to be my duty as an honorable man to make amends to the Jews, by asking their forgiveness for the harm I have unintentionally committed, by retracting so far as lies within my power the offensive charges laid at their door, and by giving them the unqualified assurance that henceforth they may look to me for friendship and good will."

Despite Henry Ford's plain words, some newspapers imputed base motives to him. The Chicago *Tribune* quoted an anonymous "Jewish financier and industrialist":

"I think that Ford has at last realized that he has been making a boob of himself. It is very likely that Ford's attacks on Jews did hurt his business."

Said the New York *Daily News:* "We respectfully suggest that the last sweet dose of love and kisses be ladled out to Mr. Ford's new-found friends by leaving the name Ford off the new car. Let it be called instead, let us say, the Solomon Six, or the Abraham Straight-8."

MILESTONES

MARRIED: Eva Tanguay, 48, plump, red-haired vaudeville comedienne, who played Cedric Errol in *Little Lord Fauntleroy;* to one Allan Parado, 25, her Hungarian accompanist, secretly, a month ago.

DIED: Benjamin Franklin Smith, 96, perhaps richest New Englander ($50,000,000), who built the world's second largest stockyard in Omaha, Neb.; in Boston. With his three brothers he started his career by buying a gold mine near Pikes Peak, Col., which was thought to be a quartz claim. General Fitz-John Porter attempted to bore into the claim. Gold-miner Smith forthwith made an opening into the outlaw shaft from below, built a fire, and smoked out the General's workers. The General promptly installed a huge fan which blew the smoke down into the Smith workings, but whenever the fan was removed the fire was rebuilt. After three weeks the General gave up, returned east.

MISCELLANY

CANNIBAL: When Fisherman Eli Kelly, drifted to the beach of Santa Catalina Island with the half-eaten body of his partner, James McKinley, in the stern-sheets of his yawl, a coroner's jury began to investigate. Cannibal Kelly, last week, gave details. The yawl had been a life boat on board the yacht of Novelist Zane Grey. They had food and drink for 24 hours. On the fourth day they made a compact that the man who died first should give his flesh to the other. In the little cabin of the yawl the two huge, gaunt, enfeebled and delirious men shook hands on it. "Yes," said Mr. Kelly, "I carried out our agreement." The jury absolved him of all blame.

FOREIGN NEWS

British Commonwealth

*By 1927 Britain appeared to be pulling out of the economic dif-
ficulties that had plagued her since the war. The slump had cul-
minated in the great general strike of 1926 which was crushed
by the Conservative Government under Prime Minister Stanley
Baldwin. Baldwin also managed to end a long and costly coal
strike and, for many Englishmen, he emerged as the symbol of
British grit and calmness in adversity. In the fall of 1926 he pre-
sided over the Imperial Conference in London which officially
sanctioned the British Empire's new title: The British Commonwealth of Nations. Included in the Commonwealth were the onetime dominions or colonies of Canada, South Africa, Australia,
India and New Zealand. On the surface things looked fine, but
Britain was still dreadfully impoverished. New problems piled
up. Baldwin did very little about them, and by the end of 1927 his
government was in trouble.*

GREAT MEN: Where does Old England stand as the New Year JAN. 3
opens? The question is best answered in terms of her great
men. A new book by Alfred G. Gardiner, a shrewd and dis-
cerning British editor, discusses the great men of his country
in a style brilliantly quotable. Quotations:
¶ On Stanley Baldwin, Prime Minister, First Lord of the
Treasury and Leader of the House of Commons: "There are
times when he seems to be a prophet coming with a message
hot from Sinai, and there are times when he suggests that
Alice has wandered, round-eyed and innocent, into the Won-
derland of Westminster. He means well, but his merits are of
the heart rather than the head. He is English to the core."
¶ On L.C.M.S. Amery, Secretary of State for the Colonies:
"If I were asked to name the most influential member of the
Government I should name the most dour, the most drab,
the least popularly attractive figure in the Cabinet. The form

Prime Minister Baldwin is "round-eyed and innocent," like Alice.

Chancellor Churchill is "loathed, distrusted, hated" and outstanding.

his fanaticism takes is that of Imperialism. He envisages a world in which the British Empire, armed to the teeth, self-contained, neither buying nor selling with mere foreigners, looms menacing and tremendous over the world. No lip service from him to that nonsense about the League of Nations."

¶ On Winston Spencer Churchill, Chancellor of the Exchequer: "The principal difference between Mr. Churchill and a cat, as Mark Twain might say, is that a cat has only nine lives. He is an Ishmael in public life, loathed by the Tories whom he left and has now returned to; distrusted by the Liberals, on whose backs he first mounted to power; hated by Labor, whom he scorns and insults. Today, in the prime of life, he is easily the foremost figure in Parliament. I see no reason why he should not one day emerge from No. 10 Downing Street" [home of British prime ministers].

JAN. 17 **ELIZABETHS:** To the Queen-Empress there have been born no children for 21 years. Yet as Her Majesty retired at Buckingham Palace one evening last week, she was pleasantly conscious that a room adjoining her bedchamber sheltered an infant princess.

Her Majesty and the rest of the royal family had partaken of an unusually frugal meal. No soup was served, and everything was cooked with as little grease as possible. Such a dinner is Her Majesty's invariable precaution against queasiness of the stomach when she is in expectancy of taking a sea voyage. The soupless royal meal was served for the benefit of the Duke and Duchess of York [later King George VI and Queen Elizabeth]. On the morrow they were to embark aboard H.M.S. *Renown* to visit Australia. In their absence Queen Mary will care for "Baby Betty" (Princess Elizabeth), their eight-months-old daughter [and later, Queen Elizabeth in her own right].

Aboard the *Renown* the Duchess of York and her two ladies-in-waiting experienced the qualm of being not merely the only three women on a very big ship, but absolutely the only women who have ever been transported—except in emergencies—aboard a British ship of war.

No maids are at their disposal. Their hair will be dressed by a marine especially educated for this duty by London coiffeurs. They must subject their washables to the deadly friction of sailor scrubbing boards.

MADCAP CHANCELLOR: Chancellor of the Exchequer Winston Churchill is an individualist of such reckless stamp that only chance kept him from the gallows until he attained the armor of prestige and power. A minor exploit of his youth was to "shinny" up the central pillar in a London music hall, wearing the uniform of his Queen (Victoria) and demand three cheers for every daughter of joy in the house. Theirs were, he shouted, the only bosoms on which the tired head of a British soldier could always find repose. By a miracle he was not cashiered.

Last week, vacationing at Rome, he praised extravagantly the Fascist régime which stamps out so ruthlessly all individualists. Said Chancellor Churchill to Fascists: "If I had been an Italian I am sure I would have been wholeheartedly from start to finish with *Fascismo*'s triumphant struggle against the bestial appetites and passions of Leninism.

"In regard to the Fascist foreign policy I may say that your movement has rendered a service to the entire world. It had been said that a continuous course toward the left, a kind of fatal ebullition toward the abyss are the characteristics of all revolutions. Italy has demonstrated that there is a way of dealing with subversive forces. She has found the necessary antidote against the Russian venom."

Finally madcap Chancellor Churchill described Signor Mussolini in unique terms: "I could not help being charmed by his gentle, simple bearing and his calm, detached poise."

FEB. 28 **LONDON ENGULFED:** A slow, yellow gas engulfed London suddenly, one morning last week. It was not poisonous but it made eyes to smart and throats to tickle. Grime laden, it soiled. Dense, it blotted out objects within arm's reach. Translucent, it diffused broad daylight into a dull, enveloping bluish glow. As it must to London, "the worst fog in half a century" had come.

Bus conductors walked ten feet ahead of their busses, connected with them by electric wires on which lamps glowed. When two bus conductors sighted each other they signaled port or starboard to the drivers whose busses did not then bump. At Charing Cross, at every major crossing, huge gasoline torches sent up roaring flames three feet high—barely visible at ten yards. Cross Channel boat service was suspended for the first time in 50 years. Their Majesties, the King and Queen of the Belgians, in London to open an exhibit of Flemish art, were unable to get back to Belgium by either sea or air until the fog cleared.

MARCH 7 **GOLDEN CROWN:** Last week at the London Hospital, Queen-Empress Mary bent for a moment over a crippled girl's cot.

Questioned the blue-eyed, tow-headed child: "Are you really my Queen? I thought you always wore a golden crown."

Said the Queen-Empress Victoria Mary: "My dear, I am sorry I have left my golden crown at home. When I go out I wear only this sort of crown"—pointing to her hat.

Then, turning to the brown-bearded man who was standing near a cot across the aisle, Her Majesty continued: "Come here, George. This little girl wonders why we are not wearing our crowns. This is the King, my dear."

MARCH 14 **"BRUTAL FACTS":** As it must to all wives, a measure of disillusionment came last week to Mrs. Stanley Baldwin, wife of the British Prime Minister. Tender-hearted, she learned that some 62 miners had been entombed during the night at Cwm (pronounced "Koom"), Wales, by a mine explosion. Soon Mr. and Mrs. Stanley Baldwin were speeding to Cwm by motor.

The local government inspector, J. M. Carey, approached, hat in hand, spoke in low voice to the Premier. The mine was full of poisonous gases. Rescue work, even in gas masks, was too dangerous. The inspector had ordered that no one should go down in the mine until the fumes of explosion should be pumped away by the electric ventilators. Any other course was madness, said Inspector Carey, but the wives and families of the entrapped men were getting restless. He could not conscientiously advise the Premier to remain with his wife in that vicinity.

Conscious of their good intentions the Baldwins stayed, went among the stricken families. To one Mr. Button, two of whose miner sons were killed by the explosion, Premier Baldwin said: "I have come to see you as man to man—not as Prime Minister. I feel very sorry for you in your great loss." Meantime, Mrs. Baldwin held Mrs. Button's hand, urged Mrs. Button from the fervor of her own faith to seek consolation in prayer.

As the Baldwins returned to their limousine a woman, the wife of a miner still trapped in the mine, pointed to the Baldwins and suddenly shrieked: "Murderers! Murderers!! You

Elizabeth, Duchess of York. She skips soup before a sea voyage. Page 84.

Mrs. Stanley Baldwin. She and her husband are threatened by miners.

won't let them rescue my Tom. You—you rich beasts!"

Affrighted, Mrs. Baldwin clung to the Premier's arm. Imperturbable, he looked at the crowd with level eyes, silently sucked at and puffed his famed pipe.

"Traitor! What about the eight hours law?" cried a burly miner. All knew that Premier Baldwin had seen through the Commons a bill extending the one-time seven-hour miners' day to eight hours.

"What about our men dying now in the mine? Why don't you put on a gas mask and go down the pit, Baldwin? Coward! Traitor! Rush him! Down him and his psalm-singing wife!"

Mrs. Baldwin paled. Then Mr. Baldwin took his pipe out of his mouth, nodded to his chauffeur. The starter buzzed, the engine roared. At a blast from the limousine's powerful siren horn the crowd wavered. "Come on! Down them!!" shouted some voices; but the limousine broke through as one young miner shouted "Baldwin! You're lucky to get away!"

Returned home to No. 10 Downing Street, London, Mrs. Baldwin was overheard to say to her daughter Betty, as she entered the door: "It was terrible! Terrible! But your father said to me at the time: 'Don't worry, we must expect little rubs like this once in a while.'"

In the House of Commons fiery Laborite J. J. Jones cried: "The miners at Cwm received Baldwin in the proper spirit!"

"Order! Order!" cried Conservatives.

"I say and I will repeat," shouted Mr. Jones, "that all the crocodile tears shed over this disaster by the Government are sheer hypocrisy. The visit of the Prime Minister with a tearful sop to men on whom the Government has imposed the eight-hour day was sheer effrontery!"

MARCH 21 **DANCING MAN:**

> He begins the day with an orange.
> His telephone number is Regent 4140.
> Six and seven-eighths is the size of his hat.
> He speaks French and German fluently and
>   a few words of Welsh.
> Unlike his father he does not like soup.
> He chews gum, on occasion.
> Squash racquets is his best game.

When asked what he would like best in the world, the Prince of Wales once replied: "Two full days absolutely alone and to myself."

Such were Walesiana collected last week from many a London source.

At Melton Mowbray, famed hunting centre of Edward of Wales, he danced one evening last week with the wife of his stud groom, with the wife of the village fishmonger, and with the sole local telephone operator, a buxom girl.

SLEEPING PRINCESS: To tea at Buckingham Palace came Sir APRIL 25 James Matthew Barrie. Perhaps because most people think irresistibly of him as his own fictional character, Peter Pan, not-quite-grown-up, Sir James enjoys, even from Royalty, something like the indulgence accorded in every British heart to Peter. Therefore, last week, though 300 guests were present at the royal tea, Sir James approached the Queen-Empress and whispered a request in her ear, as even good little boys sometimes do with their grown-up hostess.

Queen Mary did not seem embarrassed or say, "Shh!" Her face lighted, she nodded, and with a royal finger discreetly indicated to Sir James a door. He should go through, and turn thus and thus. Then he would find Nurse Knight and should tell her by the Queen-Empress' command to show him the Sleeping Princess. On tiptoe, then, Sir James Matthew Barrie came to the crib in which lay Princess Elizabeth (just one year old on April 21). Perhaps the baby, with feminine intuition, realized how near she was to Peter Pan. Dispatches told that she stirred in her sleep, wakened for an instant and looked sleepy-eyed at the smiling man in thin-rimmed glasses, white stiff collar, and impeccable frock coat who stood, still a-tiptoe, beside her crib. Then, with a small pink yawn, Her Royal Highness dismissed Sir James.

GRAVE STEP: Sir William Joynson-Hicks, Secretary of State MAY 23 for Home Affairs, took a step of such grave moment last week as to render probable a break in the diplomatic relations between Great Britain and Soviet Russia.

Sir William's act was nothing less than to authorize a raid by operatives of Scotland Yard on the five-story building in Moorgate Street, where 1,000 British and Russian clerks were employed by Arcos, Ltd., the trading organization representing in England all the Russian co-operative societies. Moreover, in this same building is housed the Soviet Trade Delegation, guaranteed diplomatic immunity under the British-Soviet Trade Agreement of 1921. Details of the raid:

Throwing a cordon about the building just at tea time, police rushed the open door, occupied the whole building in a twinkling, warned screaming typists and frightened clerks not to touch or attempt to destroy any paper, book or document, herded the women into one large room, the men into another.

At 8 p.m. curtains were drawn, and all night the silhouettes of policemen could be observed occasionally upon the blinds as the police ransacked.

Trucks backed up and carried away tons of papers. Desks and strongboxes were rifled; but the two large safes in the basement proved too much for the police. Soon workmen with safe-blowing apparatus arrived. Pneumatic drills were featured in their technique, and all the next day a purring t-t-tat-tat-tat-t-t was heard in Moorgate Street. Finally the safes were burst open, more trucks backed up, more papers were trundled away.

The Soviet Trade delegation later issued a statement to the press, reading, in part: "The way the raid was carried on gives no guarantee that documents and materials which the police might allege to have found were really there before the raid took place."

Home Secretary Sir William Joynson-Hicks, or "Jix" in popular parlance, has the name of being a passionate, implacable foe of "Communism." He and Winston Churchill have been trying for months if not years to get the Cabinet to break with Russia, against the sober judgment of Premier Stanley Baldwin and Foreign Secretary Sir Austen Chamberlain. Last week "Jix" apparently staked all on the chance of being able to produce documents sufficiently charged with social dynamite to excuse violation of Soviet diplomatic immunity.

JUNE 6 **RUSSIAN BREAK:** From the Government bench of the House of Commons last week, Premier Stanley Baldwin announced in even, measured tones that His Majesty's Government desired, with the approval of the House, to break off formal relations with Soviet Russia.

He revealed for the first time what had been discovered by Scotland Yard when its operatives raided Arcos House. The evidence cited by Premier Baldwin was released in a *White Book* bearing His Majesty's Arms, last week, and further imprinted with the title: *Documents Illustrating Hostile Activities of the Soviet Government and the Third International Against Great Britain.*

As a random example of what the *White Book* contains, observers noted a letter telling how down-and-out British subjects have been trained as Communist agitators while being given employment as sailors on Russian merchant ships. The Soviet agent in charge of this subversive activity told in early letters how "choice of the men was carefully made, preference being given to Negroes, Hindus and other oppressed nationals." In later correspondence these "oppressed nationals" were declared to have turned out to be "lazy swine, the refuse of the Labor Party, slackers and bad workers who drank or left the ships."

As a matter of course, the Conservative majority in the Commons put through a motion of confidence in Premier Baldwin's course by a count of 367 to 118. A few hours later diplomatic relations were formally severed; and the official Soviet diplomatic and trade representatives were given ten days in which to clear out of England. The Soviet *chargé d'affaires* ordered packing to start at once. [Relations were resumed by the Laborite government of Ramsay MacDonald which took office after the next general election in 1929.]

CROPPED: A French correspondent cabled on Derby Day one JUNE 13 of those small, revealing anecdotes of His Majesty George V which British newsgatherers have not the humor to appreciate.

His Majesty had strolled out to the paddock, and was regarding pensively a sleek little filly whose tail had been cropped short. A shadow of disapproval crossed the King's face as he inspected the *very* close-cropped tail.

"May I trust that Your Majesty is pleased?" quavered a groom, as the silence became oppressive.

"No," said the King slowly. "No. I do not like at all such

trimming of a horse's tail. I think it is very ugly." A still longer pause ensued. "In fact," concluded His Majesty, at last, "such a cropped tail reminds me of a woman with bobbed hair."

JUNE 27 **FABLES IN HISTORY:** The Director of Military Operations of the Imperial British General Staff was, from 1915 to 1918, Major General Sir Frederick Barton Maurice, who may certainly be assumed to know as much about the War as any man alive. Recently this great soldier and tactician picked up and read two fat volumes about the War by Chancellor of the Exchequer Winston Churchill (*The World Crisis 1916-1918*). As he read, Sir Frederick apparently began to experience a sense of scorn. Here were errors of fact, sloppiness, perversions of truth and everywhere the pink and soapy touch of superficiality. What to do?

Sir Frederick Maurice sat down and penned a long, calm, deadly review which was released last week in the July issue of that distinguished U.S. quarterly, *Foreign Affairs*. Excerpts:

"Mr. Churchill's misstatements of fact are so many and so grave that no historian will in future be able to accept any of his assertions about the War without the most careful checking of references.

"Almost the whole of an important paragraph in Mr. Churchill's description of the battle of the Marne is pure fable."

JULY 18 **POMP:** Half a million golden pounds ($2,433,000) were spent to provide, last week in London, a welcome for Ahmed Fuad I, King of Egypt. The rich standards of the Grenadier Guards dipped and swept the ground in salute. Soon the Household Cavalry moved off at a smart trot. Through a lane between applauding hands passed two sovereigns who have little in common except that they both collect stamps.

On to Buckingham Palace whirled the twice royal cavalcade. Portly Ahmed Fuad was soon shown into a suite in what is technically known as "Wing V." There the Egyptian Great Chamberlain marshalled Ahmed Fuad's numerous attendants—not the least of these being a chemist to test his food, a taster to sample it, and two of George V's physicians skilled in antidotes.

When the dinner was served, the Britannic lackeys were able to set before King Fuad a very fair example of his favorite *entrée,* tender, luscious little steaks of horse flesh.

MURDER IN DUBLIN: A lean, rather handsome young Irishman, his face prematurely stern and sad, set out last week from his home at Black Rock, near Dublin, to attend midday mass. Perhaps young Kevin O'Higgins was pondering some of his problems as Minister of Justice of the Irish Free State. At 34, he had climbed higher than most politicians are content to find themselves at 64. The noon sun poured down. A motor car, approaching at great speed, droned louder.

Brakes set with a long screech. Three men pointed black steel muzzles from their car at the lone pedestrian. Four bullets passed through Mr. O'Higgins' neck, one lodged in his chest, a sixth entered one ear and penetrated to the base of his brain. The motor car lurched, raced away.

Almost miraculously Mr. O'Higgins survived for some hours. "Forgive them all!" were his first, gasping words to those who came running at the crack of rifles. "Someone bring paper. I must make my will."

Beside him knelt an old friend, whose pencil took down nine words: "I leave everything to my wife and baby daughter." Although Mr. O'Higgins' strength was ebbing he was able to sign.

At the last he said: "There is no hope. They've got me just as they got my father. I die for my country. I go. . . ."

Kevin O'Higgins was one of those who formed the Provisional Government of the Irish Free State in 1921. "We were simply eight young men," he has said, "standing amid the ruins of one administration, with the foundations of another not yet laid, and with wild men screaming through the keyhole."

This statement did not exaggerate, and the task of taming Ireland's "wild men" fell to 28-year-old Kevin O'Higgins. At one time the new Free State had to employ an army of 40,000 men to put down that violence which had become second nature to Irishmen. Firmness was needed and Mr. O'Higgins proved himself capable of making bold decisions with the quickness of a steel trap. His enemies became innumerable. His success in quieting Ireland and restoring the police power earned him a title: "Ireland's Strongest Man."

By family connection Kevin O'Higgins stood rooted in the very fibre of the new State. His father, Dr. Thomas O'Higgins, a distinguished surgeon, was a man who simultaneously championed the highest nationalist aspirations of Irishmen and defied their tendency to base, rabble violence. The result was that a band of armed incendiaries murdered him in his own home on the night of Feb. 11, 1923. Blood and bone, Mr. O'Higgins stood for all that gives a man the right to say: "I die for my country."

AUG. 8 **SIR HARRY FLAYED:**

> *Oh, when I was twenty-one!*
> *When I was twenty-one!*
> *I never had lots o' money,*
> *But I always had lots of fun!*

The words rollick. The little Scot prances and taps them out with his cane as he sings. The Puckish smile of Sir Harry Lauder becomes as irresistible as the merry light in his grey eyes. Soon one more audience has succumbed to Scottish magic and is lilting the chorus joyously:

King Fuad of Egypt has a private taster to test his steaks of horse flesh.

Sir Harry Lauder is "a Scotchman we would send to an asylum!" Page 94.

Oh, I was a har-r-rum scar-r-rum!
And my courtin' days begun
On the ver-r-ra, ver-r-ra, ver-r-ra NIGHT!
When I was twenty-one. . . .

Could any man who has joined with Sir Harry Lauder in such a chorus shake off the spell sufficiently to speak ill of him? In Edinburgh last week at a meeting of the Town Council, Mr. Councilman Gilzean struck the table a blow with his doubled fist and shouted:

"I say that no man has done more to bring Scotch songs into contempt than Harry Lauder!"

The Council has been debating whether to confer "The Freedom of the City" on Sir Harry, and had heard several councilmen wax unctuous over his morale work during the World War. Mr. Gilzean roundly said that Sir Harry Lauder has not only debased and vulgarized the songs of his country; but that "he portrays a type of Scotchman not found in the heavens above, on the earth beneath, or in waters under the earth." Waxing emphatic, Councilman Gilzean cried: "If that type of Scotchman ever went about Scotland in the flesh, we would pack him off to an asylum!"

INADEQUATE ABBEY: Last week the Cathedrals Commission suggested that Westminster Abbey be enlarged to make more room for Britain's illustrious dead—an entirely anticipatory proposal. George Bernard Shaw, master of brilliant self-publicity, commented: "I am still alive; I am not ready for it." NOV 14

NEW SUBJECT: Last week a sleek, brilliant citizen of the U.S. became a subject of His Britannic Majesty King George V. He is Thomas Stearns Eliot, relative of the late Charles William Eliot, President Emeritus of Harvard University. Poet and critic, he is the author of *The Waste Land,* a poem which won the *Dial* prize for 1922, and *The Sacred Wood,* a volume of critical works.

Mr. Eliot, now 39, was born in St. Louis. His education was wrought at Harvard, the Sorbonne, the Harvard Graduate School, Merton College, Oxford. Today he is editor of *The Criterion,* a quarterly of pronounced modernist tendencies.

His many adverse critics, in no wise surprised by his change of nationality, hint that a certain superciliousness in his attitude toward U.S. letters caused him to feel more at home in England, where neo-literary figures abound.

International

MARCH 7 **DESTRUCTION:** Along the Germano-Polish frontier heavy earth charges of dynamite sent clods, cement and steel hurtling.

Polish frontier guards could not conceal their satisfaction —nor Germans their discomfiture. The hurtling fragments meant that the Germans were carrying out their promise to the Allied Council of Ambassadors of the League of Nations that they would destroy the German fortifications against Poland, Germany having entered the League of Nations in 1926.

MARCH 21 **MADAME:** Among events crowding a busy seven days at Geneva, following the first opening of the Council of the League of Nations in German, was the Annual report of the League of Nations "white slavery" Committee which revealed that the Panama Canal Zone is now one of the chief headquarters of this international traffic. Portugal was stigmatized because the Portuguese law still allows girls as young as 14 years to be registered and licensed. The Mediterranean lands are declared the chief source of "white slaves," and Latin America is the principal consumer region.

During the reading of the Committee's report a member of the French delegation rose to protest the Committee's translation of *tenancière* into English as "madame." *Tenancière,* he protested, meant a woman who kept disorderly premises; and *madame* is the ordinary title of married Frenchwomen. *Tiens!* Did the Committee propose to slander at one stroke all the honest wives of France?

Soon indulgent Anglo-Saxons explained that in this special connection "madame" has become *de facto* an English word, and that the Committee knew of no other sufficiently polite English word to express its meaning.

VITAL PROTOCOL: Whenever the League of Nations holds an APRIL 25 important international conference, the U.S. and Soviet Russia are invited to send "observers," and, while the U.S. usually accepts, the Soviet Government has steadfastly refused, these past four years.

The reason is that during the Lausanne Conference of 1923 (at Lausanne, Switzerland) the Russian representative, M. Vaslav Vorovsky, was assassinated. His alleged assassin was acquitted by a Swiss Court. For four years the Swiss Government has refused the kind of apology demanded by the Soviet Government. Ergo, no Soviet "observers" have come to League Conferences.

For four years earnest attempts have been made to relieve the stress of this situation, a stress inimical to the peace of the world. The Swiss have offered to sign a note apologizing "sincerely." The Russians have held out for "emphatically."

In Moscow, last week, "emphatically" was inserted in a Russo-Swiss protocol resuming diplomatic relations between these countries. [Russia joined the League in 1934.]

STRAWBERRIES: A dish of strawberries was the reputed agen- JUNE 27 cy which brought to an abrupt close, last week, the 45th session of the Council of the League of Nations at Geneva.

The strawberries were eaten by Foreign Minister Aristide Briand of France. As everyone knows some strawberries have a pollen which can produce on certain pollen-sensitive persons an irritating rash. Soon such a rash broke out upon M. Briand. Impetuous, he scratched. The rash spread, attacked the patient's eyelids, caused them to swell, to close one eye, nearly to close the other.

Finally the afflicted French Foreign Minister retired to his bed with a compress over both eyes. Into his bedroom came, daily, for conference, Foreign Minister Gustav Stresemann of Germany and Foreign Secretary Sir Austen Chamberlain of Britain. These "Big Three," putting their heads together, and occasionally calling in lesser statesmen for political consultation, virtually made up, last week, the Council of the League of Nations.

M. Briand, sitting up in bed, reputedly told Dr. Stresemann with great vehemence that France will not hasten her evacuation of the Rhineland until Germany carries out more fully her disarmament obligations. Dr. Stresemann offered to produce photographs showing the destruction of German fortifications along the Polish frontier; but returned an evasive answer when M. Briand insisted that a French military commission be allowed to investigate the destroyed defenses in question.

Later in the day, M. Briand's "strawberry rash" became so severe that he hastily returned to Paris for expert treatment. The Council then dispersed.

JULY 4 **EGGSHELL DEBATE:** An atmosphere tense with Anglo-U.S. suspicion and discord characterized the sessions at Geneva last week of the Naval Limitations Parley, nicknamed by the Swiss *"La Conference Coolidge."*

A major Anglo-U.S. point of contention last week was whether, if the British proposal to limit cruiser guns to a six-inch bore were adopted, the British could transform their fast merchant fleet overnight into a cruiser fleet by mounting these guns on the *Mauretania, Majestic, Berengaria, Olympic,* etc.

"Why those ships are only big eggshells!" scoffed British Vice-Admiral Sir Frederick Field to correspondents. He continued: "They would be a big target, with guns inconveniently placed and with no fire controls, and which any cruiser would quickly put out of business."

The correspondents hurried over to ask U.S. Admiral Hilary P. Jones about this.

"Eggshell, eh?" he snorted. "Well, give me their *Majestic* with 30 six-inch guns aboard and I guarantee to sink any 7,500-ton cruiser ever launched."

Thereafter, last week the correspondents hounded both admirals with questions about ships and eggshells, and drew from them practically infinite variations on this safe, discussible, amusing topic. Admiral Jones outdid his rival by declaring explosively, "Why the plates on some destroyers are so thin you could almost poke a finger through 'em!"

UGLY CHARGE: Although crimination and recrimination moved hot and quick last week, between U.S. and British delegates, via the press, no charge made was uglier than this: that the British Admiralty systematically lists its war boats at about five-sixths of their real tonnage, according to U.S. measurements.

Correspondents drew from a member of the U.S. delegation, who withheld his name, the statement that when Edward of Wales, and later the Duke of York passed through the Panama Canal on British warships, careful computations of the water displaced proved their ships to be nearly 12% overweight.

PUNGENT NOTES: U.S. and British delegates to the Naval JULY 18 Limitations Parley at Geneva struck last week increasingly pungent keynotes. Viscount Cecil of Chelwood, Secondary British Delegate, 1924 recipient of the Woodrow Wilson Peace Award, tireless champion of the League of Nations:

"America does not fear us; America knows there is no possibility of war with Great Britain—then why does Washington insist on limiting our navy below the strength the Admiralty states we require?"

Ambassador Hugh Gibson, dapperly dressed, is young but formidable.   *Marshal Pilsudski of Poland shouts: "Is it peace, or war?" Page 100.*

Commented Mr. Hugh Gibson, Chief U.S. Delegate and U.S. Ambassador to Belgium, to newsgatherers:

"While we are asked to trust Great Britain's purity of intention whatever her demands, it does not seem to work the same way when we make a few ourselves. There is no such thing as absolute needs. If needs were absolute then there would have been no need for a conference. So far in this conference, aside from what we consider minor details, Great Britain has not offered to give up one single thing. The 7,500-ton cruisers we are asked to take would give us a woolly-lamb fleet, a kitten fleet."

Because Hugh Gibson is a dapperly-dressed, middling-sized man of only 43, and thus "the youngest U.S. Ambassador," his appearance at Geneva as U.S. Chief Delegate was at first regarded in Europe as one of U.S. President Coolidge's solemn little pleasantries.

Gradually, as the Parley got under way, the metal of Hugh Gibson began to be manifest. No "young" diplomat ever faced more formidable opponents, among them Lord Cecil who is accounted one of the very ablest and most persuasive negotiators in Europe.

AUG. 15 **CHERRIES & PEACHES:** There was a total breakdown in Geneva last week of the U.S.-British-Japanese Naval Limitations Parley. In order to claim that their plan was really the more economical, the British stated the obvious fact that a small ship costs less than a large one, and then pointed out that their plan called for many ships individually smaller than those proposed by the U.S. delegation. Thus the British said in effect: "We want cherries and you want peaches. A cherry costs less than a peach, and therefore our plan is the cheaper."

The British carefully ignored the fact that they were asking for so very many more "cherries" (small ships) than the U.S. with its "peaches" (large ships) that the total cost of the British plan was much the greater.

Nearly all observers agreed in thinking that the U.S. public has been jolted by the Parley in two of its long-cherished beliefs: 1) that the U.S. is approximately equal in naval strength to Britain (whereas the airing of statistics at Geneva has proved Britain's long lead); 2) the belief that even if the U.S. chooses to remain weak in naval strength, Great Britain will not take advantage of this chance to make reductions herself.

Unquestionably, the ill-will generated at Geneva during the last six weeks has made Britain seem far more the "enemy" in U.S. eyes than at any time within the present century.

BRIAND'S "MIRACLE": From Warsaw straight to the Hotel DEC. 19 des Bergues in Geneva came, last week, Polish Dictator Marshal Josef Pilsudski. At the Hotel astute Aristide Briand greeted Pilsudski with a neat reference to the days when they were fellow radicals. "My old friend," he said, "we see now how useful it is to be a Socialist. Here you are Premier, Marshal and Dictator of your country, while I hold the record for the number of times [ten] I have been Premier of mine." Seemingly the Marshal (a Socialist turned Autocrat) minded not this sally.

After luncheon—at which the Dictator wore both his sword and spurs—both statesmen settled quietly to the business which had brought Marshal Pilsudski to Geneva; the Polish-Lithuanian frontier crisis.

The next day the session began with Pilsudski and Lithuanian Prime Minister Augustine Valdemaras bristling silently at one another across the Council's horse-shoe table, while the proposed details of settlement were droningly read. Suddenly Pilsudski interrupted in a hoarse voice: "Gentlemen, I have not heard the word peace mentioned. I came here to hear that word. If I do not hear it, I will return to a place where the word war may be heard."

When an instant of astonished silence had ensued, the Marshal stamped to his feet, flung a blazing glance about him, and shouted: "I AM GOING!" Amid confusion, cries, expostulations, Pilsudski was persuaded back into his seat. Then, leaning forward, he suddenly shot out a long pointing arm and finger at M. Valdemaras. "I have a definite question to put to the honorable representative of Lithuania," he rasped, then shouted: "IS IT PEACE, OR WAR?"

Bewildered, M. Valdemaras managed to reply: "If he really means that he wants peace, I will say 'peace.'"

"That is not enough!" cried Pilsudski and furious recriminations burst between the two Dictators each excitedly shouting snatches of French mixed with Polish or Lithuanian. It was, of course, M. Aristide Briand who eased between them, speaking as a father to naughty children. "You both mean the same thing!" he said. "You have got to stop. You both love each other. It is absolutely necessary."

Both dictators subsided. Within twelve hours the technical "state of war" along the Lithuano-Polish frontier, which has existed since 1920 (when the Poles seized the Lithuanian city of Vilna which they still hold), was declared terminated by a resolution of the Council of the League of Nations—both Lithuania and Poland concurring.

Belgium

JAN. 31   **EMPRESS' FUNERAL:** Over a thousand Belgians braved a raging blizzard in Brussels last week, trudged on foot four miles behind a coffin draped with the flags of Mexico and Belgium. Thus they paid homage to a lady great in sadness, Marie Charlotte Amélie Augustine Victoire Clémentine Leopoldine, daughter of the late King Leopold I of the Belgians, once Empress of Mexico.

Her story: At 17 she was the radiant bride of the Archduke Maximilian whose brother was Emperor Franz Josef of Austria-Hungary; at 23 Empress of Mexico, set beside Maximilian upon that throne by the Emperor Napoleon III of the French; at 26 a distracted woman, kneeling before Napoleon III, begging him to deliver her husband from the revolted Mexicans, crying when Napoleon III declared he could do no more: "My Fate is what I deserve! A granddaughter of Louis Philippe should never have trusted herself to a Bonaparte!"

Thereupon she fainted, and, when she recovered was found to have lost her reason so that she did not know her husband was murdered a year later (1867). Mercifully, through the 60 years of her madness (up to her death at 86, last week) she was always expecting the Emperor Maximilian to return to her, would sometimes don court regalia in expectation of his coming, and say, "He will come soon. He will come very soon now."

Lady of sadness, Death came to her in a white wintry robe. Eight young officers bore her coffin to the royal crypt in the Laeken Château, near Brussels. Albert, King of the Belgians, and the Royal Family paced behind it slowly to the sad measures of Chopin.

OCT. 24   **A MOTHER:** It was 8 a.m. in Brussels. The debauchees of the previous night were asleep. The famed fountains exuded sparkling water in the sunlight as passers-by bought their morning newspapers and hurried to their *café au lait* at nearby restaurants. There was a faint bustle in the air as the capital began to get into its business stride.

Suddenly a great *boom* disturbed the comparative quiet—the sound of artillery fire. *Boom!* Coffee cups stopped halfway to open mouths. *Boom!* Newspapers fell to the breakfast table. *Boom! Boom! Boom!* Inert bodies squirmed between the sheets. *Boom! Boom! Boom!* Alert businessmen and women resigned themselves to a long count—they hoped it would be a very long count. *Boom! Boom! Boom!* Twenty-one blank shots were fired. Ears strained for the next. The pause grew longer and longer, but the next boom never came.

Then all Brussels knew that a baby daughter had been born to Crown Princess Astrid, wife of Crown Prince Leopold of Belgium, to whom she was married last year. Had 101 booms startled the city, it would have signified the birth of an heir presumptive to the throne of the Belgians.

"Ah, well," muttered the Belgians with an expressive Latin shrug, "the next will be a boy." [The next child was a boy—Prince Baudouin, who was born in 1930 and became King of Belgium in 1951 after the abdication of his father, King Leopold III.]

Bulgaria

BOMB, OLD STYLE: In the realm of Little Tsar Boris III, who MARCH 21 sometimes finds poison in his dessert, assassins still throw bombs with long sputtering fuses in the good old way. The bombee, if an experienced official, has at least a sporting chance of snuffing out the fuse before explosion happens. Therefore, last week, when a bomb hurtled past Chief of the Secret Police Ikonomoff as he was entering his house at Sofia and rolled ahead of him down the dark hall, the worst was not necessarily to be feared.

Experienced, adept, Chief Ikonomoff did not flee out into the street, but sought to protect his household by darting forward to extinguish the bomb.

Unfortunately, Chief of the Secret Police Ikonomoff was not able to find the bomb for which he searched. The black iron sphere became a white cloud of gas which pushed out the walls of the Chief's house and drove iron splinters through him. Mercifully he died an almost instantaneous death.

China

The Chinese Nationalist Movement, under its leader Chiang Kai-shek, had by 1927 become the dominant force in a country where local warlords still operated in most areas. Chiang's stronghold was Canton in the south, and from there he launched in 1927 a massive military campaign that yielded a great deal of China to the Nationalists, along with such major cities as Hankow, Shanghai and Nanking. One result of China's growing nationalism was a mounting resentment of outsiders.

JAN. 17 **INCIDENT AT HANKOW:** Chinese outnumber foreigners in China more than a thousand to one. Yet in China the yellow men have hewn the white man's wood, drawn his water and emptied out his slops. Only recently have Chinese begun collectively to realize that they need do these chores only as long as they wish.

The Chinese Nationalist movement has surged up from Canton across half China and last week at Hankow this new and surprising thought flared up in a chattering mob of Chinamen.

The mob advanced toward the British quarter. A year and a half ago a similar mob was fired on and dispersed for doing the same at Shanghai. But then the Canton Nationalists were impotent. Today they hold half of China. Therefore the British marines who stood with fixed bayonets to guard the British quarter received the command: "Under *no* circumstances fire."

The mob advanced, gibbering, flinging stones. The marines used their rifle butts as clubs, cracked a few crowns, but gently. For four hours the game of bluff and bruises continued. Once 20 coolies, armed only with sticks, bore a British marine to the ground, tore his rifle from him, plunged the bayonet into his heart. Still no shot was fired. Then, suddenly, a troop of Chinese soldiers from the Nationalist stronghold across the river arrived and dispersed the mob with a few shots. The commander blandly explained to the British that he had been delayed.

No fool, the British Consul knew that he lied. The riot was a Nationalist warning.

Two days later a larger mob stormed the barricades of the British concession, screaming: "Down with British Imperialism! Kill the Britishmen!"

This time too many Chinamen were pouring over the barricades. Lest the mere presence of the marines provoke bloodshed they were withdrawn to British warships in the harbor. Lest the Union Jack incite to violence the British Consul hauled it down. A page of history turned. The gunboats could have raked Hankow, the marines could have shot down the mob—but an idea spiked the guns. John Chinaman, slop emptier, had bluffed the white man.

ON SHOOTING CUSTOMERS: At Washington, U.S. President FEB. 14 Coolidge and Secretary of the Navy Wilbur prepared stealthily to deal with the Chinese. Lest it be thought that the U.S. was rushing too many armed forces to China, they caused the transport *Chaumont* to sail from San Diego, Calif., loaded to the scuppers with U.S. marines last week, but announced that she was merely sailing for "a secret destination in the Orient."

British statesmen, not so subtle, baldly admitted that 12,000 British troops were being rushed to China last week—whereby Nationalist Foreign Minister Eugene Chen promptly broke off negotiations concerning the safety of Britons and their property in China; and took the unprecedented and insulting course of ignoring the British Government and cabling over its head an appeal to the British Labor Party. Chen declared that "the British decline in Far Asia" will continue "until British Labor is entrusted by England with the task of substituting the statesmanship of peace and productive work for the Tory statesmanship of imperialism, war and Byzantine glory."

Though the British Government could, of course, take no official notice of Chen's deliberate insult, an explosive retort was made *ex officio* by Chancellor Winston S. Churchill of the British Exchequer. "All we want to do in China is trade with China," said Churchill. "We regard the 400,000,000 of Chinese as potential friends and customers. Almost the last thing you usually do with a potential customer is to shoot him. The last thing to wish is that the potential customer should shoot you."

NANKING: The strategic railway running northward from Shanghai was cut last week when the Nationalists captured Nanking, a 2,000-year-old walled city of 400,000 inhabitants which was the capital of China five centuries ago. The effect of cutting the railway at Nanking was to bottle up the defeated Shantungese troops who were trying to escape northward, leaving them at the mercy of their Nationalist conquerors. Marked disorder and looting broke out. Soon insurgents had broken into the U.S., British and Japanese consulates, robbed, glutted.

Several women servants at the Japanese consulate were stripped and subjected to carnal violence. The Japanese consul, who was sick in bed, barely managed to escape with his life, saved nothing but a portrait of his Emperor, the sublime Son of Heaven.

The U.S. consul, his wife and their children hastily set out with other refugees for an eminence known to ancient Chinese poets as The Purple Mountain and to moderns as Socony Hill (for the oil company with heaviest U.S. investments in China). Arrangements had already been made that U.S. and British warships in the harbor would lay a barrage to protect this valuable property—the signal for the barrage to be a rocket.

U.S. Consul John Ker Davis, eleven U.S. marines and 24 refugees barely managed to gain Socony Hill, under a running fire from Chinese snipers. One marine was wounded, but was able to walk, continuing to return the Chinese fire. At Socony Hall, Mrs. Davis, the other women refugees and the children crowded into a spacious bathroom, lay down on the floor. The children, unconcerned, counted the bullets pinging into Socony Hall.

Consul Davis parleyed with the Chinese attackers, buying them off from hour to hour, until those at Socony Hall had no more money. Then said a Chinese: "We don't want money, anyway, we want to kill."

Davis shouted: "Men, get your guns! Guard the women! Send up a rocket!"

Soon U.S. and British shells began to whine over Socony Hall. Subsequently a U.S. landing party took off the refugees from Socony Hall, and it was later announced that all U.S. citizens at Nanking had been accounted for.

The Rev. John E. Williams, Vice Chancellor of Nanking University, was the sole U.S. citizen killed, last week, in China. An earnest and simple Christian, he was held in affectionate esteem by thousands of Chinese.

How Dr. Williams met his death was told by an eye-witness, Dr. A. J. Bowen, Chancellor of Nanking University. He said: "I was crossing the campus with our university librarian when we noticed what we thought to be Northern troops looting and burning the home of Dr. Daniels, also a faculty member.

"We walked toward the Daniels home, when we were accosted by seven or eight soldiers wearing the uniforms of the Southern (Nationalist) army. The soldiers stopped us and demanded our valuables, which we handed over. Dr. Williams, who spoke the language like a native, then stepped up and protested at the action. The soldier immediately shot Dr. Williams through the temple, killing him instantly, after which he robbed him, taking everything of value, even stripping the clothing from his body.

"After finishing robbing us and murdering Dr. Williams, the troops walked off unconcernedly, chatting with each other as though they had shot only a pig or a dog."

CONQUEROR: At precisely two o'clock, one afternoon last week, a long grim cavalcade of motor cars entered Shanghai from the South. Armed men, a hundred strong, rode in these automobiles—modern equivalents of a bodyguard of cavalry. A slim but unmistakably commanding Southern Chinese, clad in a uniform entirely unadorned, rode in the third motor car. This was the great Conqueror of half China, the Nationalist War Lord Chiang Kai-shek.

Thoroughly modern, businesslike, Chiang Kai-shek had ready a short typed statement for the press: "Right must triumph. The Powers cannot keep China suppressed no matter how many warships and soldiers they send here. We will use the economic boycott against any nation which still desires to keep intact the treaties which have oppressed China in the past and validated the foreign concessions. The Chinese people are unable to feel contented so long as the present situation obtains."

These statements, firm, clear, dispassionate, were little more than a notation of the fact that China has been fired by the Nationalist program, "China for the Chinese," to a pitch seriously menacing the long supremacy in Chinese affairs of the Great Powers.

Life came to Chiang Kai-shek 39 years ago in a tiny village in Chekiang Province. He ran away from being apprenticed to a merchant and embraced the career of arms, winning a scholarship at the Military Academy of Yuan Shih-kai, in far-Northern Chili. Later, he was sent by the Manchu Government to study at the Imperial Japanese Military College, Tokyo (1906).

When the Chinese Revolution burst (1911) he, a stripling of 23, was given command of a brigade by the Revolutionary party at Shanghai, and for two years he took advantage of his new position to live a life of drinking, gaming and debauch. Suddenly he abandoned these practices.

With the zeal typical of a converted sinner Chiang threw himself into active fighting in the cause of the great Dr. Sun Yat-sen, late "Father of the Chinese Republic." Dr. Sun was at this time experiencing reverses, having been driven from Canton, his capital, by his own War Minister. Soon Chiang Kai-shek with 10,000 men had materially assisted in driving the traitor War Minister out of Canton, and back to his walled stronghold Waichow, a city deemed impregnable.

The question was, how to capture Waichow. Dr. Sun's generals declared the task impossible. Chiang Kai-shek asked to be admitted to lay his plan before the great Dr. Sun.

Sun was an old man then. He may have already decided that Chiang should be the sun to rise out of his own setting. When the young general entered, Dr. Sun rose dramatically to his feet, scanned carefully the face of Chiang Kai-shek and exclaimed: "Ah! Here is the second Sun Yat-sen. He shall one day take my place! Explain your project, Oh young and rising Sun."

Chiang Kai-shek explained his plan. It depended on his ability to fire his 10,000 soldiers with sufficient enthusiasm to follow him in a direct frontal attack on the walled city of Waichow during which they would nearly all most certainly be killed.

Chiang led the attack. Nine thousand one hundred of his ten thousand men were killed; but he captured Waichow. Strangely he did not lose but rather gained prestige after this prodigious butchery of his own troops, for he had himself fought in the thick of it.

The reformed sinner, now a mighty hero, retired after his victory to a Buddhist temple for three months, a vacation period of meditation which he has several times since repeated. The year 1922 found him in Moscow, acting as military liaison officer for Dr. Sun, who had despaired by then of receiving aid from any other Great Power for his project of conquering China in the name of Nationalism.

When Sun died (1925), Chiang Kai-shek became the outstanding Nationalist leader, though still little known in the Occident. Withal, though he is careful to wear no distinguishing mark on his uniform, Chiang is a conqueror of dominating mien, not a comradely Bolshevik back-slapper. He has publicly disavowed Bolshevism; and he is much more dangerous to the Great Powers than if he were a Bolshevik. His purpose is to accomplish, by *any* means (including Bolshevism where prudent) all that is implied by the threadbare but kindling phrase "China for the Chinese."

HEROES: To delighted correspondents at Shanghai, Lieutenant Commander Roy Campbell Smith, U.S.N., told last week APRIL 11 with infectious gusto how, as Commander of the destroyer *Noa,* he had ordered the bombardment of Nanking in order to save the lives of the U.S. Consul and other U.S. citizens besieged in the city.

The spectre of Commodore Dewey, and his ringing command, "You may fire when you are ready, Gridley!" kindled in the correspondents' imagination as their pencils raced to take down the words of Lieutenant Commander Smith:

"Well now, when I saw the Consul's rocket [page 105], I said to myself: 'Here's where I get either a medal or a court martial.' So I leaned over the rail and said, 'Let 'er go, Benny!'"

It was ascertained that "Benny" is Lieutenant Benjamin F. Staud of Pittsburgh, who pulled the lanyard firing the first U.S. gun to send a shell spinning over Nanking. Commodore Dewey's "Gridley" was Charles Vernon Gridley of Logansport, Ind. Proud U.S. citizens balanced and weighed upon their tongues "Benny" v. "Gridley"; and "Gridley" v. "Benny." Each seemed unforgettable.

DISGRACE: While U.S. and British guns were thundering at Nanking, Lieut. K. Araki of the Imperial Japanese Navy went ostentatiously unarmed into Nanking with a small detachment of Japanese sailors, likewise unarmed, in an effort to rescue the Japanese Consul in which he was successful.

Last week Lieutenant Araki reached Shanghai and reported to his Rear Admiral. Then he went to his cabin on the Japanese flagship, took pen and paper, wrote: "In order to insure the safety of Japanese residents at Nanking, I endured, from the Chinese, insults which no Japanese can tolerate. The lives of the Japanese refugees could be saved, but I am ashamed that the honor of the Japanese navy has been disgraced in my person."

Soon Lieutenant Araki composed himself for a night's sleep. At dawn, as the bugle blew for hoisting the Japanese ensign, he arose, mounted the bridge, faced the sun, as it rose over Japan, and shot himself.

APRIL 25 **COUNTER-REVOLUTION:** The Nationalist Generalissimo, Chiang Kai-shek, suddenly called a meeting of conservative Nationalists at Nanking. They voted to impeach the whole Nationalist Cabinet at Hankow on the ground that it is "Red," sparing only Foreign Minister Chen. Him they dubbed "misguided but loyal to Nationalism."

This keen blow by Chiang Kai-shek lopped off the Communist faction of Chinese Nationalism which has fattened at Hankow on Russian support. Thus did Chiang Kai-shek become *de facto* Nationalist Dictator and a proven foe of Communism.

CHIANG RESIGNS: "The Conqueror" Chiang Kai-shek returned AUG. 22 last week, abased and fallen, to his home and birthplace, the little village of Fenghwa, 100 miles south of Shanghai. He came in the dense blackness between midnight and dawn—for in China one who has "lost face" does well to hide his features. A faithful secretary would say only: "General Chiang Kai-shek is with his family here and is going into retirement indefinitely, seeking rest following a year of superhuman efforts to further the nationalist cause."

Addressing himself to "The Chinese People" General Chiang reviewed the initial brilliant success of the nationalist movement and its present heartbreaking disintegration. "Our revolution got into difficulties because of communism," declared General Chiang, and then mourned that his own ruthless anti-communist activities had been interpreted by many Nationalists as aggrandizement so that "My nationalist comrades subsequently in almost all cases lost confidence in me." Chiang Kai-shek went on to claim that the Nationalists have now been purged of Communism largely through his own efforts; but concluded that so much bitterness existed among nationalists against him personally that "I am willing to sacrifice my own position in order to see the revolution succeed."

While these high principled statements probably came honestly the immediate cause of his resignation last week was simply the recent series of defeats which his armies have suffered in their attempt to take Peking.

CHIANG'S MARRIAGE: Two thousand pompously arrayed DEC. 12 Chinese witnessed the marriage, in Shanghai last week, of the defeated but honorably esteemed Marshal Chiang Kai-shek.

Chiang loomed last week as the most matrimonially romantic of modern Chinese conquerors, because he has openly persisted in wooing a lady known to have refused him at first. In China such a refusal causes the suitor to "lose face," a disgrace so abysmal that many Chinese have committed suicide rather than endure it. Usually this contingency is circumvented by having the proposal of marriage conveyed through intermediaries; but Chiang Kai-shek has been obliged to risk his "face" because his fiancée was that intensely Westernized "modern woman," Miss Soong Mei-ling, Wellesley, '15.

Like her brother, T. V. Soong, Harvard '15, she has been closely identified with the Hankow Nationalist Government in which he was Finance Minister. In person she is charming, in mentality alert, in speech sometimes caustic. Observers, knowing her passionate Nationalist zeal, wondered if she married Chiang Kai-shek, last week, with intent to rouse him from retirement to renewed leadership of a Nationalist military force. [Competing Nationalist factions soon felt the need of Chiang's leadership, and in 1928 he returned to capture Peking and resume his campaign of uniting China.]

France

JUNE 27 **DAUDET JAILED:** There is a kind of human happening, ridiculous and yet sublime, which occurs in France alone. Of this sort was the taking into custody last week by some 3,000 police, soldiers and firemen, of famed Royalist editor Léon Daudet, who had barricaded himself in his office to resist arrest and was guarded by 980 stalwart young Royalists armed with canes.

The hour was 7 a.m. As the Prefect of the Paris police, M. Jean Chiappe, marshaled his forces, *tout Paris* knew that Premier Raymond Poincaré and his Cabinet had been up most of the night trying to decide whether they would permit the forcible arrest of M. Daudet. After all, his crime was only "defamation."

And whom had he defamed? Only those who said that his son, Philippe Daudet, had committed suicide. What was the harm? What if Editor Léon Daudet *had* printed defamatory statements in his news organ, *L'Action Française*, to the effect that "my Philippe, my little Philippe was *assassinated* by the police!" Should a loving father be jailed for defending the name of his dead son?

Almost every newspaper in Paris answered *"Non!"* The President of the Republic was hourly besieged by telephone, telegraph, letter and *pneumatique* (messages shot through Paris by pneumatic tubes) to pardon M. Daudet. What to do? At last the Cabinet decided that Editor Daudet simply *could not* be allowed to succeed in resisting arrest. Therefore M. le Préfect Jean Chiappe was summoned, just before dawn, and instructed to accomplish the arrest of Léon Daudet—without bloodshed.

A task so formidable demanded formal garments. At 7 a.m., then, Préfect Chiappe took up a stance before the office of *L'Action Française* impeccably attired in a trim cutaway, wearing a monocle, a tall sleek hat, carrying a cane. Behind him were ranged four fire engines, three extensible scaling ladders, a quadruple rank of Municipal Guards, police seemingly innumerable and two squadrons of the Guard Republican mounted on prancing horses.

Very modestly M. le Préfect Jean Chiappe advanced and rapped with his gold signet ring on the door of *L'Action Française*. "I want to see M. Daudet," he said.

Replied the door-guardian: "Wait but one moment. Our leader will speak with you publicly from the balcony."

Amiable, M. Chiappe retired a few steps, waited until portly, but dynamic Léon Daudet bustled forth upon his balcony.

Then, quoth "Romeo" Chiappe to "Juliette" Daudet, in a clear, loud voice: "M. Daudet! I speak to you as to a man and a Frenchman. You do not wish bloodshed and I think you know as well as I do that in the mood of your followers there will be bloodshed. Give yourself up. The blood which you may cause to flow will not bring back that of the boy for whom you mourn."

On the balcony, M. Daudet raised his hand with a gesture spacious and commanding. "M. le Préfect," he cried in a strong resonant voice, "though you are charged with performing an inhuman act you have spoken humane words. I do not wish that blood should be shed by my fault. I do not wish that civil war should break out in our country. I surrender for the sake of France. I surrender for the memory of my boy, knowing full well that the men who are behind me could create bloodshed and trouble. I do not wish that others should feel the grief I have known. I surrender to the cry of *Vive la France.*"

Soon, one by one, the 980 Royalist youths who had stood ready to defend Editor Daudet filed out, were allowed to go unarrested. M. Daudet himself rode away with Préfect Chiappe in a limousine. They went first to Editor Daudet's house, picked up his wife, then motored to the Prison Santé. There Mme. Daudet made arrangements to have her husband supplied with his favorite viands from a neighboring restaurant; and brought him, later in the day, a set of Greek and Latin classics with which he proposes to amuse himself during his five months' jail term.

JULY 4 **"VIVE L'AUDACE!"**: The inimitable, irrepressible, M. Léon Daudet, editor of the Parisian Royalist newspaper *L'Action Française,* escaped last week from the Prison Santé. It was a group of keen-witted, although sometimes foppishly clad, Royalists who filched M. Daudet deftly out of jail and spirited him into hiding.

Their plan was simple, shrewd. At noontime, while Minister of Interior Albert Sarraut was lunching, a young Royalist entered a telephone booth in the Ministry of Interior. He called the Prison Santé, asked for its Director, M. Catry, and mimicking the voice of an assistant of Minister Sarraut, ordered that M. Léon Daudet and two other prisoners should be instantly released from jail.

Director Catry, no fool, suspected trickery. After hanging up he waited a few moments, then called the Ministry of Interior. Meanwhile several dozen other Royalists had called all the Ministry's telephones except that in the booth. Therefore the call of Director Catry was switched to the only phone that was not in use, that at which stood the mimicker, who, for a second time, ordered M. Daudet's release, rebuked M. Catry.

He, no longer suspicious, went to Editor Daudet's cell and released him. M. Daudet burst into tears, kissed M. le Directeur Catry, and rushed out into the street to mount a taxi. Even the taxi driver was a royalist in disguise.

Not until two hours later did Paris learn the news. Even dyspeptics chuckled, and men of spirit openly roared at one another over café tables: *"Vive Daudet! Vive l'Audace!"*

JULY 18 **DAUDET AFTERMATH:** A Parisian telephone operator had just been put in jail. And how, then, could she perform her duty to the babe which had nestled at her breast a few hours before? In jail! And what was to become of her four elder children, none as yet in their teens? In jail! And why was Mme. Montard in jail?

Members of the Chamber of Deputies were loud in shouting, last week, that no sufficient reason existed. Mme. Montard had simply chanced to be employed as local switchboard operator for the Royalist newspaper *L'Action Française* when its staff decided to get their editor, M. Léon Daudet, out of prison by mimicking the voice of a high official and ordering his release. Mme. Montard, by handling these hoax calls, became, in the eyes of the police, a conspirator. She was arrested, led into the grey depths of *La Prison Santé*.

Soon epithets rang and adjectives cooed, as MM. les Deputés expounded their grand theme: The Sanctity of Motherhood. By tens, and finally by hundreds, the Deputies demanded that the Government order Mme. Montard released.

Royalist Léon Daudet's Great Escape almost topples the government.

Premier Poincaré, shaken by a hoax, is magnanimous, chagrined.

Premier Raymond Poincaré, great War President of France, faced an extremely trying dilemma. Obviously the woman could not be kept in jail; but the Cabinet had lost much of its prestige when M. Daudet escaped, and to back down tamely now would be to lose still more "face." Therefore the Premier stood adamant when a motion of censure against the Government was introduced. If the Chamber wanted to unseat him—so be it! But MM. les Deputés quickly came to their senses, supported the Cabinet, 351 to 110. Soon the

Government, magnanimous, prudent, ordered Mme. Montard released.

Meanwhile the police, to their intense chagrin, continued powerless to find the secret hiding place of M. Daudet who contributed daily an impudent, secretly written article to *L'Action Française,* reviling and ridiculing the Cabinet.

DEC. 5 **32,000 BARS:** "How m'ny bars you shink there are in Paris?" is a question which numerous U.S. tourists have often asked each other tearfully toward dawn. Last week the Temperance League of France answered this by no means foolish question with crisp statistics. For every 75 inhabitants of Paris there is a retailer of alcoholics—in all 32,000, counting cafés, bars, brasseries, cabarets, and *boîtes de nuit* ("night boxes"). Throughout France more than 500,000 such establishments exist, one for every 81 French persons.

Germany

JAN. 10 **GUILT VANISHING?:** Article 231 of the Treaty of Versailles reads in part:

"The Allied and Associated Governments affirm and Germany accepts the responsibility of Germany and her allies for causing all the loss and damage to which the Allied and Associated Governments and their nationals have been subjected as a consequence of the War imposed upon them by the aggression of Germany and her allies."

Germans read in the *Berliner Tageblatt* last week an unofficial message from Senator William Edgar Borah, the Chairman of the U.S. Senate's Foreign Relations Committee:

"I hope to see the sole War guilt deception rejected once and for all. It is to nobody's advantage to maintain a false benefit, which only serves to preserve rancor and to retard the confidence and friendly relations which we should seek to further and restore in every way. There is no sole guilt for the War."

SEPT. 26 **IMPERIAL VAPORINGS:** Wilhelm II, onetime German Emperor, received in his château at Doorn, Holland, a correspondent of a Copenhagen newspaper. The onetime Kaiser, now a grey-bearded old man, has seemingly lost none of his arrogance, none of his pomposity, none of his commanding dogmatism; for, complaining, he said to the Danish newspaperman: "I could show the road to peace, but the world prefers regarding me as a scapegoat to consulting me as an adviser."

Bent, his withered left arm hanging loosely by his side, the fallen All Highest went on: "While ministers with olive branches in their hands are discussing peace, I see jealousy among the nations steadily increasing. Besides transocean flights, secret duration flights are made by planes heavily loaded with bombshells, so that one must consider the possibility of being attacked suddenly."

Then, assuming his psychic powers—an alleged natural gift in which he takes great pride—he predicted dire war: "I am even certain that many of those powers talking about disarmament do so in order to inspire greater confidence, thus disguising their purposes. According to my opinion, we shall go through another and more awful war at the latest in 1937, a war which will last only a few days and possibly only a few hours.

"In the same moment that war is proclaimed giant fleets of airplanes, airships and U-boats will be informed by wireless. Merchantmen will be destroyed immediately and a nation unprepared for war will be exterminated within 48 hours. On land and sea new and pernicious gases and explosives, unknown in Germany, will be employed and annihilate the weaker nations within a moment."

TANNENBERG MONUMENT: Erect and martial, President OCT. 3 Generalfeldmarschall Paul Ludwig Hans von Beneckendorff und von Hindenburg arrived at Tannenberg, East Prussia, there to unveil a War memorial to the soldiers who fell in the historic Battle of Tannenberg (at which, in 1914, Hindenburg helped defeat a Russian army).

More than 100,000 people gathered to witness the ceremony. Six miles of veterans lined up to do honor to their old military chief. Some of them were resplendent in plumed helmets and gold-braided tunics of imperial days.

Clad in his marshal's uniform, with the baton of his rank

in his left hand, the aged Hindenburg, almost 80, passed through the cheering throng. He is grim, cool, calm, yet genial enough on occasion.

Germans recall a story about their President that exemplifies his peculiar wit. One of his old friends is alleged to have asked him:

"What do you do when you get excited?"

"I whistle," replied the President.

"But I have never heard you whistle."

"I never have."

Said he to the dense mass of people around him:

"The Tannenberg national monument serves primarily as a memorial in commemoration of those who fell in freeing their Fatherland from enemy invasion. Not only in their memory, but also in honor of my living comrades, I feel it is my duty here on this occasion to say the following:

"The charge that Germany is guilty of the greatest of all wars, we, the German people, repudiate in all its phases. Not envy, hate, nor eagerness for conquest caused us to resort to weapons. War was a last resort for us, and the requiring of the greatest sacrifices of the entire people was the last means of maintaining our prestige against a host of enemies."

DEC. 19 **GRAVE CHARGES:** Dr. Wilhelm Marx, Chancellor of the Republic, returned indignant, last week, from a trip through those sections of the Rhineland still occupied by Allied troops. In Germany the Chancellor is expected always to retain his dignity, never to lose his temper. Therefore Dr. Marx stated to the German press with chill reserve the following grave charges:

1) Target practice by Allied artillery in the occupied Rhineland is so negligently conducted as to menace the lives of many inhabitants.

2) Autumn maneuvers by 1,000 French Negro troops and other Allied forces were recently carried out in such manner as to trample down whole fields of ripe grain without compensation to the owners.

3) More than 700 native Rhinelanders have been arraigned before Allied courts-martial on "trifling charges," this year, and some have been punished by whippings.

Italy

DEPORTATIONS: Pallid busts of the Caesars keep a spectral JAN. 3
watch in the great high-ceilinged room which Signor Mussolini [in his fifth year in power] calls his office. There, upright
at his massive desk, he transfixed newsgatherers last week with
a calm smoldering glance, answered their questions about the
new Proscription Law. Was it not, hinted the representatives
of the press, a little persecutory to deport non-Fascist offend-
ers to "penal islands" for "political and social crimes"?

The brow of *Il Capo del Governo* contracted as he formu-
lated a definition. Soon it boomed from his heavy lips: "This
measure for the deportation of incorrigible political and social riff-raff, including loan sharks, cocaine sellers, white slave
traffickers and perverters of children will be a social purge
ridding the country of many pernicious influences. There will
be no irresponsible or arbitrary deportations. A commission
of appeal is examining thoroughly every case, referring it in
the last instance to myself, who decides each one on its merits.
There is no work for them on the islands, but they will be well
treated. They are in the charge of my Black Shirt militia."

WOMEN: At night Signor Mussolini lies between silken sheets MARCH 14
in a huge, carved bed at the Villa Torlonia. A domed and
gilded ceiling canopies above. From the sumptuous *milieu* he
rose up refreshed one morning last week and spoke biting
words to French feminist Vahdah Jeanne Bordeaux, who interviewed him after breakfast on the topic "Women."

Benito Dixit: "Women are trusting, confiding little animals. When a man tells a woman that he loves her, she makes
it a point to believe him, no matter how many times she may
already have been deceived. She believes him because she is
an idealist, and being loved is an ideal condition. She believes
him because she is romantic, and the state or condition of
loving and being loved is a romantic one. Oh, when it is a
question of imagination, women are far superior to men.

"Women cannot create. In all of the arts, from the beginning of time, women have done delicious small things, but
when they have attempted grandeur they have failed igno-
miniously. For example, what woman has ever created a great
painting?

"Women are to man what men desire them to be—woman is to me an agreeable parenthesis in my busy life; they never have been more, nor can they ever be less. Today, I have no time to punctuate my life with other than work, but in the past, now the long ago past, when I was free to pick and choose my style of writing, I often found the parenthesis a pleasant way to punctuate.

"Flirtations should be indulged in as frequently as possible up to the age of 40, then a man should settle down to more staple amusements, such as work.

"What more agreeable than the enthusiasm a woman knows how to awaken in a man? What more charming, thrilling than the first kiss; what brings a more profound sigh of relief than the last?

"The power behind the throne? No, woman is not that. No great man has ever been inspired to greatness by a woman's unseen power."

MARCH 28 **BREAD:** Snooping Fascists, at Naples, followed a hearse. Snifting, they inhaled the aroma of fresh bread. Soon the mortician was handcuffed, his hearse found to contain 60 pounds of finest pure white loaves. Weeping, imploring, the wretched culprit was dragged away, was jailed. He had broken the law forbidding the baking, transport, or sale within Italy of bread whiter than the "economy loaf" imposed by Signor Mussolini—a loaf either of whole wheat flour, or of white flour mixed with coarser grain.

APRIL 25 **CAGED BRAVO:** Signor Benito Mussolini, The Head of the State, The Leader of *Fascismo,* permitted a fair trial last week to onetime Socialist Deputy Tito Zaniboni who was arrested at his hotel bedroom window calmly puffing a cigaret and training a high-power rifle upon the balcony of Signor Mussolini's office, from which *Il Duce* was shortly to deliver his Armistice Day address. A special military tribunal sat upon the case last week in the grim Roman *Palazzo di Giustizia;* but the prisoner faced only the normal Italian criminal law. Recent legislation providing the death penalty for attempts on the Premier's life is not retroactive and would-be-assassin Tito Zaniboni faced, last week, a maximum penalty of 30 years in jail. His bravado was prodigious.

The military judges, sitting in stiff gold braid upon the bench beheld a wiry, dynamic little prisoner who hurled lightnings of defiance. "What more do you want? What more do you want?" he shouted as the presiding judge strove to compel at least an orderly confession. It was useless. Signor Zaniboni was not to be suppressed.

"Mussolini is an imposter!" he went on. "As the illegal *Capo del Governo* (Head of the State) he is stamping upon Liberty and the Constitution. *Ah! Libertà Bella,* you are trampled, you are ravished! Will no one but Zaniboni cry 'Long live Liberty!'?"

"Signor Zaniboni," rapped the Court, "confine yourself to facts."

"Ha! Facts!" roared Signor Zaniboni. "Well, it is a fact that if the police, instead of arresting me at 8:30 had done so at 12:30 my project would have been completed. What more do you want?"

"Do you mean, Signor Zaniboni, that you would have fired with intention to hit and kill *Il Capo del Governo?*"

"Hit? Of course I should have hit him! I hate *Fascismo!* I will always hate it! I wanted to restore the government of the State to my King by killing this imposter. What more do you want? I alone am guilty!" [Zaniboni and a general whom the state convicted as an accomplice were both given a maximum sentence of 30 years in prison.]

WORK GUARANTEED: What is the essential doctrine of *Fascismo*? It is direct, constructive, continuous action by the People under the guidance of the State. This gospel of *action*, dynamic, propulsive, was expounded last week by Signor Benito Mussolini in a great document designed as the ground plan on which the new social order must arise. Fascists hailed the proclamation as their *Charter of Labor*, as the first *magna charta* guaranteeing to a people not rights but duties. MAY 2

The Charter of Labor, promulgated last week, lays down the following general principles:

1) The Marxian theory of class war to be explicitly abjured in favor of the Fascist theory of class cooperation.

2) Labor is declared "a social duty," and property "accomplishes a necessary social function."

3) In a word, all bargaining between employer and em-

ployed will be collective by compulsion, with the State as compulsory arbiter.

4) Absolutely forbidden are: lockouts, strikes, sabotage. The employer must employ. The worker must work. None may damage the engines of production.

5) Capital is guaranteed the right of Property and the right to undertake capitalistic enterprises on private initiative.

6) Labor is guaranteed a six-day week; extra pay for night work; full pay on national holidays; compensation in case of discharge.

7) Employers and employed to be equally and mutually responsible to the State for maintaining maximum factory production.

8) Penalties: fines, suspension of employers from management, discharge of workers from employment.

JUNE 6   **LOOKING FORWARD:** The Chamber of Deputies passed through two momentous hours last week. Benito Mussolini came and spoke from the tribune in reasoned, winning fashion. "The precise, fundamental duty of Fascist Italy," he roared, "is to reach a maximum strength with her armed forces on land, sea and air. Hence we must at a given moment be able to mobilize 5,000,000 men thoroughly armed, we must strengthen our navy; while aviation, in which I believe more than ever, must be on such a large scale and so powerful that the noise of its motors must surpass any other noise, and the area of the wings of our airplanes must obscure the sun from our land."

The audience applauded fiercely when *Il Duce* cried at last:

"Five years ago I thought that after five years I would have finished the major part of my work. Now I see I have not. I am convinced that, despite the gradual creation of a directing class, despite the discipline of the people, I must assume the task of governing the Italian people for 10 or 15 years more, if necessary, not because I am lustful for power but because it is my precise duty. (A pause, arms folded, then, challengingly) My successor is not yet born!"

JULY 25   **SMART BRUNO:** The Fascist-controlled press of Rome displayed last week a little story, perfect as a gem, concerning small Bruno Mussolini, 9, younger son of *Il Duce*.

Bruno's schoolteacher, it seemed, was recently examining him in grammar and desired to elicit the information that, in Italian, a verb may take the imperative mood in the second or third person but not in the first.

"Now Bruno," said the examiner, "tell me in what person one cannot command."

Bruno, obviously puzzled, showed himself the smart son of a smart sire by replying:

"There are two persons one cannot command, the King and my father."

Japan

TENNO DIES, TENSHI LIVES: Commerce halted and impending JAN. 3 Death hushed the people of Japan last week into a dread dull stillness. Their Emperor lay dying at Hayama. They knew that the shades of his 122 imperial ancestors were assembling at Tokyo in awful conclave round the Imperial Shrine in the Chiyoda Palace. It was as though the people of the U.S. should suspend all activity, believing that Washington, Lincoln, Pierce, Arthur and the 23 other dead Presidents had gathered, majestic ghosts, at the Capitol.

Dusk came. As lamps were lighted the Emperor received an ounce of liquid food administered through a tube. He was approaching the last stages of pneumonia, and his lungs have always been weak. At his bedside a physician administered oxygen whenever he seemed sinking. The pulse, constant for some time, became too fast to count.

At midnight hope was abandoned. At 1 a.m. Death was a matter of moments. At 1:25 a.m. His Imperial Majesty, Yoshihito Harunomiya, found rest at last. A Shinto arch-priest, bearded and stately, heralded the *Tenno*'s death to his ancestors at Tokyo. Thousands who had gathered to pray believed that the arch-priest might even have talked with the Sun Goddess from whom the Emperors are traditionally descended.

Immediately after Yoshihito *Tenno*'s death (Japanese ordinarily refer to the Emperor as *Tenno*—Heavenly King—or *Tenshi*—Son of Heaven), his eldest son Hirohito (since 1921 Prince Regent on account of his father's invalidism) assumed imperial rank in a room adjoining the death chamber. He will not be crowned until 1928, since the period of mourning in the Imperial Household will be one year. Nonetheless, Hirohito *Tenno* received last week the Privy Seal and various imitations of the sacred symbols of his office—the sword, the mirror and the beads.

The 25-year-old Son of Heaven, his visage grief-stricken, repeated, as he assumed his rank, a traditional formula:

"Confronting the imperial death unexpected, we are bowed in grief. The throne, however, cannot be left vacant even for a day. We hereby accede to the mandate of the gods, accepting the imperial throne of Japan."

JAN. 10 **"MOURNING SQUEAKS":** With the death of His Imperial Majesty Yoshihito there began last week the usual sacrifices of loyal subjects in his honor. Hundreds of young girls cut off their hair and burned it ceremoniously in the temples. Stalwart youths pierced veins and painted in blood devout ideographic prayers for the *Tenno*. Finally Baron Mansasuke Ikeda, lifelong companion of the *Tenno,* set up a portrait of the "Heavenly King" in his house near Tokyo, cried, "I followed you in life, I follow you in death," and shot himself.

Meanwhile the respected Rintaro Nishimura, hereditary hearse-maker to the Imperial House, arrived at Tokyo from Kyoto, the ancient Capital, with 50 workmen and began work on the great two-wheeled cart in which the *Tenno*'s remains will journey to the grave. No one else knows the secret of constructing the wheels of the funeral car so that they will emit the traditional "mourning squeak." At the hubs a mechanism capable of emitting loud groans will be installed. Finally the hearse will be made of unvarnished cypress, oak, teakwood and fir, 12 feet high, 23½ feet long, the whole polished to glassy smoothness.

A committee of the Diet reported favorably last week the funeral budget bill, providing for a total expenditure of 2,980,-000 yen ($1,490,000) on the state funeral which will be held late in February. Among other expenses will be the permanent support of the oxen used to draw the Imperial Hearse, since these animals never thereafter will perform labor of any kind.

SYMBOLIC CRANE: Solemn priests of the Shinto faith entered AUG. 8 the private apartments of Her Majesty, the Empress Nagako, at Tokyo last week, and reverently wound about her waist an *obi* of purest white silk some twelve feet long. Previously this girdle had been purified and made sacred at the Imperial Shrine. Its presentation to the Empress was in the nature of a symbolic prayer that she might give birth in a few short weeks to a manchild, her first.

Since there is a possibility that the man-being, a sublime and God-begotten "Son of Heaven," already exists, the ritual of last week should have been accompanied by loud banging of brazen instruments and public demonstrations. Because the Court is in mourning for the Emperor Hirohito's late father, these festivities were omitted. Spontaneous rejoicing burst forth, however, when it was announced that a crane had been seen to flap sedately three times around the Imperial Palace: a man-symbol, according to Japanese.

GIRL: To the Empress Nagako of Japan was born a sister to SEPT. 19 her first child, Princess Shigeko Teru-No-Miya. Once again the Imperial Stork had failed to heed the gods of Shintoism and the call of the great Lord Buddha for a son and heir to the august Imperial throne.

This is little less than a tragedy to the Japanese royal house. Girls in the Orient have no social standing or importance of their own. Therefore, a girl may not succeed to the august throne of *Jimmu Tenno,* occupied by the present dynasty for 2,587 years. Actually, the line of succession is not endangered by the carelessness of the Imperial Stork, for Hirohito has three brothers. [A son and heir, Crown Prince Akihito, was born in 1933.]

Mexico

Mexico was in the midst of turmoil. The regime of President Calles was pressing its plan to expropriate U.S. oil holdings. It was carrying out a stringent program of anti-Catholic legislation which had been written into the 1917 Constitution and was accompanying the campaign with violent anti-clerical propa-

*ganda. And, with a Presidential election set for 1928, Calles,
who had hand-picked a successor, was taking effective measures
against the other candidates: they were being hunted down and
shot by government troops in a bloody purge.*

JAN. 10   **WAITING:** Titles to approximately 80% of all U.S.-controlled
Mexican oil lands were on deposit last week with the Mexican
Government, which has promised to issue "operating concessions" to the owners in accordance with the new Mexican
laws. All Mexican oil lands whose owners did not surrender
their titles and apply for concessions by last week are now
technically the property of the Mexican State.

It remains to be seen whether the Calles Government will
dare to seize these lands, in defiance of the protests of Secretary Kellogg. The U.S. State Department intimated last
week that it would wait for a concrete instance of seizure before taking action.

FEB. 7   **ENFORCEMENTS BEGIN:** One hundred and seventy-nine permits to U.S. oil companies operating in Mexico were canceled
by the Calles Government last week, under the so-called con-
fiscatory Mexican laws pertaining to land and oil. The U.S.
oil operators affected by these cancellations prepared to begin
litigation through the Mexican courts to prevent actual seizure of their properties. The immediate effect of cancellation
of permits was to throw some 3,000 Mexican laborers who
had operated the wells out of work.

FEB. 14   **VIRGIN:** Mexican peasants are quite apt to see an apparition
of the Blessed Virgin almost anywhere, and forthwith convert
the spot into a shrine. Even a *châlet de nécessité* became by
this means a place of worship in Sonora. Last week a group
of workmen were interrupted in preparing to dynamite a large
rock near Guadalupe, by a mob of peasant women who insisted that the Mother of God had once sat upon that very
rock. Agnostics, the dynamiters were unimpressed. Passionate, the women clung to the Virgin's rock, defied the workmen to blow them up. At last policemen charged the women,
dragged them to a safe distance, held them ungently until the
rock was dynamited to atoms.

President Calles. His daughter defies him by getting married in church.

General Gomez. Even without his mustachios he is shot. Page 132.

NATALIA INTO WIFE: Señorita Natalia Calles, daughter of FEB. 28 President Plutarco Elias Calles, is a devout Roman Catholic. So is her dashing sister, Ernestine. So is their mother. But President Calles has said: "No influence, national or international, including the grunts of the Pope, will cause the Government to vary its attitude [toward suppressing the Catholic clergy]."

Therefore, the Calles womenfolk were in a delicate position, last week, on the eve of Señorita Natalia's wedding to Señor Carlos Herrera, a minor government official. Would big, burly Papa Calles insist that his daughter should have only a civil marriage, demand that she live out of wedlock in the eyes of Roman Catholics?

Papa-President Calles resisted tears, supplications. Señorita Natalia Calles was united in wedlock exclusively by the Mexican civil power. Then, on separate trains, the bride and bridegroom sped to San Antonio, Tex. At Mexico City the Papa-President clamped down his censorship, forbade Mexicans to print that at San Antonio a Mexican bride and groom achieved union through the Holy Roman Catholic Church.

EXECUTIONS: In Mexico City the U.S. Embassy made formal APRIL 18 protest last week to the Mexican Government at the murder in Mexico during the past month of three U.S. citizens: George Holmes, slain in the state of Chihuahua; Edgar M. Wilkins, killed in Jalisco; and Frederick C. Combs who was done to death in Sonora.

Since these were by way of being "routine assassinations," and since so many other U.S. citizens slain in Mexico are un-avenged, it was especially notable that the police of Guadala-jara seized seven Indians last week and executed them as the slayers of Edgar Wilkins.

The police called attention to the fact that Mr. Wilkins had been killed by seven knife wounds, each of which has now been avenged by the execution of a Mexican Indian. Further, the police explained that when a gang of Indians sets out to commit murder each must strike a blow, by custom, that all may be equally guilty and none tempted to betray the others.

MAY 2 **ATROCITY:** In Mexico City, huge identic headlines screamed from *El Universal Grafico* and *El Excelsior,* news of an atroc-ity unparalleled. War Minister Joaquin Amaro gave out the story verbally, in lurid fashion:

"As the Guadalajara-Mexico City Express neared La Barca, in Jalisco, a train ran at full speed upon two rails from which attacking Indians had removed the spikes, and crashed to a sudden stop.

"The object of the attack was the soldier train guards, but the infuriated hillsmen dealt death to everyone in the line of fire. Of the passengers in the two second-class cars, numbering over 100, scarcely one escaped injury or death. These wooden cars were perforated as though cardboard, by bullets from the high power rifles of the peasants.

"The battle was in semi-darkness, for the moon had not yet risen and the train cars were not lighted. Toward the end of the ghastly scene the moon began to rise, and in the ob-scure light the commanding form of a priest in priestly robes could be seen urging on the hillsmen to the work of destruc-tion. Amid the shrieking of women, crying of children and shouts of desperation of the men on the doomed train, the battle went on. It was an uneven fight to the last. Then the work of destruction began. The safe was broken open in the express car and the contents, amounting to $200,000 in gold and silver coin, was extracted.

"Apparently the work was deliberately planned as a crusade of vengeance for the execution two weeks ago of Catholic plotters in Guadalajara. The Rev. J. M. Vega, a priest well known in Guadalajara, who led the hillsmen, spoke to passengers while the pillage was continuing: 'The hand of God has descended upon this train. The Almighty has smitten it.'

"It is to appeals like this," said the War Minister, "that the Mexican Indians respond."

From a Cabinet Minister, such a Deadwood Dick account was white hot news. The Mexican Government informed newsgatherers, late in the week, that it possessed proof of the ordering of the atrocity by the Mexican Episcopate of the Roman Catholic Church. Next day the Archbishop of Mexico, the Most Reverend José Mora y del Rio, one other archbishop and four bishops, were escorted by police to a train which left for the U.S. border.

TROUBLES SCOTCHED: The week was the most hopeful in MAY 9 many months for Mexico. In Mexico City, President Plutarco Elias Calles called in newsgatherers who found his heavy, brown features alight. He pointed with honest satisfaction to the Spanish translation of a paragraph from President Calvin Coolidge's speech a fortnight ago in Manhattan. In their original English, the words of President Coolidge read:

"I am glad to report that the Mexican Ambassador has recently declared to me that Mexico does not intend to confiscate our property, that she has shown diligence in capturing and punishing those who have murdered our citizens, and expressed the wish, which we so thoroughly entertain, of keeping cordial and friendly relations."

President Calles commented "Ah-h-h . . ." rumbling complacently. Then he spoke for 20 minutes. Excerpts:

"The attitude of President Coolidge seems to me to be serene, cordial and conciliatory. As I have clearly said before, in the entire range of the revolutionary policy of Mexico and its expression, in the laws, there is no spirit or proposition of confiscation." [American oil properties in Mexico were confiscated in 1938.]

THE RELIGIOUS SITUATION: Roman Catholics in Mexico AUG. 15 who are resisting the enforcement under President Calles of the anti-religious Mexican Constitution were sharply reminded last week by U.S. Secretary of State Frank B. Kellogg that they can expect no official aid or comfort from the U.S.

Since the Coolidge-Kellogg policy of "hands off religion" has thus been strongly re-affirmed, who does stand ready to champion the Roman Catholic cause in Mexico?

Barring the possibility of a *coup d'état* by one of the Roman Catholic insurgent leaders in Mexico, the first opportunity for an orderly change of government will be the Mexican presidential election of 1928. The present reactionary Mexican group headed by President Calles will put Señor Calles' old and strong friend, onetime (1920-24) President Alvaro Obregon into the race, but who is the chief pro-Catholic candidate?

Although several "opposition" candidates will take the field, none seems so likely to fire both the army and the populace in his support as does General Arnulfo R. Gomez, the Zone Commandant of the State of Vera Cruz, and virtually a local dictator there.

To exalt himself still further, General Gomez has released a photographic poster of himself captioned *"El Hombre Sin Vicios"* ("The Man Without Vices"). A glance at this shows General Gomez to be unquestionably dashing and sleek, with impeccably upturned "Kaiser" mustachios. He proclaims himself in favor of "complete religious toleration," and is on good terms with many U.S. citizens who have financial interests in Mexico. Thus he should poll a large Roman Catholic vote and knows where to find campaign funds.

The great complexity of the religious situation arises from the fact that many Mexicans are actually of a different religious complexion from that which they profess or even from that which they suppose to be their own. Thus many anti-Roman Catholic statesmen have secret leanings toward the Holy See and often have Roman Catholic wives. On the other hand, numerous peasants who ardently profess themselves Roman Catholics barely understand a few rudiments of that faith. The result is hopeless confusion.

The public observance of Roman Catholic rites was at first brutally suppressed wherever possible. A second phase ensued during which wealthy Roman Catholics were able to bribe the authorities and hold secret rites. At present a third stage seems to be setting in, due to the wearing down of Government zeal for enforcement and to the numerous scandals arising from the discovery that high officials have not only taken bribes to permit masses but have sometimes even attended these very masses themselves.

MEXICAN BANDITRY: A Southern Pacific train last week SEPT. 5 chugged swiftly over the rails in the State of Nayarit, Mexico, belching steam and smoke into the night air and spewing fine cinders over the countryside. Sleeping soundly in comfortable Pullmans were eleven U.S. citizens on their way back to the U.S.

At 4 a.m. up rode a large group of skulking bandits with an eye to the robbery and a will to violence. Madly they raced along with the swaying train, their horses' hoofs beating a drum rumble on the arid land. Half a hundred shots screamed through the air and clattered against the sides of the cars, some of them piercing the woodwork and windows. But all in vain; booty was denied them.

Inside a Pullman a girl awoke with a scream, rolled over with a moan, exclaiming, "I'm shot!" She was Miss Florence M. Anderson, Los Angeles schoolteacher, returning home from a summer course at the National University, Mexico City. Her friend, Miss Louise Rider, also of Los Angeles, summoned help and administered first aid. It was found that Miss Anderson had been shot in the left side toward the back, the slug piercing her intestines.

At Mazatlan, the first stopping place, she was removed from the train to a hospital and operated upon. She died next day. Fifteen others were killed or wounded in the attack, none of them U.S. citizens.

REVOLT: Last week the Mexican presidential campaign broke OCT. 17 out in bloody revolt and boded well to be settled on the battlefields rather than in the ballot boxes. As the week wore on the summary executions of one of the two opposition candidates and many supporting generals seemed to hold promise of a complete annihilation of the opposition to the candidacy of General Alvaro Obregon, one-armed, onetime President of Mexico, whom the Calles administration is tacitly supporting, just as the Obregon administration, when it was in power, tacitly supported President Plutarco Elias Calles.

The immediate cause of the attempted revolution was the opposition of Generals Francisco Serrano and Arnulfo Gomez to the re-election of General Obregon, they being the only candidates standing against him.

Within a single day after the first shot had been fired General Serrano was captured, tried by summary court martial and shot as a traitor. Rumors to the effect that General Gomez had suffered a like fate subsequently proved to be false, he being annoyingly at large. But with General Serrano died no less than 13 generals and private citizens, convicted of aiding him.

Two days later General Alfredo Rueda Quijano, and 13 legislators, were similarly shot. General Quijano pleaded at his trial that he had been duped, but it made no difference. He was led out into the sunshine, nonchalantly gallant. A large crowd gathered to see his end and more than 1,000 troops were assembled to do him a last gruesome honor. He was marched to a pile of stones and ordered to stand with his back to it. But this did not suit him and he elected to be shot with his back to a wall.

With head erect, refusing to be blindfolded, he faced the firing squad of six soldiers commanded by an officer. One last glance at the sun he took before he resigned himself to the inevitable. But as his glance swept downward he saw three U.S. newspaper correspondents and, recognizing them merely as foreigners, he waved his hand cheerily, calling out in English to them "goodbye."

Then the volley of six rifles speaking as one sounded as the officer let his sword fall as the signal to fire. General Quijano dropped to the ground, his body convulsing. On orders from the officer, a soldier approached the quivering form and put the muzzle of his rifle against the general's head, pulled the trigger. Thus died General Quijano, brave to the last.

The heavy hand of the Calles forces had discouraged the revolters for the time being and had driven them into the mountains and had therefore rendered them comparatively innocuous. This being so, General Alvaro Obregon remained as the only aspirant to the Presidency.

POLITICAL DEATHS: General Arnulfo Gomez, onetime presi- NOV. 14
dential candidate, fell into an ambush prepared for him by
General José Gonzalo Escobar, who personally made the
capture. A few hours later he was executed by a firing squad
in the hamlet of Teocelo, Vera Cruz. Shortly afterwards,
Federal troops also shot General Adalberto Palacios, Colonel
Salvador Costanos, Major Francisco Meza Perez. Their
bodies were all shipped to Mexico City, where their relatives
claimed them. Each showed a bullet hole through the temple.

MORE DEATHS: At his execution, General Adalberto Palacios NOV. 21
joined laughingly in a joke that was causing some merriment
to the spectators of his approaching death. As he was lined up
against a wall with Martinez Pulido, the latter asked him for
a loan of a few pesos, which he placed on his sombrero,
promising them to the soldiers on condition that they shot
him through the heart. "Be sure and pay them back," said
General Palacios as he made the loan. Then he rebuked
the laughing spectators, saying: "This is no laughing
matter."

In Mexico City the emaciated corpse of General Arnulfo
Gomez was laid, amid great weeping and hysteria, in its last
resting place. At the same time what purported to be the
true report of the manner of his capture and death was circulated.

Surrounded by troops, General Gomez, making a futile
effort to draw his gun, fell on the slippery ground. Seeing that
his game was up, he surrendered, and, fearing that he was
about to be summarily shot, begged for his life, offering to
take any punishment other than death.

Holding on to the sleeve of his captor, Señor Gomez was
taken to the village of Teocelo, where at 1 o'clock in the
morning a court martial was held and his death sentence pronounced. Just before the first rays of the sun appeared in the
east he was divested of his U.S. bulletproof waistcoat and
led out to meet his death. He presented a strange appearance.
Gone were his Kaiser-like mustachios—he had shaved them
off to prevent recognition.

According to eyewitnesses, as he was placed with his back
against the customary wall he showed considerable signs of
fear. He first asked that his eyes be bandaged, for it was bad

enough to be shot—let alone see the leveled rifles pointing at his heart. His request was promptly complied with. Then, leaning against the wall for support, he asked that the command to fire be silent.

Ever ready to heed the wishes of a man condemned to die, the commander signaled to the soldiers to fire by dropping his hat. The staccato cracks of firing rifles cut the still air of a calm morning and General Arnulfo Gomez sank to the ground—his career and presidential aspirations ended.

BOMBS: While passing through the Chapultepec Gardens, Mexico City, on his way to a bull fight, General Alvaro Obregon, onetime President of Mexico, one-armed Presidential candidate, good friend of President Calles, was halted by a smallish auto (Essex) swinging in front of his powerful limousine.

Immediately two small black objects came hurtling through the air to be followed by two deafening detonations and a number of revolver shots. The glass left the general's car abruptly, some of it burying itself in his face; otherwise he was unhurt, as were his companions. Before they had time to recover the speedy Essex disappeared.

Another car immediately gave chase and eventually caught up with the fleeing would-be assassins. A duel of shots was exchanged, in which two of the bombers were seriously wounded; a third was arrested, unharmed, while a fourth escaped. [He was captured later, and all four were executed.]

DEC. 5 **NO GRIEVANCE:** On the day after the execution of his would-be killers, General Alvaro Obregon said, in the course of a campaign speech in Mexico City: "The men who tried to assassinate me confessed that they did not know me personally and had no personal grievance against me. They explained that the crime was inspired by their fear that I, if re-elected president, will continue the policies of President Calles. This attempt shows that we must be alert against clerical reactionaries who demonstrate their intention to continue to the utmost their activities in combating our cause, even to most reprehensible methods." [Obregon was elected President in 1928, but he was assassinated by a Roman Catholic fanatic before he could take office.]

Monaco

REORGANIZED: "Going to Monte? Really? You know it is JUNE 23 FRIGHTFULLY *passé*."

Such has been the comment of smart folk, for several seasons, to anyone who proposed a visit to once smart Monte Carlo. Of course the crowds at the Casino tables have been as large as ever—but unfashionable. What to do?

The chief stockholders in the Casino have been puzzling for some time. They are now trying an experiment: Elsa Maxwell.

Miss Maxwell is very large, very mirthful, very well known in the U.S. colony at Paris. Her *entrée* is still tolerably smart. She is just the woman, decided the stockholders, to freshen up "Monte," to get the right people going there again.

Dispatches told last week that Miss Maxwell is now in Monte Carlo, at a salary of $50,000 per year, and possessed of a bonus of 400 shares of Casino stock. Officially, it is announced, she will "reorganize Monte Carlo."

Nicaragua

HERO COACHMAN: Death, clad in an assassin's cloak, sprang JAN. 3 last week at Señor Adolfo Díaz whom the U.S. has recognized as President of Nicaragua. The President was riding alone in his carriage at 11 p.m. when two men armed with machetes rushed upon it from an alley. Quick-witted, Señor Díaz leaped out of the left-hand door of his carriage as the men wrenched open the right-hand door. A machete hurtled, split the leather of the President's left heel, bit into his flesh. The coachman, faithful, sprang from his box, fell upon the attackers. Maddened, they felled him, slashed off his hands, his nose, gouged out his eyes.

As policemen arrived the two attackers fled, unidentified. President Díaz rushed to the coachman who had saved his life, lifted the man into his carriage, climbed onto the box himself, drove furiously to the nearest hospital. Not until the dying coachman had been attended to did President Díaz notice the pain in his heel, discover that he had been wounded.

This barbarous, indefensible attack on President Diáz evinced the hatred which he inspires among Nicaraguan Liberals. They see in him a corrupt Conservative, a puppet set up by the U.S. and elected only under duress by the Nicaraguan Congress. They have mobilized an army to overthrow him and have proclaimed as a rival president, Dr. Juan Sacasa, who has been recognized by Mexico.

INTERVENTION: The armed feud between President Adolfo Diáz of Nicaragua (recognized by the U.S.) and President Juan Sacasa of Nicaragua (recognized by Mexico) was crucially affected last week when Rear Admiral Julian L. Latimer landed U.S. Marines from his flagship the U.S.S. *Rochester* on the Mosquito (Eastern) Coast of Nicaragua.

Rear Admiral Latimer was not called upon to inspect the "rights" of the situation. Curt, he commanded President Juan Sacasa to disarm his troops or withdraw them from the Puerto Cabezas area. Secondly, he ordered the local mahogany growers to pay taxes only to the Conservative Government of Adolfo Diáz. By these acts it appeared that the hopes entertained by Dr. Sacasa and the Mexican Government that he should continue President had been blasted.

In the U.S., the Chairman of the U.S. Senate's Foreign Relations Committee, William Edgar Borah, growled that the Administration seems to be looking for grounds on which to commence "a shameless, cowardly little war with Mexico."

JAN. 17 **MARINES POURED IN:** Last week Senator Borah called on President Coolidge and immediately thereafter trumpeted to newsgatherers that he believes the Administration has recognized as President of Nicaragua a man who has no just claim to that office, and further that the Administration is intervening in Nicaragua against Dr. Juan Sacasa, Liberal, the rightful President of Nicaragua in Senator Borah's opinion.

Senator Burton K. Wheeler of Montana cried last week:

"We are simply bullying the Nicaraguan people because it is a small nation, and we are doing it to protect men who obtained concessions from the Diáz Government that was set up there at the point of the bayonet. Should we have landed American marines in Italy when Mussolini overthrew the Government and set up a Dictatorship? Should we land marines in Russia to protect American property and lives in Russia?"

Aboard his flagship, the *Rochester,* anchored off Puerto Cabezas, Rear Admiral Latimer calmly directed the marines as they maintained "a neutral zone to protect American lives" in such a way as to cut off the Liberal adherents of President Juan Sacasa from their chief base.

Meanwhile President Adolfo Díaz welcomed another detachment of U.S. marines which arrived "to protect the U.S. Legation" at Managua, Capital of Nicaragua.

Actual fighting between the Sacasa (Liberal) and Díaz (Conservative) forces continued in the interior. Since false reports of success were sent out on both sides, the true state of the civil war remained obscure, but a total of at least 500 combatant Nicaraguans were killed last week.

The forces rushed to Nicaragua by the Navy Department brought the number of U.S. warcraft in Nicaraguan waters up to 15, and the number of officers and men available up to 4,680—enough to wipe Nicaragua off the map.

MORE MARINES: There was one U.S. marine in Nicaragua FEB. 28 late last week for every 200 Nicaraguans. But, by repeated definition, the U.S. was not at war with Nicaragua; and, indeed, no Nicaraguan dared to shoot a U.S. marine.

TREATY PROPOSED: Some 6,000 U.S. marines held all the MARCH 7 important Nicaraguan cities except Matagalpa and Granada last week. The instant was ripe for President Díaz, synchronous with U.S. financial interests, to propose the further subordination of his country to the U.S.

At Managua, President Díaz presented to Parliament a proposed treaty with the U.S. While marines stood on guard about the Parliament House the treaty text was commended by a vote of confidence and cabled to Washington. It provides: 1) that the U.S. undertake to preserve peace in Nicaragua and the continuity of the Nicaraguan Government; 2) that accordingly the right of intervention in Nicaragua be extended to the U.S. by mutual consent; 3) that a U.S. financial adviser and receiver-general of revenues assume the task of rehabilitating the finances of Nicaragua with dictatorial powers; 4) that a loan of $20,000,000 from exclusively

U.S. sources is declared indispensable for rehabilitating Nicaragua; 5) that all military paraphernalia now possessed by Nicaraguans be handed over to a new constabulary, trained by and under the command of U.S. officers for ten years; 6) that all the foregoing considerations show that the arrangement Nicaragua desires, so far from forming part of an imperialistic scheme of U.S. aggrandizement in Central America, is nothing less than a highly humanitarian project sought by Nicaragua and not by the U.S.

APRIL 11 **PIQUANT GUNS:** Nicaraguans know better than to fire at 6,000 U.S. marines who patrol, police and "neutralize" their country; but last week some of the marines began to fly about Nicaragua in airplanes, and Nicaraguans embraced enthusiastically the opportunity to snipe undetected at these planes from cover.

After two planes had been hit, Admiral Latimer ordered the U.S. planes to mount machine guns and use them when fired upon. Since the U.S. is not at war with Nicaragua this development was piquant.

President Diáz announced last week that, aided by a $1,000,000 loan placed in Manhattan, he will be able from now on to pay his Conservative soldiers 50¢ a day. As an earnest of this the Conservative troops were reported to have received a flat payment of $2.50 each last week, pending the arrival of promised U.S. gold.

MAY 16 **NO WAR:** President Calvin Coolidge appeared to Nicaraguans last week to have assumed frankly and even conscientiously the role of Dictator in Nicaraguan affairs. The President's personal representative in Nicaragua, one-time Secretary of War Henry Lewis Stimson, conferred with the leaders of both warring Nicaraguan factions and meted out to them peace terms.

Nicaraguan President Adolfo Diáz, recognized by the U.S., has been consistently in such close harmony with U.S. nationals that it was only necessary for Presidential Representative Stimson to be firm with the Liberal faction of Nicaragua.

Accordingly, Mr. Stimson conferred with the Liberal military leader, General José Maria Moncada last week at Tipitapa, while some 50 U.S. marines stood guard. Next day

General Moncada informed the Associated Press that, since the U.S. was threatening to disarm his troops by force, he would do all in his power to persuade his men to hand over their arms to U.S. marines without fighting.

MARINES KILLED: Six thousand two hundred rifles, 272 machine guns, and 5,000,000 rounds of ammunition were surrendered last week to the U.S. forces in Nicaragua by the Liberal and Conservative armies, heretofore engaged in a civil war. Colonel Henry Lewis Stimson, personal representative of President Coolidge, supervised this operation, cabled: "The civil war in Nicaragua is now definitely ended." MAY 30

Next morning, at 1 a.m., a band of about 300 Liberal soldiers, not yet disarmed, offered resistance in the hamlet of La Paz Centro to a platoon of U.S. marines commanded by Capt. Richard Bell Buchanan. For two hours and a half the engagement continued. Captain Buchanan fell, wounded in the chest and arms, and died some hours later. Fourteen Nicaraguans were killed. The rest scattered, but not until Private Marvin Andrew Jackson, U.S.M.C., had been instantly killed by a shot through the brain.

"TRANSITION TO PEACE": A Manhattan lawyer who had disarmed the Republic of Nicaragua in 60 days with the aid of U.S. marines arrived last week at the White House and reported to the President. Officially Lawyer Henry Lewis Stimson had held no rank or office, though styled by courtesy "Personal Representative of President Coolidge." Actually, with the President behind him, and with Congress not in session, Mr. Stimson had wielded power of life and death. By persuasion and threats of force he had compelled the embattled Conservative and Liberal Nicaraguan armies to lay down their arms and submit to U.S. control of Nicaragua until 1928, when the U.S. guarantees to supervise an impartial election. JUNE 6

RULE BY BANKERS?: Señor Toribio Tijerino, onetime Nicaraguan Consul General at New York, recalled last week to Manhattan newsgatherers the $1,000,000 loan negotiated between the present Nicaraguan Government (upheld by U.S. marines) and the Manhattan firms of J. & W. Seligman & Co., JUNE 20 and the Guaranty Trust Co. Said Señor Tijerino: "The loan contract was entered into with the knowledge and approval of the State Department of the United States. Without risking or spending one cent, without making an investment of any kind, the New York bankers have taken absolute control of Nicaragua. Its transport system, its currency and credit and, by those means, the government of Nicaragua itself, is in the hands of J. & W. Seligman & Co. and of the Guaranty Trust Co. of New York."

AUG. 1 **MARINES RESCUED:** When 39 U.S. marines and 48 Nicaraguan constables were attacked last week at the remote town of Ocotal, by 600 armed Nicaraguans, only one eyewitness came forward with a complete and factual albeit hair-raising account. This personage, Señor Arnaldo Ramirez Abaunza, chief municipal official at Ocotal, wrote:

"The hour is 1 a.m. I hear shouts of 'death to the Americans' in the streets. Six hundred or maybe 1,000 strong, the forces of General Augusto Calderon Sandino surround the Americans under Major Gilbert Hatfield and attack from all sides. The fighting becomes general. American sharpshooters keep the corners clear. A Browning and two Lewis guns rake the yard. Anyone so imprudent as to cross meets death.

"The hosts of Sandino sweep on, attempting to capture the park, to use the stone wall for protection. It is now daylight—the Americans have not retreated an inch. The constabulary maintain their positions. The American sharpshooters are piling up the dead.

"Sandino sends a note to the heroic Major Hatfield, intimating that as he (Hatfield) has no water, he will eventually have to surrender. Hatfield replies: 'Received your message, and say with or without water, a marine never surrenders. We remain here until we die or are captured.'

"Five airplanes are seen at 3 p.m. They approach in battle formation; then they get in line, flying low, and open fire with their machine guns. They drop bombs on Sandino's army, which now is beginning to retreat.

"On the floor I see a marine dead—the only casualty among the Americans. In the park and inside the houses are Sandino's dead. In one place I count 21."

Later, Marine officers reported that 300 of General Sandino's men were killed and 100 wounded. These surprisingly large casualties were accounted for by two or three hits by powerful U.S. bombs among the massed attackers whose bodies were instantly mangled and blown to fragments.

A Latin American comment which was not more than typically censorious appeared in the leading newspaper of Mexico City, *Excelsior*: "May President Coolidge sleep peacefully after the assassination of 300 Nicaraguans who committed the error of defending their country, violated by an invader!"

In Washington, D.C., the Administration's view was presented by U.S. Secretary of State Frank Billings Kellogg. He recalled that General Sandino was indeed the only Nicaraguan commander who refused to disarm his forces; but Mr. Kellogg drew from this refusal the conclusion not that General Sandino is a "patriot," but instead the decision that he is "an outlaw whose acts have no political significance." The Secretary backed up this postulate by stating that General Sandino's men have recently sought to maintain themselves by foraging upon the property of U.S. citizens and others in Nicaragua. Thus they would fall directly within the scope of U.S. marines sent by President Coolidge "to protect the lives and property of U.S. citizens."

General Sandino retired into hiding after his defeat, but soon sent a message of defiance: "Whoever believes we are downcast by these casualties, misjudges my army, for today we are more impatient than ever to seek out the traitors of our country, determined to die if we cannot secure liberty."

Rear Admiral Latimer, who was in Washington last week, said: "Sandino has no political significance in Nicaragua— no more than Jesse James had in the United States." [The Marines remained in Nicaragua until 1933. They never did catch General Sandino. He came out of hiding when the Marines left, but was murdered in a political ambush.]

Rumania

The aging King Ferdinand, who had been on the throne of Rumania for 13 years, was near death. His oldest son and logical successor, Crown Prince Carol, had been forced to abdicate in 1925 because of his notorious liaison with his mistress, Magda Lupescu. Carol's young son, Prince Michael, was next in line to succeed his grandfather. The real power, meanwhile, was Premier Jon Bratiano.

JAN. 24 **"IMPOSSIBLE":** A bell tinkled, the doorbell of a secluded mansion near Paris in which reside the abdicated Crown Prince Carol of Rumania and Mme. Magda Lupescu, now *enceinte.* Soon Carol received in his study a bearded Rumanian, M. Cezianu, who said: "I ask you, in behalf of the King, that you immediately renounce Mme. Lupescu and return to Bucharest."

According to M. Cezianu, Carol answered:

"Impossible! At no price could I accept that condition. I know the love and affection that the King really has for me. I know the sentiment that caused him suddenly to change his formal decision not to see me again. I have friends who always have defended me before the King, and I sincerely thank them, as I thank the King, my father."

FEB. 7 **3 WOMEN, 3 CHILDREN:** The abdicated Crown Prince Carol of Rumania was sitting quietly on a divan at his Paris home one morning last week. Beside him sat a red-haired Rumanian Jewess, Mme. Magda Lupescu. A prying world knows that they reside together and that she is *enceinte.* A pea coal fire glowed upon the hearth and Carol read aloud, in thoughtful domesticity, from the morning newspaper.

Suddenly came a sound at the casement window. It was pushed open, and a seven-year-old boy climbed onto the sill. He was supported by a weary, drawn-faced woman, Mme. Zizi Lambrino, one-time morganatic wife of Prince Carol. The tow-headed boy was their son, Mircea.

"Papa! Papa!" he cried, "Mama and I want you to come home with us! We love you, Papa!"

Carol, vexed, rushed to the window, banged it shut and telephoned to the Prefect of Police. He demanded protection against such picketing by his morganatic wife and her son whose legitimacy he does not recognize. Soon two Parisian detectives were patrolling Carol's yard. When little Mircea came next day with his mother and shouted "Papa! Papa!" from the gate, the detectives told him to move on.

Simultaneously a very beautiful woman and a handsome child of five were en route to Italy from Rumania in a private car attached to the famed Simplon-Orient Express. She was Helen, Princess of Greece and Rumania, consort of the abdicated Prince Carol. The boy was their five-year-old son, Michael, now Crown Prince of Rumania. Carol has not returned to reside with them since November, 1925, when he left Rumania to attend the funeral of Alexandra, late Dowager Queen-Empress of Britain.

Zizi Lambrino and son, Mircea. "Papa!, Papa!," he cries to Prince Carol.   *Princess Helen and son, Michael. They escape the winter in Italy.*

As the Simplon-Orient Express drew into Venice, newsgatherers watched to see if the royal salon car would remain coupled when the express puffed out toward Paris, toward Carol. Through a lady-in-waiting Princess Helen intimated her plans to the press: "Her Royal Highness declares absolutely false all rumors to the effect that she will meet the abdicated Crown Prince Carol while on her present trip. The sole intention of Her Royal Highness in leaving Bucharest is that her son, the Crown Prince, may escape the extremely rigorous winter of Rumania. From Florence she and our little Crown Prince will go to spend the rest of the winter at Rapallo."

JULY 11 **BACK TO BRATIANO:** The course of Rumanian politics is an orbit, often fiery as a comet's tail, yet at present circular and without end. Just as the earth's solar year extends eternally from January to January, so the Rumanian political cycle starts when M. Jon Bratiano becomes Premier, and is not full rounded until he has resigned and then resumed that office. Therefore, politically speaking, it was "January" in Rumania last week, for M. Bratiano had just resumed the Premiership once more. He has been absent from office—*not* from power—for some 15 months.

The day of Jon Bratiano begins when his valet awakens him at 9 a.m., presenting a light Parisian breakfast of coffee and rolls. Although punctual about this breakfast hour, M. Bratiano is, thereafter, the acme of exquisite and sophisticated ease—of nicely timed delay. "I try to put off until tomorrow," he has said, "the mistakes which people tell me I ought to make today."

Born luckily to place and power, Premier Jon Bratiano has held and builded upon both. He and his brother Vintila, and brother-in-law Prince Babu Stirbey (intimate of Queen Marie) control the State. They dominate Rumanian banking, oil, manufactures. Their large estates are worked by peasants in a manner all but feudal. Because they have used their power to systematically exploit Rumania, a tide of public indignation periodically rises, and before it M. Bratiano resigns the Premiership, announces that he has "retired," and proceeds to lie in wait.

Fourteen months ago such a tide of resentment was at the flood. It might have led King Ferdinand of Rumania on to better fortune for his dynasty, had he dared to brave Jon Bratiano then. Instead Ferdinand I, weak, invalided, accepted M. Bratiano's resignation as Premier without comment, and meekly called one of the Bratiano henchmen, General Fofoza Alexander Averescu, to the Premiership.

Thenceforward the Rumanian cycle has moved smoothly—with General Averescu masquerading as a defender of the citizenry but actually obedient to oligarchs Jon and Vintila Bratiano. These gentlemen resolved, recently, to resume power, sensing that popular resentment had guttered down.

At once, King Ferdinand requested General Averescu to resign, an unusual proceeding for a constitutional monarch.

The King then called to the Premiership Prince Babu Stirbey. Of him the fact should be noted that Opposition leaders openly and vulgarly couple his name with that of Queen Marie. The last act, the final returning of the cycle upon itself, came last fortnight, when Prince Babu Stirbey dissolved Parliament, then resigned and was succeeded last week by Jon Bratiano as Premier.

MICHAEL I: The new King of Rumania, Michael I, five years AUG. 1 old, was playing solemnly by himself on the lawn of the Little Pelesh. To this small château, some 50 miles from Bucharest, he had been brought last week, following his investiture, and barely 18 hours after the death of his grandfather. Even as His Majesty rolled over lazily on the soft turf, statesmen were busy in Bucharest drafting his first proclamation.

"SOLDIERS!" the proclamation began—a classic opening, and one much used by the late Napoleon Bonaparte. A shrewd opening, too, for it would attest that the boy-king's first thought was for his army. Excellent!

"SOLDIERS!—After a reign, brilliant and glorious for the race, the fatherland, and the army—a reign conducted with great sacrifice and stern decision—our great and beloved king has closed forever his eyes, which never ceased to contain unlimited affection. Under his leadership you have conquered, you have forged the national unity of all Rumanians, and, with laurels gathered on the battlefields, you have crowned his brow and your own.

"SOLDIERS, we are confident that all, from the chiefs of the army to the humblest soldiers, will give proof of that spirit of discipline which is the pride of the army, and that you will remain worthy of the confidence which your country has placed in you, devoting all your strength and souls to the fatherland and throne.

(Signed) MICHAEL."

Since everyone knew that King Michael's signed proclamation had been drafted by Premier Jon Bratiano, the ruling oligarch of Rumania, it was perhaps "natural" and "fitting" that the boy-king's first state paper should thus bristle with elderly, drawing-room conceits. It was like Jon Bratiano,

63, to approve phrases such as "laurels gathered on the battlefields," and "eyes which never ceased to contain unlimited affection." What did phrases matter to the Dictator? A man-king approaching his second childhood had simply been replaced by a boy-king in his first.

When the English governess of little Michael ran to wake him with news of the king's death and first addressed her charge as "Your Majesty," his large, serious eyes betrayed a vague puzzlement.

"Has my name changed?" he asked. "Why do you call me 'Majesty'?"

Smiling, the governess explained the nature of what had occurred. Still Michael was doubtful. "They will let me play just the same, won't they?" he was said to have said.

AUG. 15 **ENFANT TERRIBLE:** Scandalous reports concerning His Majesty King Michael I, aged 5, were circulated last week by newsgatherers returning from the funeral of King Ferdinand I. After snooping about Rumania for a fortnight, the Associated Press correspondent stated positively that:

1) The Dowager Queen Marie of Rumania calls her grandson, the King, "Mad Mickey" because of his "mischievous, impulsive nature."

2) King Michael "loves to play with fire and his tutors are afraid that some day he will burn down the entire palace with everybody in it."

3) "Probably his worst trait," the Dowager Queen Marie says, "is that he loves to tease dogs and cats." He has been bitten several times by dogs, notably last summer, when the palace doctors gave him so much Pasteur treatment that he was sick for a fortnight. "Even this," says his grandmother, "has not cured him of his love of teasing them. He takes roguish delight in teasing even his own favorite cocker spaniel, Brown Mumbo."

DEC. 5 **VINTILA AFTER JON:** Death sped unseen across a white-walled courtyard, passed up a marble stair, and seemed to pause, irresolute, last week, in the bedchamber of Rumania's greatest man. The room, warmed by a great tile stove, was cozy; and Prime Minister Jon Bratiano, 63, clung hard to warmth and life. He could not speak, for inflammation brought on

by blood infection had gagged his throat. Blood poisoning
had set in. The great statesman who had doubled the area of
Rumania during his eleven premierships was told that Death
would surely claim him before dawn.

Jangling telephones brought to Jon Bratiano's death bed,
at 3 a.m., the three Regents of Rumania, also Dowager Queen
Marie, Princess Helen (mother of 6-year-old King Michael),
and all the Cabinet Ministers, headed by the Premier's brother, Vintila Bratiano.

As Queen Marie approached her old and loyal friend, she
asked in French: "Do you feel better?"

Tears started from M. Bratiano's eyes as he made a supreme
effort and managed to gasp: "Yes, Your Majesty. How good
and gracious it is of you to come here at such an hour!"

Jon Bratiano died at 6:45 a.m., without having resigned his
Premiership. At 6:50, Finance Minister Vintila Bratiano left
his dead brother's bed-chamber and hastened to present the
Cabinet's resignation to the three Regents. They at once
"commanded" him to assume the Premiership. Soon there
was a new Premier Bratiano—with all Cabinet posts re-
distributed exactly as before. The abdicated onetime Crown
Prince Carol of Rumania (father of Baby King Michael) continued to reside in his country villa near Dinard, France.
[Carol, divorced by Princess Helen in 1928, returned to Rumania in 1930 and proclaimed himself King. He was deposed
in 1940 and fled the country with Mme. Lupescu, whom he
married in 1947. He died in exile in Portugal in 1953. Michael,
who succeeded his father to the throne in 1940, was forced
to abdicate in 1947 when Rumania went Communist. He
became a businessman in Switzerland.]

Russia

*Even before the death of Lenin in 1924, a conflict for power
within the Communist hierarchy had been raging between Joseph Stalin (in 1927 TIME spelled it Josef), General Secretary
of the Party, and Leon Trotsky (in 1927 TIME spelled it Trotzky), who, as War Commissar, had been instrumental in estab-
lishing Lenin's regime. After Lenin's death, Stalin increased*

his control over party machinery and gradually edged Trotsky aside. The final break between the two came in the fall of 1927.

MARCH 14 **ORATOR ORATING:** In Trades Union Hall, Moscow, a huge, blood-red disc above the stage, bearing the Hammer and Sickle, emblems of Soviet Russia, was hung. A vast crowd surged—peasants in blouses, urban workers in tight, shoddy store clothes. They had come to hear the first public speech in four months by Russia's greatest orator, famed Leon Trotzky. All knew that M. Trotzky had been silent perforce, following the crushing of his section of the Communist party by Dictator Josef Stalin. When Comrade Trotzky slipped upon the stage last week, pale, wiry, magnetic, there was stamping, applause and cheers for 15 minutes—proof enough that Leon Trotzky is still great, though subservient to Dictator Stalin.

Choosing words carefully, avoiding internal politics, yet speaking with his wonted fire, Comrade Trotzky said: "The lands bordering the Pacific will be the scene of the world's most important events. Europe does not relish this any more than it relishes the fact that the United States has become the most dominant power in the world, expanding northward through Canada and southward through Nicaragua."

FOUNDRYMEN'S QUESTION: A slow rain drizzled over some hundreds of workmen assembled in the great open courtyard of the Moscow Railway Shops. The men had come from lathe, forge and foundry to hear a campaign speech by Dictator Josef Stalin—for elections to the Moscow Committees or "Soviets" began last week. Soon the rain was trickling from Dictator Stalin's hat and soddening his coat. Cried a worker: "Comrade Stalin, will there be war this year?"

"No," replied Dictator Stalin. "No, Comrade, there will be no war this year. A war danger does exist, but our enemies are as yet unprepared and the workers of the world do not wish to fight Russia. Because our policy is directed to peace, it is difficult to pick a quarrel with us. No breaking off of relations with England is likely, no war this year."

ENTER KERENSKY: At the invitation of an Assistant U.S. Attorney, one Kenneth Simpson, there arrived in Manhattan from Paris last week Alexander Feodorovich Kerensky, to stop with Mr. and Mrs. Simpson at their Park Avenue residence.

Through an interpreter M. Kerensky, who speaks no English, said: "I never think of a return to power. My episode is over. But I am continuing and will continue until the last the struggle for human freedom. Russians must settle their own internal affairs." [Kerensky had been Premier of Russia briefly after the fall of the Tsar. Then the Bolsheviks seized power and he was replaced by Lenin in 1917. He later moved to the U.S.]

THRICE-SLAPPED CHEEK: Five thousand Russians paid MARCH 21 $6,000 to hear famed Alexander Feodorovich Kerensky, onetime Russian Dictator, speak at the Century Theatre, Manhattan. Amid furious excitement a half-ton bronze candelabra was uprooted and flung down in the lobby by the pressure of the crowd. Bolsheviks yelled. Tsarists brandished canes. Both factions detest M. Kerensky because he is more radical than the Tsarists and less radical than the Bolsheviks.

Soon a pretty Tsarist girl, who has Americanized her name into "Miss Catherine Bary" and become a designer, mounted the stage with a bunch of roses which she extended toward Speaker Kerensky. As he bent forward to accept them she struck him three times across the left cheek with her gloves, screamed in Russian: "By your order my fiancé was shot in Russia! I do this to avenge him!"

"Let her go," said M. Kerensky through an interpreter to the police. Then, in Russian, to the audience: "Oh, you poor little monarchists. You have lost your manhood. Not one of your ex-officers dares to come upon this stage! Instead you send a woman."

Soon, amid pandemonium, 25 Russians were ejected, including Andrew Tolstoy who was marched roughly into the street by a Patrolman Higginson. "He says," the patrolman told reporters, "that he is related to some Wop Count that's dead, and used to write books."

With his audience thus quelled the onetime Dictator spoke: "The Tsarists were the first to come sniveling to us, swearing loyalty to the Revolution. The Bolsheviks stole the freedom of the Russian people. Both are enemies of Russia. . . . Someday a new freedom. . . . Help for the cause. . . . Dawn. . . ."

JUNE 13 **TROTZKY v. STALIN:** The severance of Anglo-Soviet relations by Great Britain brought on at Moscow last week a political crisis. Dictator Josef Vissarionovitch Stalin was again openly criticized for the first time since last fall by his incessant rival, Lev Davidovitch Trotzky. The Stalin-Trotzky feud was seemingly quenched when Comrade Trotzky was forced to sign a pledge that he would not oppose or criticize the Stalin majority group. Last week this pledge seemed less than "a scrap of paper" as M. Trotzky stood up before the *Comintern* and thundered opposition to Josef Stalin with all the moving fire of his famed spell-binding prowess. He urged that warlike "reprisals" be taken against Britain, demanded that pressure be brought on the Chinese Nationalists to proclaim a Chinese Soviet Republic, and generally flayed Dictator Stalin for not pushing with sufficient energy the Communist program of world revolution. Amid the stress of last week, the *Comintern* dared not antagonize Comrade Trotzky further than by passing a stiff resolution of censure against him.

Observers felt that M. Trotzky had given the Soviet régime a final black eye before the world by insisting on just those "orthodox" Communist policies of impractical violence and "world revolution" which the shrewd Josef Stalin is seeking to hold in check.

AUG. 22 **TRAITORS:** Black secrecy had reigned for ten days within the thick, awesome walls of the Kremlin. There the Central Executive Committee of the Communist party was in the process of expelling Comrade Lev Davidovitch Trotzky from its ranks. Comrade Trotzky, creator of the Red Army and onetime chief defender of the Communist Fatherland, was assumedly being read out of the party councils—and with him Comrade Gregory Zinoviev, zealous apostle of "The World Revolution of the World Proletariat." The struggle between these two fiery Opposition leaders and cold, relentless, stubborn Dictator Josef Vissarionovitch Stalin had reached its ultimate crisis, for the Stalin-controlled press was daily flaying Comrades Trotzky and Zinoviev as "traitors."

Amid extreme suspense the Central Executive Committee handed down a joint 5,000-word decision which was puzzling.

For whom was it a victory?

On one hand it declared: "The joint plenary session has accepted in foundation a resolution for the expulsion of Trotzky and Zinoviev from the Central Committee."

But the resolution went on to say: "The Opposition have found it necessary to give way and to renounce a number of their errors and to agree basically to proposals of the plenary session by giving a declaration. In view of this declaration, the plenary session has decided to withdraw the question about exclusion of Trotzky and Zinoviev from the Central Committee and to admonish them with severe blame and a warning."

What did these so contradictory decisions portend? Soon the dean of U.S. correspondents at Moscow, Walter Duranty of the New York *Times,* cabled an opinion:

"All signs now indicate that the Communist Party has emerged stronger than ever from what appeared to be the gravest crisis in its history. Here is the real secret of the events of the past week. The stage was all set for a split—one might almost say it actually occurred—and then suddenly, almost miraculously, it was averted."

TROTZKYISMS: To an unofficial delegation of the American SEPT. 5 Federation of Labor, visiting Moscow last week, Leon Trotzky, onetime Soviet War Lord, shock-headed and wild of eye, declaimed upon the ideals of Bolshevism and the counter-wailing tendencies of U.S. bourgeois democracy.

Said he: "I deny the existence of an American democracy. Under the externals of a political democracy the United States is ruled by a most concentrated capitalistic dictatorship."

Admitting that there was neither free speech nor a free press in Russia, he added that in the U.S. liberty of the press was only the freedom to buy for two cents a newspaper produced by bourgeois journalists in the pay of the hated capitalists.

"The United States is the most perfected expression of capitalism," he cried, "while the Soviet is the first rough sketch of the Socialist state."

Then a note of warning shot into his speech, like a drop of hot red ink into a bucket of cold clear water. Rasped he: "We are the same old revolutionaries, and if our enemies

Joseph Stalin: "No, Comrade, there will be no war this year." Page 147.   *Leon Trotsky: "I deny the existence of an American democracy."*

think we have grown sleepy and lazy through administration, they will get a rude shock. All humanity is divided into two camps, the proletariat and the imperialistic bourgeoisie, and those who attempt to turn us back to capitalism will be received with hard knocks.

"We shall continue to struggle for proletarian dictatorship, which is humanity's sole true way to freedom."

Thus said Trotzky, enemy of capitalism.

OCT. 10   **TROTZKY OUT:** For continuous outspoken opposition to the ruling oligarchy, headed by Josef Vissarionovitch Stalin, the Presidium of the Central Committee of the Third International last week deposed Lev (Leon) Davidovitch Trotzky and his aide one Vuyovitch.

Summoned before that august Bolshevist body, the former potent War Minister accused M. Stalin and Nikolai Bucharin, editor of the *Pravda,* of placing the question of their survival above all principle. He called them usurpers, Bonapartist dictators, without authority from the masses.

In answer to this defiance the Presidium formally ousted M. Trotzky, explaining its action as follows: "The presidium deems Trotzky's and Vuyovitch's remaining in the Communist International impossible because of their violent struggle against the organization by means of underground printing plants coupled with inciting malicious slander against Soviet Russia abroad. To preserve unity in Lenin ranks, to counteract the undermining activities of the oppositionist rebels, the presidium of the Communist International unanimously decided to expel Trotzky and Vuyovitch from the Communist International's executive body."

Leon Trotzky, né Bronstein, was born 50 years ago, son of bourgeois Jewish parents. In Odessa, he received an excellent high school and university education. Aged 17, he became a revolutionary, working for the downfall of the Tsarist régime. Like all Russian revolutionaries, he spent long terms in prison, and longer terms in exile in a dozen different countries, including the U.S., where he lived for a time in the Bronx, New York City.

When the Tsar abdicated in 1917, M. Trotzky left the U.S. for Russia, but was arrested and taken ashore by the British at Halifax and kept in jail until the Provisional Government of Russia demanded his release. He entered Russia a few weeks later at about the same time as Lenin, with whom he worked in preparation for the famed November revolution that set the seal of Bolshevism over all the Russias.

Since the death of Lenin in 1924, Leon Trotzky has been pushed more and more into the background. A sick man, he was indefatigable in support of an active Bolshevising policy designed to please the younger rank and file of the Communist Party.

It is the consensus that Leon Trotzky is the most brilliant of all the Soviet leaders, not even excepting Lenin. In stature small and unimpressive and in appearance like a university professor, he is a striking orator with a rare gift for metaphor. As an organizer, he probably has not an equal in all Russia. Fearlessness in debate has at once been his strength and his weakness; for by it he conquered and because of it he was conquered.

DECENNIAL: All week long, not only in Russia but in many NOV. 21 countries throughout the world, the tenth anniversary of the founding of the Bolshevist régime was celebrated.

Moscow, festooned in red, was the centre of proletarian manifestations. Here 30,000 field-grey soldiers marched past Mikhail Ivanovitch Kalinin, so-called President of the Union of Socialist Soviet Republics, who took the salute from the top of the Lenin tomb in Red Square. Behind the troops came 250,000 picked workers, preceded by a monster, two-headed green dragon. One of the heads represented, monocle & all, Sir Austen Chamberlain, British Foreign Secretary; the other, Prime Minister Benito Mussolini of Italy, with the Fascist swastika above his forehead.

Hour after hour the procession wended its way through the square. A short speech by M. Kalinin was the signal for the singing of the *International,* which was taken up by the miles of parading populace. Simultaneously, the Kremlin guns roared salvos of blank shells for six minutes, their blue smoke spiraling upwards around the pinnacles of St. Basil's Church. All this to celebrate the achievement of ten years of Bolshevist rule.

What is this achievement?

Everywhere there is a shortage of houses, huge families sleeping in small rooms, and as many as 100 people eating at a neighborhood kitchen. Children are taught only what they wish to learn, for there is no such thing in Bolshevist philosophy as forcing a child to do something that he or she does not want to do—hence the reason why 100,000 vicious ragamuffins roam the streets today.

The successors of the Tsar's secret agents are so secret that members of the force are even unknown to each other. The visitor would find many theatres and cinemas. He would be surprised to find them always crowded with enthusiastic audiences. He would be even more surprised to discover that, in order to get a seat, he must bargain with a ticket scalper. All seats are the same price (it would be most uncommunistic to charge more for a box than for a seat in the gallery).

Approaching Red Square in Moscow, the U.S. observer would see a flamboyant sign in Russian characters: "RELIGION IS THE OPIUM OF THE PEOPLE." Yet, in the streets he would frequently see black-garbed Russian Orthodox priests. Some big churches are closed because the people cannot afford to keep them up, but most of the churches are still open. The U.S. citizens would, therefore, come to the conclusion that the Soviet Government, while actively discouraging religion and paying not one kopeck to the support of the churches, nevertheless tolerates worship.

Turkey

"DANCE!": President Mustafa Kemal Pasha [later referred JAN. 17
to as Ataturk] of Turkey, tireless Westernizer, scowled last
week as he entered the new Hotel Erkraf at his grubby capital,
Angora, and found the dance floor all but deserted, though
the band was playing a fox trot according to his orders, and
officers with their wives were numerous.

A lieutenant explained: "It is the ladies' fault. They decline to dance."

"Silence!" roared Kemal Pasha, and the band stopped
amid a hush. Then, loudly apostrophizing his officers, the
Dictator-President cried: "Comrades, I cannot imagine that
there is in the whole world a woman capable of refusing to
dance with a Turkish officer. Your profession is the most
glorious and the most honorable. The whole country counts
on you. So, I repeat, I cannot imagine that there is a woman
capable of refusing to dance with a Turkish officer. Now I
order them to dance. Go on the floor. Dance."

Thereafter no lady declined. All danced, defying ancient
Turkish custom.

THE YOUNG TURKS: The Young Turks of today are trying FEB. 21
harder and with more success than any other backward
people to catch up with the march of civilization.

Polygamy is dying out in Turkey because the Young Turks
simply cannot afford plural wives, and so are generally content with their new Civil Code, based on the Civil Code of
Switzerland and absolutely forbidding polygamy.

Young Turkey is compact, and the dictature of Mustafa
Kemal, the *Ghazi* ("The Victorious"), is absolute. There
is not the occasion for internal strife and wholesale massacre
that there once was. The Turkish Civil Service still remains
lamentably corrupt; but the Departments of Justice and Education have been so improved as to be unrecognizable. The
new Swiss-type Civil Code is supplemented by a new German-
type Commercial Code; and a Penal Code based on that of
Italy has been promulgated. The immense project of scrapping outworn Turkish law (based on the Koran) and substituting Western statutes thus stands today, accomplished.

Before the Young Turk era it would have been as unthink-

Mustafa Kemal Pasha: "I order the women to dance. Dance."

Tewfik Rushdi Bey: "Pork is good" —even for Mohammedans. Page 156.

able for men to sit under women teachers as for U.S. college students to find their professors replaced by puppy dogs. The mind reels, and all but refuses to grasp that Young Turkey is following the *Ghazi* in a program as "revolutionary" as though President Coolidge should suddenly demand the nationalization of the railways, and hurry on from that, in a few months, to abolition of private property.

The explanation of the voluntary Turkish social revolution is that Turks see the Coolidge type of nation as a desired goal capable of swift and glorious attainment. Moreover, the *Ghazi* has made Turkish women abandon the veil. Could King George V, Premier Stanley Baldwin and the British Parliament cause British women to go about stripped to the waist?

MARCH 14 **EVASION:** From the Turkish city of Trebizond (equivalent to a U.S. Fundamentalist stronghold) news came last week that pious women have found a way to circumvent the recent law that all Turkish women must go about with their faces naked. Since the Government of President Mustafa Kemal Pasha has ravished from Turkish womenfolk the veil, Mohammedan "Fundamentalists" in Trebizond adopted last week the umbrella. Determined to protect modesty, they walked in rain or sunshine with only eyes peeping above umbrellas held flat against face and body.

DYING BELIEFS: "Pork is a good food. One of the best. Reli- JUNE 15
gion may forbid it, but that idea will die with the older gener-
ation. While pork has been avoided with horror for genera-
tions as 'unclean,' it is now being eaten by our younger gen-
eration."

Such were words spoken last week in Constantinople by the
great Tewfik Rushdi Bey, perhaps the most wholesomely
feared and respected Near Eastern statesman.

The present eating of pork by Mohammedans, he continued, is but one example of the voluntary acceptance of new
customs by the people, once they had been jolted from old
ruts of thought by such laws as another recent one compelling
the substitution of the hat for the fez.

"The time will come, later, when any Turk can wear any
hat he chooses or none!" said Tewfik Rushdi Bey with emphasis. "But the fez was a symbol and had to be abolished
because it represented a psychological state that was wrong."

CENSUS: Profoundest silence lay over all Turkey like a pall of NOV. 7
death. Not a train ran. Not a boat sailed. Not an airplane
flew. Not a factory hummed. Not a siren shrieked, nor a
whistle blew. Men neither toiled nor did they sweat. In
the cities the streets were deserted. Street cars did not run,
shops were closed, automobiles were garaged. From Constantinople at the Golden Horn, along the length of the Bosporus,
flanked by its minarets and white domes, diurnal scene of a
thousand scurrying ships, all was silent as the graveyard.

The Turkish Republic was holding its first census. From
the first streak of dawn to the last shadow of dusk all citizens
were ordered to remain within their doors; none might ven-
ture out unless with an official permit. All day long 50,000
census takers, accompanied by police and soldiers, counted
heads, took names, ages, religions, professions, native lan-
guages spoken, examined for health and applied simple educational tests, while the suspicious populace, quietly submit-
ting to the inquisition, wondered if all the counting of heads
was to assist the taxgatherer in his unwelcome rounds.

For two years the Government prepared for the event and,
in order to overcome the passive opposition of the people, it
was decided to hold the census on Friday, Moslem rest day,
and to keep every man, women & child at home.

<pre>
   ╭─────────────────────────────╮
   │   SPORT   │
   ╰─────────────────────────────╯
</pre>

JAN. 24 **SWIM:** Some in grease and some in bathing suits, some young, some old, all fat, all strong, all surrounded by tug boats, press boats, ferryboats, launches, shouted at by coaches, fed by trainers, 96 able swimmers got into the cold water at Catalina Island, one day last week and turned their numerous, goggled, and determined faces toward the unseen California mainland, 22 miles away. Day faded. Lights came out on the shore. Now and then on the bow of a tug a trainer lit a red flare to show that his swimmer was out of the race. Slowly, doggedly, the rest splashed on.

Like music over the water came the sound of their splashing to the ears of William Wrigley Jr. It was an inspiration, no less. He was advertising his real estate development at Catalina. He was showing himself to be a patron of sport.

Most of the best distance swimmers in the U.S. had taken his dare. There was Henry F. Sullivan who swam the English Channel in 1923, and Jean McKenzie who refused to wear any bathing suit. There had been some trouble about these nude ones—preachermen declared that if the bodies of these athletes were exposed to view there must be something indecent about the race.

On went the splashers. They sucked food through rubber tubes. They listened to the cheerings of their followers. The red flares of surrender were going up often now. Only two of the men—George Young, 17-year-old Canadian, and huge Norman Ross of Chicago—still faced the mainland. Between three and four miles from shore Swimmer Ross sighed *finis* and groped for the gunwale of his boat. That left George Young alone, and he succeeded. After 15 hr., 44 min., 33 sec., he reached Point Vinvente, Calif., losing 25 lbs. in the $25,000 venture.

APRIL 11 **"PLAY BALL":** Northward from Florida and Texas, eastward from the storm-drenched purlieus of Los Angeles they go—

500 leather-cheeked, great-knuckled athletes, members of the 16 "big" league teams, presumably the best baseball players in the world. For two months they have been practising.

A large share of impartial attention is bestowed this year upon the Philadelphia Athletics, attracted mainly by what seems a striking change of policy on the part of Manager Cornelius McGillicuddy, conveniently called "Connie Mack." This ancient, able, angular seer of baseball, who shares managerial honors with John J. McGraw of the New York Giants, led his Philadelphia club to its first American League pennant in 1902. He repeated the feat in 1905, 1910, 1911, 1913, 1914. At the conclusion of the 1914 campaign, he found that his winning habits had had a deadening, unprofitable effect on his public. Philadelphians were sure that Mack's team would win; were spending their money to witness sports in which the element of chance was more noticeable.

So Mr. McGillicuddy called together most of his gleaming stars, said a kind farewell, sold them to other club owners. With a slight fraction of this pelf he combed sandlot, high school, college, obscure league; purchased the economical services of several bright-faced lads; settled to the business of developing another winning team.

In 1925 it seemed that the old manager's patience was about to reap its reward. His youngsters, however, proved not quite stanch enough to turn the trick; finished second to the world champion Washington Senators. Last year they were again good without being quite good enough, ended third from the top. Experts liked their 1927 chances.

Then came winter with its noisy charges of scandal [the case involved a belated charge that the Cleveland Indians had thrown a game to the Detroit Tigers in 1919] unproved, dismissed. Uneasy magnates shifted in deep leather chairs, wondered if the charges would have lasting effect on the paying public. The market was glutted with disengaged ball players of note. At this point, Mack surprisingly stepped in. Disregarding his time-honored custom of selling privately developed stock to others, he signed for his own account several ripe—if not overripe—oldsters. It was whispered that, at 64, he was finally, definitely, desperately out to win another championship.

Will the addition of Cobb and Collins give Connie's team

that extra ounce of punch needed to land them on top? Will the skill, experience of these fading stars compensate for their shortened wind and brittle legs? Will the aged manager, used to handling willing youth, be able to cope with concentrated temperament, prevent it from disrupting his already capable machine? The answers would soon be found.

APRIL 18   **LOGGERHEADS:** At El Paso, Tex., Joe Parelli and Billy Hallas, wrestlers, climbed into a ring, each prepared to force his opponent's clavicles to the mat. Scuffling for a hold, the two grunters permitted their respective skulls to collide with great force. Unconscious—"even for wrestlers," as Sports Writer McGeehan put it—both fell and lay where they had fallen. The referee was puzzled; noted that Hallas was resting on his back; Parelli on his side; proclaimed the comatose Parelli winner.

JULY 11   **AT WIMBLEDON:** The interest of Spaniards in matters of sport follows the King. Therefore, last week, the presence of King Alfonso at Wimbledon was almost equivalent to a royal cheering section for the great Spanish net star Señorita Lilli de Alvarez. She, warmly beautiful, vivacious, and compellingly feminine, came up, last week, in the women's singles finals against Miss Helen Wills.

They played the first set without either young woman ever coming within 20 feet of the net. Miss Wills, smashing like clockwork, seemed to have regained and even surpassed the magnificent speed and rallying power which she possessed before her operation for appendicitis. During the second set, at 3-3, Señorita de Alvarez suddenly switched from back-court play to a furious storming of the net which had about it the flavor of a battle cry: "For King and Country!" Soon Señorita de Alvarez led by one game and fairly scintillated pleasure.

Putting her strokes like pistol shots, Miss Wills took the eighth game, the ninth, the tenth. Then she was women's singles champion at Wimbledon—and, by popular consent, women's singles champion of the world. Not since Miss May Sutton (now Mrs. Bundy) won at Wimbledon, 20 years ago, has a U.S. woman worn this supreme tennis crown.

As Miss Wills and Señorita de Alvarez walked off the

court, the new champion chanced to be a step behind at the gate. Señorita Lilli de Alvarez smiled in friendly fashion, stepped aside, and gestured for Miss Wills to pass. "Queens first!", she said.

"BAWBY" AGAIN: Fifty-seven years ago, the cathedral town JULY 25 of St. Andrews, Scotland, went daft over a youth of 19 whose name was Tom Morris Jr. With his long-necked clubs, lumpy balls and tam o'shanter, he had gone over to Prestwick on the west coast and, for the third year running, whipped all the golfers in the land for the British Open Championship. They gave him the champion's belt, to keep permanently. The next year they did not bother to hold the tournament.

St. Andrews erected a statue of Tom Morris Jr. making an iron shot. The statue's legend reads: "Sure and Far." Not until 1926, when he won the British Open with a 291 did another young man come along who really played them "Sure and Far." Last year Robert Tyre Jones Jr. of Atlanta looked very much indeed like another Tom Morris Jr. Aged 25, he appeared to carry on where Tom Morris Jr. left off.

Hence the unusual crowds last week at St. Andrews, cradle of golf. They banked the fairways with solid walls of humanity, 20,000 strong. The galleries followed "Bawby" Jones. Excursion trains stopped to watch him. Clergymen, grandmothers, policemen, cripples made shift to get a view.

Entering the treacherous "loop" stretch of the old course, where the holes criss-cross among wiry gorse and whins, he played four holes in twelve shots. He finished the round in 68, tying the course record. He clicked off his next round in 72. His pluperfect form lapsed to mere perfection in a third round of par 73. He finished with another 72, six strokes ahead of the previous tournament record.

One dismayed Scotsman growled, "Ye're nae a gowfer at a'—ye're juist a machine." Another said: "The gr-reat-est gowfer in the wur-rld." Carried on Scottish shoulders to his hotel, Gowfer Jones hastily sought privacy. The terrific strain had ended in an attack of nausea. When it had passed he said: "To be a champion at St. Andrews is quite too much for me."

AUG. 1 **A MATTER OF OPINION:** Prize fighting is popular because, watching it, civilized people are vicariously purged of their primitive inclinations. In the Stone Age, a fight was simply a fight, with no non-physical exchanges before or after. Today a fight stimulates the popular art of debate. Psychologically speaking, the meeting of the country's two second-best physical fighters last week in the Yankee Stadium, Manhattan, was one of the most successful affairs of its kind ever conducted by society.

Of the principals, one was a 194½-pound man, aged 32, of Irish descent—Jack Dempsey. Thick-lipped, splay-nosed, laconic, he was to demonstrate whether or not he could again transform himself into a smashing feline whirlwind in the boxing ring as he could from 1919 to 1926 when he was world's champion heavyweight.

The other was a 196-pounder of Lithuanian descent, Jack Sharkey, aged 25. Heavily good-looking, bright-eyed, garrulous, he was to prove himself formidable enough to deserve a chance at overpowering the man that whipped Dempsey last autumn, World's Champion Gene Tunney.

They drove their fists into each other savagely, scarcely bothering to protect themselves. Eighty thousand people, swarming around them in the night, bellowed with joy. Several million people, listening to an excited radio announcer at the ringside, rocked with excitement. It was, said the announcer, a furious fight, fast and even.

Some thought Sharkey hit oftenest. Others said Dempsey hit hardest and forced the fight. Sharkey seemed the livelier, Dempsey the stronger, when, in the seventh round something happened. The man nearest the two fighters at the time, Referee Jack O'Sullivan, described it later:

"There is no question about the punch on Sharkey's left leg by Dempsey's right. It was a sweeping blow which glanced off the leg and it was followed by Dempsey's left to the solar plexus, which was the decisive blow as I saw it. Before the solar plexus blow was delivered and after the right landed on Sharkey's left leg, I was stepping in toward the men, saying: 'Watch your punches, Jack.' Then, realizing there were two Jacks, I said: 'I mean you, Dempsey.' Then Dempsey hit the solar plexus blow. Sharkey dropped his right hand and Dempsey hit him a left on the jaw."

Sharkey fell on his anguished face. Referee O'Sullivan counted ten seconds, declared Dempsey the winner. Under the regulations this decision was final. Though he complained loudly after coming to, Sharkey entered no formal appeal from the decision. He bore no tell-tale bruise; did not seek medical examination.

A "roll call" of ringside sport writers revealed a distinct preponderance of opinion that claimed a foul. Among those voting "no foul" were Mayor Walker of New York City; Champion Tunney. Grantland Rice, usually calm, said: "Dempsey struck Sharkey two foul blows."

Receipts of the fight totaled about a million dollars, taxes included. Of this—

The U.S. got	$ 98,502
New York State got	49,251
Dempsey got (reputed)	352,000
Sharkey got	210,426
Promoter Rickard got (balance)	273,350

People present included the Maharajah of Ratlam, India, wearing diamond-studded earrings, followed by pickpockets and detectives; Jack Kearns, onetime manager of Dempsey, followed by an odor of perfume.

Having beaten Sharkey, Dempsey went on to challenge Gene Tunney in an attempt to regain the heavyweight championship of the world. Their meeting, billed as the fight of the century, whipped up enormous excitement. In it occurred the famous "long count" incident that fight fans still argue about. TIME *chose to tell its story in the words of Graham McNamee, the most popular radio announcer of the day.*

THE BIG FIGHT: "Good evening, Ladies & Gentlemen of the OCT. 3 Radio Audience," said announcer McNamee. Fifty million people purred contentedly at being thus addressed. All leaned forward eagerly.

"This is a big night. Three million dollars' worth of boxing bugs are gathered around a ring at Soldiers' Field, Chicago. Burning down at us are 44 1,000-watt lamps over the ring. All is darkness in the muttering mass of crowd beyond the spotlight. The crowd is thickening in the seats. . . . There's Jim Jeffries . . . Mayor Thompson in a cowboy hat . . . Irvin Cobb . . . John Ringling . . . Tex Rickard in a beige fedora. . . . It's like the Roman Coliseum.

"Here comes Jack Dempsey, climbing through the ropes . . . white flannels, long bathrobe . . . friend in a long green coat. . . . Here comes Tunney . . . (blast of cheering from the crowd). . . . He's got on blue trunks with red trimmings. . . . They're getting the gloves out of a box tied with pretty blue ribbon. . . . The announcer shouting in the ring . . . trying to quiet 150,000 people. . . . Robes are off. . . ."

The Bell.

"Jack leads with a long left and misses . . . boxing quietly. . . . Gene is stabbing Jack off . . . oh-o . . . Jack wandering around Gene. . . . Dempsey drives a hard left under the heart. . . . Jack pounded the back of Tunney's head with four rights. . . . Gene put a terrific right . . . hardest blow of the fight . . . Gene beginning to wake up . . . like a couple of wild animals . . . Gene's body red . . . hits Dempsey a terrific right to the body . . . Jack is groggy. . . . Jack leads hard left. . . . Tunney seems almost wobbling . . . they have been giving Dempsey smelling salts in his corner. . . . Some of Dempsey's blows make this ring tremble. . . . Tunney is DOWN . . . down from a barrage . . . they are counting . . . six—seven—eight—"

Lilli de Alvarez: warm, vivacious, but a loser at Wimbledon. Page 159.

Gene Tunney "is DOWN. *They are counting . . . six—seven—eight—."*

Theodore J. Carron and Henry Koenig, listening at different radios in Detroit, dropped dead from excitement. Charles F. Brown died in Watertown, N.Y. James K. Chilson and George K. Johnson died in California.

"NINE and Tunney is UP . . . backing away . . . now out-boxing Dempsey . . . Jack trying to get Tunney where he can hit him . . . following . . . motions Gene to come in and fight. . . . Dempsey comes in like a wild man. . . . Dempsey is DOWN from a hard left to the jaw. He is UP . . . Dempsey's eyes are getting worse. . . . TUNNEY LOOKS MAD . . . drives hard on Dempsey's eye, and it is a very, very bad eye. Dempsey is very, very tired . . . Dempsey is almost down. . . . FIGHT IS OVER."

Spencer W. Crowell at Algona, Iowa, and Robert J. Glick of Shamokin, Pa., died during the terrific suspense when the VOICE failed to announce the decision.

"I think Tunney is still champion. . . ."

Announcer Graham McNamee could scarcely be expected to grasp immediately the technical detail here involved, through which Dempsey protested to the Illinois Boxing Commission that he had won the fight. Dempsey knocked Tunney down. By the rules of the contest he should have walked immediately to a neutral corner and waited until his antagonist arose or was counted out. Instead he stood over him: went to the wrong corner. Thus five seconds were lost before he reached the neutral corner and the actual count began over the prostrate Tunney. Tunney rose after the ninth second. A boxer is knocked out after ten seconds. Actually, Tunney was down 14. Tunney insists that his head was clear after the first few seconds and that he could have risen within the first ten seconds; that, grasping the situation, he waited for the extra respite to arise stronger, steadier.

SWAT: Cheering, screaming frantic fanatics flooded George OCT. 10 Herman ("Babe") Ruth with the wildest ovation ever accorded a baseball player. In the eighth inning of a New York game against Washington, Ruth hit a ball pitched by left-handed Thomas Zachary into the right field bleachers. The home run was Ruth's 60th of the season.

Said Frederick G. Lieb, sage baseball writer: "It is doubtful if anyone in that crowd will ever live to see another baseball player hit his 60th home run in a 154-game season. I saw Ruth hit his 59th in 1921 and never thought I would score the game in which that record would be broken."

Ruth's record this year is chiefly owed to another member of the Yankees. Directly behind Ruth on the batting list is Louis Gehrig. He too is a home-run hitter (47 for 1927). With Gehrig next at bat, pitchers dare not give Ruth a complimentary base on balls, hoping to dispose of his successor easily. Ruth in 1927 received fewer bases on balls than in 1921, more chances to hit. [Ruth's record stood until 1961 when Roger Maris, also a Yankee, hit 61 home runs—but in a season of 162 games.]

NOV. 7 **ROCKNE OF NOTRE DAME:** Since Knute K. Rockne came as coach to University of Notre Dame in 1919, his team, playing desperately difficult schedules, has won 64 games; lost 6; tied 2. Many regard him as the greatest coach of football.

Various reasons for his success have been advanced. But he has no secret of success, no formula. He knows what to do; tells his players and they do it. Among the things he tells them: "Don't be a mollycoddle"; "See everything"; "Eat no chocolate, cocoa, greasy fried potatoes, pork or bananas"; show "brains, courage, coordination, fire of nervous energy"; "No star playing, just football."

Rockne, in his tenser moments, looks like an infuriated bulldog. Sometimes he talks that way. His talks to the team have made Notre Dame the best advertised college in the land. [Notre Dame ended its 1927 season with seven victories, one tie, one loss.]

MISCELLANY

RABBITS: In northeastern Colorado, men armed themselves with clubs, flocked to Fort Morgan, ranged in a wide-flung line over the prairie, herded 2,000 wild rabbits—pestilential to crops—into a wire enclosure, waded among them, slew all, eagerly looked forward to another field day, the "mammoth bunny slaughter" of the nearby Brush Civic Club, occasion for an annual holiday in northeastern Colorado.

STORK: In Delavan, Wis., Mr. and Mrs. William Storck announced the arrival of a daughter, their 17th Storck in 22 years.

THE THEATRE

"OH, PLEASE!"—Beatrice Lillie makes all men laugh in *Oh,* JAN. 3
Please! The vehicle is a rickety contraption, a musical comedy about an actress who invades the home of the President
of the Purity League while his wife is on leave of absence.
Gowned in a Turkish towel, she warbles her hopelessly ridiculous songs, wrestles with Purity League President Bliss, flops
on her other end with the *savoir faire* and polite restraint of
a duchess, with a twinkling in her two eyes merrier than all
the unbridled hilarity in the audience.

"EARL CARROLL'S VANITIES"—Following the "Fifth and JAN. 17
Grossest of All" comes the International edition of *Earl Carroll's Vanities.* The hordes in the chorus look much like their
predecessors, are engineered about into similar stage designs
by the same swinging hooks, rising platforms, whirling chan-
deliers a-dangling with girlies. Julius Tannen and his oddly
trained seal are also on hand. But the best part is still Moran
and Mack, lackadaisical, lethargic, ridiculous dialogue come-
dians.

"ZIEGFELD FOLLIES"—For 21 years Florenz Ziegfeld has AUG. 29
produced the *Follies* according to one formula: to frame the
most beautiful show girls discoverable against the most gor-
geous backgrounds conceivable. His formula has never failed.
But as nothing subscribes more unreservedly to the law of
diminishing returns than a succession of splendors, this last
superbly heralded *Follies* achieves only another anticlimax.
Though Eddie Cantor (eyes big as baseballs) paces the stage
with a repertory of "wisecracks," the tone of metropolitan
criticism seemed to be, condescendingly: "The Ziegfeld
Follies is the world's most beautiful dumb show."

"BURLESQUE"—Last week loud applause came to a young SEPT. 12
actress who found herself bowing to bravos as featured player

of the season's first hit, while her ears still rang with the jazz jingles she crooned only two years ago in the smoky staleness of a nightclub. Barbara Stanwyck came that suddenly to the apogee of Broadway nights.

At first she sang in a cabaret and imitated stage celebrities. Then she had an understudy part. Now her name is in white lights. She is cast as a slangy lady of the burlesque wheel, who is unfortunately in love with a no-account, shiftless husband (Hal Skelly), a "comic hoofer" without "a laugh above the hips," without timbre to respond to her affection.

Though he shuffles off with a chorine, she cannot bring herself to marry a princely cattle rancher of the prairies, whose great heart and expansive properties are spread at her feet. She finds herself completely subject to her first, trashy love, follows him through his glimmer of success and his nights of degeneracy.

Barbara Stanwyck with Hal Skelly. Suddenly she is bowing to bravos.

Mae West. Her new play is clean, her fans disconsolate. Page 168.

In the last scene, the audience sees them together as they appear to audiences on the burlesque circuit, doing a waltz buck while a brazen orchestra shatters her sentiment into cheap, broken rhythms. "Can you make it?", she asks under her breath of her tottering spouse, snapped out of a month's debauch for this merry function. "I can—if you'll stick, kid." "I'll stick—always," she answers, and as the curtain falls the audience knows that she belongs forever to the blah of her man, to the hurdy-gurdy of the footlights.

Burlesque is a stunning, crafty show.

"THE LETTER"—When the curtain rises the sound of a shot OCT. 3 is heard and a cry from Hammond. Leslie fires again.

Hammond: "Oh, my God!"

He falls in a heap on the ground. Leslie follows him, firing and then standing over him, fires two or three more shots in rapid succession into his prostrate body.

Thus begins the Somerset Maugham play in which Katharine Cornell makes anything but merry as Leslie Crosbie, murderess. But for the acting of the star, the evening would have been unimpressive. Miss Cornell is one of the few great players in the land who will risk the sympathy of the spectators by playing women they wouldn't want around the house.

Claudette Colbert: so much sex appeal she seems miscast as a lady.   *Helen Hayes. "Coquette" is aglow with her stunning performance.*

"THE MULBERRY BUSH" discusses divorce with some sagac- NOV. 7 ity, some wit, and rare indelicacy. Claudette Colbert, adding to her role such an atmosphere of skillful sex appeal that she seems almost miscast as a lady, acts the wife.

"THE WICKED AGE"—Mae West betrayed her public. *Sex,* NOV. 14 which she wrote and in which she acted, was very dirty and very dull. She went to jail for it. Her new play is about bathing beauty contests. The greasy gathering that assembled, itchingly expectant for the first performance, was disconsolate. Her cheap, shiftless talent is useless to them now. She has cleaned it up.

NOV. 21 **"COQUETTE"**—What seems reliably like the finest play of the season arrived last week aglow with a stunning performance by Helen Hayes. By her playing she joined immediately the tiny group of actresses who make the theatre a land of wonder, tears & pure delight. Ably seconding her is Elliot Cabot, who plays a rough villager with whom the fickle lady of the play falls surpassingly in love. Her southern father shoots the villager. For the gay, lying lady, suddenly swept off her feet by the truth of passion, there is no resource but death.

DEC. 5 **"FUNNY FACE"**—Three noble contributors to musical comedy have collaborated for the third time, and for the third time with thorough excellence. George Gershwin writes music; Fred and Adele Astaire dance it. They began together with *For Goodness Sake,* repeated with *Lady, Be Good!* and in *Funny Face* furnish the smartest and best of the new musical comedies.

MILESTONES

MARRIED: Vilma Banky, cinemactress, to Rod La Rocque, cinemactor; in Los Angeles.

DIED: Ernest R. Ball, 48, composer of "Mother Machree," "Love Me and the World Is Mine," "When Irish Eyes Are Smiling," "Let the Rest of the World Go By," "Will You Love Me in December As You Did in May?" (lyrics by New York Mayor James John Walker) and many another tune; of heart disease, suddenly; at Santa Ana, Calif., while on a vaudeville tour.

MISCELLANY

GAFFER: In Paris, one Gilbert Nicolas Leclerc, peasant of Limoges, France, old, bearded, pious, hobbled last week into the *Moulin Rouge,* internationally famed revue and dance hall. M. Leclerc came seeking his daughter, Jeanne, who had run away to Paris from tedious Limoges. M. Leclerc found his *petite* Jeanne and begged her to come home. She refused. "I cannot survive your dishonor," he said. Drawing a revolver he shot himself through the heart.

ORANGE-EATER: In Cincinnati, one Howard Stribbling, 20, of Columbus, Ohio, ate 62 oranges, spat out the seeds, broke his own Ohio record; won $20, a straw hat, a walking stick. His masked rival, one "Hoggie," ate 53, was satiated. Orange potentates rejoiced.

MUSIC

"INTERMEZZO": Vienna, the Gay—Vienna, rival of Paris, JAN. 24 was last week preparing joyfully to revive its famed opera ball, after four years of "interruption." Its committee was resolved it should miss no facets of the sparkle of days before the War.

As distinguished prelude to this gayety, there occurred the Vienna première of *Intermezzo,* newest opera by Richard Strauss, now 62. He, its composer, has lately been unkind to Vienna. Only last month, he refused to conduct the Viennese Opera unless the government granted him a huge salary, complete autocratic powers, a once royal palace for the duration of his life—this at a time when the Viennese are living on rations. But Vienna could not do without him. He alone could be the central jewel of a reconstructed crown.

The creations of Richard Strauss are never treated casually, for his work is intensely personal and his personality is provoking. Looking upon the philosophical brow, dreamy eyes, sensitive lips, effeminate chin, one marvels how this musician can grate so on the world.

His melodious yet powerful *Don Juan,* an early work, remains his most popular tone poem. *Salomé,* his third opera, first produced in 1905, was a literal sensation. Because of the realistic power with which the composer treated the theme, for which he chose Oscar Wilde's necrophilistic version, U.S. presentations were banned for some time. But victrola records were allowed to popularize the "Dance of the Seven Veils"—and in Europe the opera at once took front rank. *Der Rosencavalier,* with its infectious burlesque, wit and sparkle, stays his best liked opera, perhaps his best to date.

Intermezzo's libretto, based on personal spats seldom so openly revealed, will cause some shrugging of shoulders, some sharper comment. Those who question the taste of such autobiography forget, possibly, that the world left him poor while he was creating some of its richest musical treasure; that critics derided when first he wore his heart on his sleeve; that such experiences leave strange marks on sensitive natures.

FEB. 21 **VIRTUOSO:** They say nothing can move sophisticated Europe. Last week in the Salle Gaveau (Paris concert hall) a fair-haired little boy in a blue sailor suit put his violin under his chin and played Mozart. He did not seem to notice that women were weeping, that men were looking at their waist-coat buttons. After his last number, he could not help notic-ing that hats were flying up in the air, that the room was ring-ing with deafening cheers; that women were throwing violets at him. Startled, he ran off the stage. His mother protected him from men and women who came plunging through back doors crying, "He is a love!" "He is divine!"

Yehudi Menuhin. The little boy in a sailor suit is "A love!," is "Divine!"

Deems Taylor. His new opera gets a tumultuous reception.

His name is Yehudi Menuhin. He is ten. He was born in New York, raised in San Francisco. His parents came from Palestine. Paris critics said: "Not since the child Mozart, seated on a pile of music on a piano stool. . . ."

FEB. 28 **NEW OPERA:** The Metropolitan Opera House hummed its loudest and busiest. The most brilliant gathering of the year had assembled to hear the first U.S. opera commissioned by Metropolitan Director Gatti-Casazza, *The King's Henchman.*

Edna St. Vincent Millay, poetess with a dramatic sense, had written the libretto; Deems Taylor, composer of concert music, onetime music critic of the N.Y. *World,* composed the score.

What "native" theme did they use? Indians? Witchcraft? Skyscrapers? No, the most native to U.S. spirit, decided Miss Millay, is the old Saxon legend. The Saxon is nearer than the redman; the turbulent warrior dearer than the Puritan to our age. Theirs was a forthright, swaggering, romantic spirit. Mr. Taylor wrote his music true to the hunt, the forest, the clash of sword, the misty superstitions, the feudal ideals of loyalty. The story parallels Wagner's *Tristan and Isolde*—a king, a vassal sent a-wooing.

At the end of the première performance the yellow curtains folded. A moment of silence, then storms of applause and 37 curtain calls. No one fled for his limousine. This ovation was sincere. Critics hailed a triumph: *The Henchman,* they said, was more than the greatest U.S. opera; it took rank with the great music of the world. [*The King's Henchman* was performed at the Metropolitan only 14 times. It was last played there in 1929.]

"PERFECT TENOR": To rise to the position of leading singer of the Metropolitan, musicians of this Continent usually strive for European reputation first. Edward Johnson, by birth Canadian, "trouped it" on the other side under the name Eduardo Giovanni. Playing whatever parts fell to him, this Signor Giovanni finally won his reward. Last week, Director Gatti-Casazza assigned him five leading tenor roles to be sung within eleven days.

That is an unusually strenuous schedule, demands phenomenal memory, perfect physical condition. Tenor Johnson satisfies these requirements. As Romeo, in *Romeo and Juliet,* he appears in medieval doublet and hose. One notices at once why he has been called "the perfect tenor." His waistline is where every true Romeo's waistline should be, where most tenor waistlines are not.

Another of his roles is Avito in *L'Amore dei Tre Re.* For this, he fits himself snugly into the insolent costume of the Florentine prince, again doublet, hose, cloak and hat with a plume. In a third, Pelléas in *Pelléas et Mélisande,* the period

Edward Johnson lives his roles intent-ly, sings five of them in 11 days.

George Antheil. His ballet is "a moun-tain out of an antheil."

is the same. Only the color schemes vary. Romeo is purple; Avito, grey; Pelléas, blue. The wig is always the dark, bobbed one that goes with almost anything.

Since he dresses himself so many ways, does he ever forget which medieval garment to wear and sing to the fair Méli-sande what is for the ears of beautiful Juliet only? The execu-tives of the Metropolitan Opera will assure you he does not; that they know of no singer in their distinguished company who lives his roles more intently. [After his retirement as a singer, Edward Johnson served as General Manager of the Metropolitan from 1935 to 1950, when he was succeeded by Rudolf Bing.]

APRIL 25 **NOISE:** George Antheil, U.S. born, European-educated, pre-sented for the first time in his native land his *Ballet Mécanique,* which nearly precipitated a riot on its première in Paris. The young composer's theory is to express the U.S. in its own terms of steel, machinery, physical strength, without em-ploying jazz. To this end he has created a symphony of per-cussion instruments, ten mechanical pianos, several xylo-phones, assorted bells, wind machines, aeroplane propellers, etc., abjuring completely more lyrical aids.

The critics of the Manhattan newspapers derided, ignored. Said Critic Samuel Chotzinoff of the New York *World*: "This is making a mountain out of an antheil." The stately *Times* disdainfully neglected to mention the concert in its critical column at all, rating it simply a news story, another sensational sideshow of the arts.

To many, this reception seemed unfair. Composer Antheil knows the classics, admires Beethoven and Handel above all others, appreciates them intelligently. He is an accomplished musician himself on orthodox instruments. His departures, though radical, are too sincere to be dismissed with a sniff for the show-off. He is, first of all, an earnest young man. Had Manhattan waxed indignant, as did Paris when the mistake was made of facing the propeller toward the audience and thereby nearly blasting them into the street, the youthful creator might have derived satisfaction. The manner in which Manhattan dismissed his work means the kiss of death for the percussion symphony, in the U.S. at least.

"DIXIE": Southern notables assembled last week at Fletcher, JULY 11 N.C., to sing a song and unveil a tablet to the song's author, Daniel Decatur Emmett, who, though he never took his stand or lived or died south of the Mason & Dixon line, nevertheless composed both the words and music of "Dixie." Son of Ohio and buried there, Composer Emmett is the adopted son of all "Dixieland."

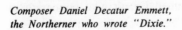

Composer Daniel Decatur Emmett, the Northerner who wrote "Dixie."   *Composer Franz Schubert. Should his "Unfinished Symphony" be finished?*

Composer Emmett never regarded "Dixie" as his ablest creation. He personally liked better his now-forgotten "Old Dan Tucker." Emmett, runaway son of a blacksmith, sang and banjoed in the country's earliest traveling minstrel quartets, barnstorming from hall to hall with striped calico shirts, ruffled sleeves, flaring collars. One Saturday night, on tour, his minstrel leader asked him to compose a new "walk around" (stage march) for use the next day. Emmett frowned at the hurry order, went to his hotel, rummaged out of his trunk the rough draft of a tune he had thought up some years before. The words for the tune had been suggested to him by a grumble he had often heard on the lips of circus performers "up North" when nippy autumn nights set in: "I wish I was in Dixie land."

To the original draft Minstrel Emmett put a few new touches, rhymed "cotton" and "forgotten," changed the tempo, handed his chief what he felt was a botched job. But next evening, the audience swayed to the new tune, caught the words easily, especially the "hoorays." It was one of those songs that people sing leaving the theatre. Soon the whole country sang it.

OCT. 17 **FINISH SCHUBERT?:** To help celebrate the centenary of Franz Schubert's death, the Columbia Phonograph Co. has offered prizes to the composers who submit the best fragments completing Schubert's famed "Unfinished Symphony." Of such efforts Ossip Gabrilowitsch, conductor of the Detroit Symphony Orchestra, disapproves. Last week he wrote to the Committee in charge: "Several weeks ago the Committee invited me to become a member of the Artists' Advisory Board. Believing the purpose was a dignified tribute to the memory of the great composer, I gladly accepted. I am now informed of the competition for completing Schubert's masterpiece. This seems, to me, like adding a pair of arms to the Venus of Milo. I request that my name be eliminated."

DEC. 5 **AGAIN, FARRAR:** A small block advertisement appeared in Manhattan newspapers. Geraldine Farrar would give a recital—and in no time every seat in Carnegie Hall had sold itself. It was a subdued, dignified Farrar who appeared last week—save for one terrible moment when backing off stage, she stepped on her train and sat down Ka-Plop. Her hair has turned grey since her great days at the Metropolitan. Her methods were in all ways softer, more delicate than those of five years back. But still it was the old Farrar, winning, by sheer charm of personality, an audience that was on its feet to greet her, to rush to the front when the program was done, to give thunderous ovations after each number. Critics had unqualified praise for her taste, for the intelligence with which she used a voice no longer fresh and glowing, with which she has approached a new and supreme art.

MILESTONES

MARRIED: Norma Shearer, 22, famed cinemactress; to Irving Grant Thalberg, 26, executive director for Metro-Goldwyn-Mayer; in Hollywood. The ceremony was prolonged by the bride's unfamiliarity with responses in the Hebrew.

DIED: Isadora Duncan, 47, famed *danseuse;* in Nice. One end of her red scarf caught in the front wheel of her motor; she was dragged from her seat and instantly killed. On her bier, her chauffeur laid a huge bouquet of flowers representing a month's earnings.

DIED: Clarence Shepard Day, 82, onetime Governor of the New York Stock Exchange: son of the late Benjamin H. Day, founder of the New York *Sun*; father of Author Clarence S. Day Jr. [whose 1935 bestseller, *Life With Father,* became a hit play on Broadway], in Manhattan, of pneumonia.

MISCELLANY

LEG: At Waterloo, Iowa, one Mrs. Marlow Tharp found that her wooden leg did not fit becomingly. She refused to pay the salesman, whereupon he boldly unstrapped the leg from her body and ran. Petulant, frustrated, she called the police.

REVIVALIST: From Flagpond, Tenn., one Rev. George Bennett, revivalist, started home from a revival, full of grace. At him, out of darkness, strode a menacing figure, armed with a pistol, a pint flask.

"Ah reckon," said the highwayman, "that you'd bettuh drink down dis yere drap o' White Mule."

"But I never drink," murmured the Rev. M. Bennett, elevating his arms. "Do you not know that—"

"Ah wasn't inquirin' abaout yo' pussenal habits, Misiter Preacherman. Ah was jest a-tellin' you' dat dis yere White Mule's a-goin' ter do yo' a right smart o' good."

With the pistol burrowing into his ribs, the Rev. George Bennett raised the flask, bubbling, gasping, choking with fury.

"Oh Lord, Thou seest that I have no choice—harrumph! Arggh!—in this—Klohchch!—iniquitous procedure. Smite, O Lord, thine enemies—Graowchch! Ugh! Urgle-urgle-phew!" The Rev. Mr. Bennett seethed with anger, staggered. The highwayman was not content until the flask was nearly empty.

Such, at least, was the story told by the Rev. George Bennett when he stumbled, angry and shy $10, into his home at Erwin, Tenn., very late one night last week.

AERONAUTICS

APRIL 25 **PARIS PRELIMINARIES:** Both shores of the Atlantic buzzed last week with the activities of men determined to fly between New York and Paris. The standing offer of Raymond C. Orteig, Manhattan hotel man, of $25,000 to the first successful performer, had little to do with the case. These sums would hardly pay interest on the total investments involved. Fame, promotions, above all Adventure—were the real stimulants.

Abroad, five bands of Frenchmen were thus stimulated, the most notable being headed by Ace Coli and Ace Nungesser. But shortage of capital hindered the French preparations.

In the U.S., expeditions tested their planes, accumulated final equipment.

Engineer Giuseppe M. Bellanca of the Columbia Aircraft Corp. had conditioned an elderly yellow-winged monoplane with one Wright motor, and engaged Pilots Clarence D. Chamberlain and burly Bert Acosta, onetime auto speedster, to test this ship's endurance. Up they put from Mitchel Field, L.I., with 385 gallons of ethylated (high power) gasoline. All day they droned back and forth over suburbia, circled the Woolworth Building, hovered over Hadley Field, N.J., swung back to drop notes on Mitchel Field. All that starry night they wandered slowly around the sky, and all the next day, and through the next night, a muggy, cloudy one. Messrs. Acosta and Chamberlain swallowed soup and sandwiches, caught cat naps on the mattressed fuel tank, while on and on they droned, almost lazily (about 80 m.p.h.) for they were cruising against time. Not for 51 hr., 11 min., 25 sec., did they coast to earth, having broken the world's record for protracted flight (45 hr., 11 min., 59 sec. set in France in 1925). In the same time, conditions favoring, they could have flown from Manhattan to Vienna. They had covered 4,100 miles. To Paris it is 3,600 miles from Manhattan.

Commander Richard Evelyn Byrd, U.S.N., and his comrades in polar flight last year—Floyd Bennett, and Lieut. George O. Noville—have a new triple-motored Fokker. Its wings spread 73 feet. It shines and is beautiful, but it will not fly to Paris soon. Last week, Commander Byrd and his aides soared aloft in the *America* which, as it returned to earth and taxied along the field, lowered its heavy nose and flopped over abruptly in a heavy somersault. Lieutenant Noville suffered an injured pelvis, Officer Bennett a cracked thigh, Commander Byrd a broken wrist, Designer Fokker a bad shaking, the *America* a splintered propeller, crumpled nose and fuselage.

DEATH IN A MARSH: Imagine a gigantic yellow bird, with MAY 9 wingspread of 67 feet, weighing some 6,000 pounds, carrying an additional load of 11,000 pounds. Imagine that bird losing necessary flying speed a few feet above the ground, trying to land in a marsh at 70 miles per hour.

In such a bird, last week, were Lieut. Commander Noel Davis and Lieut. Stanton Hall Wooster, crack flyers of the U.S. Navy. They were making their last test flight in the tri-motored *American Legion,* preparatory to attempting a non-stop jump from the U.S. to Paris. Loaded with enough gasoline to cross the Atlantic, their plane roared along the ground at Langley Field, near Hampton, Va. Gradually, almost painfully, it rose to a height of some 50 feet. A row of trees, planted years ago by an industrious pioneer, now rose up to thwart these air pioneers. Lieutenant Wooster turned the beak of the *American Legion,* slightly, ever so slightly. With that turn, the plane lost flying speed. A landing was now imperative. Marshes, mud flats, duck ponds yawned below. Upon a small patch of green, Lieutenant Wooster made a perfect landing—an almost unheard-of-feat with a plane loaded so heavily. The yellow giant skidded across the green marsh into the muddy waters of a shallow duck pond, wherein the giant's beak stuck. Its tail completed a semicircle. In its cockpit lay Lieutenant Wooster with his neck broken, Commander Davis with his face crushed—both lifeless in a gloomy pool of water and gasoline.

NUNGESSER & COLI: At Le Bourget (Paris airport) hundreds MAY 16 of humans were squatting, dancing, shouting on a flat and barren plain in the dead of night. Revelers in evening clothes uncorked champagne bottles. Suddenly, at 3:15 a.m., the plainsfolk scampered and cheered as a huge, ghostly bird, the biplane of Captain Charles Eugene Jules Marie Nungesser and Captain François Coli, emerged from its hangar. Its engine was tested—roared magnificently. Captains Nungesser and Coli gave it a final inspection. Soon they kissed relatives, mechanics, engineers; climbed aboard, while French soldiers with bayonets kept the crowd at a distance.

Dropping its landing gear to lessen its load, the *White Bird* skirted the southern coasts of England and Ireland, pointed its nose toward Newfoundland. It had no wireless. It was flying north of the usual steamship lanes. An angry wind from the west was beating in its face, slowing its speed. Expecting to reach New York in 35 hours, it carried only enough gasoline for 40 hours flying.

The world waited—40 hours, 50 hours—no ship had seen or heard the *White Bird* since it soared along the Irish coastline. Captains Nungesser and Coli were either floating on the Atlantic's waves or resting in peace on its bed. [No trace was ever found of pilots or plane.]

JUNE 6 **"OUTSIDE LOOP":** Imagine sitting upright on top of an enormous flywheel, 2,000 feet in diameter. You are strapped to its outer rim. The wheel is in motion, whirling you forward and downward at a speed which increases from 150 miles per hour to 280 miles per hour when you are upside down, beneath it.

Lieut. James ("Lucky Jimmy") Doolittle performed a similar revolution in his 420-horsepower Curtiss biplane last week, when he completed the first "outside loop" in aviation history. Two flyers attempted this stunt in 1912 and were killed. Lieutenant Doolittle began his loop above Dayton, Ohio, at an altitude of 8,000 feet, flying at 150 miles per hour. His great dangers were the collapse of his plane or the breaking of straps which held him in the cockpit. Even though his plane held together, Lieutenant Doolittle came out of the loop with bloodshot eyes and a slight hemorrhage of the lungs. At one point he had attained a speed of 280 m.p.h. The usual loop-the-loop stunt, an "inside loop" during which the plane rises and is on its back at the top of the loop

—brought death to two Army flyers at Clover Field, Santa Monica, Calif., last week. The wings of their plane collapsed in coming out of a loop at an altitude of 2,000 feet.

FOUR MEN IN A FOG: "We are going to land," scribbled JULY 11 Commander Richard Evelyn Byrd on a slip of paper. He crawled back through the fuselage of the giant Fokker monoplane, *America,* handed the paper to Lieut. George O. Noville who was lying on the floor, exhausted, temporarily deafened by the roar of the motors. "It was just as if he were handing me an invitation to tea," said Lieutenant Noville. The paper was shown to Lieut. Bernt Balchen who was piloting the plane, and to Bert Acosta who was so deaf and so miserable that he did not seem to care what happened.

For five hours, they had been flying over France, lost in a fog that obscured land and the tips of the *America*'s wings.

Their earth inductor compass had fits of running wild, their radio had become disabled, they were fast running out of gasoline—when suddenly at 3 a.m. they saw the seacoast and the flicker of a lighthouse beacon beneath them. That was the moment when Commander Byrd scribbled: "We are going to land." It was safer to drop into the sea than to crash into unyielding, unknown, fog-blanketed land, he decided.

So Lieutenant Balchen piloted the *America* into the waves, as gently as possible. The impact hurled Commander Byrd, watching at his cabin window, into the sea. He saw Lieutenant Noville climbing out of another window, dazed and unable to hear his shouts. He swam to the cockpit, helped Lieutenant Balchen extricate himself from the wreckage. Everyone yelled for Bert Acosta—he was not in the cabin—but soon he appeared out of the dark waves. Two days later, a Paris surgeon discovered that Mr. Acosta had a fractured collarbone, the only serious injury of the crash.

The four men in a fog inflated their pneumatic tub, paddled 200 yards to the shore of the little fishing village of Ver-sur-Mer. Aroused from sleep, the villagers aided in dragging the *America* into shallow water, bringing ashore the three Wright Whirlwind engines which had not once whimpered during the flight. Although the distance between Roosevelt Field, L.I., and Ver-sur-Mer on the coast of Normandy is

3,477 miles, yet Commander Byrd estimated that the *America* flew some 4,200 miles during its 42 hours' journey.

Virginia has been proud of its Byrds ever since William Byrd fought Indians in 1683. Today there are three famed Byrd brothers—"Tom, Dick and Harry." Harry F. Byrd is Governor of Virginia. Capt. Thomas D. Byrd, U.S. Army retired, served with distinction in the World War. Commander Richard Evelyn Byrd, 37, is the outstanding scientist-aviator in the U.S.

Adventurous at 12, he took a trip around the world, during which he was forced to eat parrots and monkeys while quarantined in the Philippines. He entered the Navy via Annapolis. His services to aviation include the invention of the bubble sextant (giving flyers an artificial horizon), the perfection of the sun compass and the drift indicator. He was flight leader of the MacMillan expedition to Greenland in 1923. Everyone knows the story of his flawless flight from King's Bay, Spitzbergen, to the North Pole and back in 16 hours on May 9, 1926. Last week he hinted that his next exploit would be a trip to the South Pole. [Byrd flew over the South Pole in 1929, and during his 1933-1935 expedition spent 19 weeks alone in a shack some 700 miles from the Pole.]

AUG. 29ᐧ **TOPSY-TURVY:** Tired of craning his neck over the edge of his plane to see the earth, Aviator Fisler (German) turned his plane over at Zurich and peered at the earth for eleven minutes. The upside-down flying record was claimed. Herr Fisler flipped his plane over, landed safely. He was not dizzy.

FLYING TRAINS: The country has broken out in a rash of airplane companies. The latest project is a New York-to-Chicago airway; there to connect with the Chicago-and-San Francisco planes, already operating. The fare will be $400; the flying time 32 hours.

Alluring reports of various concerns picture the passenger stepping into a deeply upholstered cabin; sailing smoothly, swiftly above the realms of way stations; ordering luncheon from a white-coated and obsequious steward. Actual facts from the Aeronautical Chamber of Commerce of America indicate that the solid citizen is skeptical of airways. Last

year only 7,651 citizens paid for tickets on U.S. flying trains.
Airway travel is roughly three times as fast as railways;
costs three times as much. There are eight passenger airways
now operating. The figures:

| | AIR | | RAILROAD | |
	Time	Fare	Time	Fare
Chicago to San Francisco	22 hr. 40 min.	$200.00	68 hr.	$79.84
New York to Boston	3 hr. 5 min.	30.00	5 hr. 30 min.	8.24
Portland to Los Angeles	11 hr. 15 min.	113.50	39 hr. 30 min.	40.88
Salt Lake City to Los Angeles	7 hr. 15 min.	60.00	30 hr.	28.05
Chicago to Minneapolis	5 hr. 50 min.	40.00	12 hr.	14.66
Cheyenne, Wyo., to Pueblo, Col.	3 hr.	25.00	8 hr.	8.16
Detroit to Grand Rapids, Mich.	1 hr. 45 min.	18.00	4 hr.	5.49
San Diego to Los Angeles	1 hr. 10 min.	17.50	3 hr. 30 min.	4.55

FIRST GIRL: The weather persistently spat drizzle and squall in OCT. 24
the face of the proposed flight, holding the aviatrix and her
co-pilot, George Haldeman, at Roosevelt Field, L.I. Then,
Miss Ruth Elder took off to fly the Atlantic—weather or no
weather.

Storms battered them southward from the start. Five
hundred miles out they were sighted by a passenger ship. They
were seen no more that day, that night. Crowds waiting at
Le Bourget field, Paris, turned away, glum, morose.

Meanwhile, the *American Girl* bucked storms. Flying
high, flying low, sleet and wind cut into her. Once Miss Elder,
unafraid, climbed out onto the tail of the ship to balance it.
In perilous spells she relieved her co-pilot at the levers. Then
the oil pressure fell. Part of the gasoline supply had been
dumped to lighten the ship in its fight against the storm. They
knew that their time was short.

After five hours of scouring the sea for help, they sighted
the Dutch tanker, *S.S. Barendrecht,* bound from the Azores

to Rotterdam. Circling low they dropped a message on the ship's deck. "HOW FAR ARE WE FROM LAND AND WHICH WAY?—RUTH ELDER."

On the deck, in large letters, Capt. Goos painted the answer: "TRUE SOUTH, 40 WEST, 360 MILES, TERCEIRA, AZORES."

Only 520 miles from the Portuguese coast the *American Girl* came down close to the tanker *Barendrecht.* Even if the oil system had functioned, the gasoline supply was too low to negotiate the distance. The pilots crawled on to the wings of the plane, bobbing precariously on a choppy, fresh-blown sea. Soon both were hauled to the deck of the tanker.

Captain Goos tried to haul up the *American Girl,* too, but gasoline ran over her hot engine, took fire. The flames shot into a towering pyramid, higher than the rescuing ship. An oil tanker avoids flames. The *American Girl* was abandoned. Said Miss Elder: "It was like watching an old friend drown."

At Horta, island harbor of the Azores, pilots Elder & Haldeman were welcomed by the entire population (about 3,000). Mrs. George W. Mackey, wife of Western Union Traffic Manager Mackey, lent Miss Elder an evening gown for a reception in her honor. Later, she replied "indeed not" when asked if she were too tired to dance.

NOV. 7 **PRIVATE CAR:** Mrs. James A. Stillman flew from Grand Anse, Quebec, to Pleasantville, N.Y., 450 miles. She has opened a charge account with the Fairchild Aviation Corporation (Canadian) and will commute between her residences at $100 an hour.

MILESTONES

SUED FOR DIVORCE: By Helen Menken, actress (*Seventh Heaven, The Captive*), Humphrey Bogart, actor (*The Cradle Snatchers, Saturday's Children*). She charged cruelty.

DIED: John Drew, 73, called last week by his nephew John Barrymore "The world's greatest actor"; at San Francisco, Calif.; of rheumatic fever. As death approached, Mr. Drew said: "This is but another act and I am playing my part."

MISCELLANY

GLASSES: In Asta, Italy, one Giovanni Noverre made a wager. He then drank a glass of water, another five glasses, (roughly, the outside limit of a healthy person's capacity), another 14 glasses, another 23 glasses, then very slowly nine more, then seven more taken in gulps and sips; finally he raised the 60th glass, poured it drop by drop down his gullet. After this glass, his wager won, Giovanni Noverre fell down and died.

ART

"GREATEST": In New Haven last week Lorado Taft, U.S. APRIL 11
sculptor who was born the year before the Civil War began,
declared, "As Americans we have a perfect and inalienable
right to our ignorance of art." He then explained that since
the American sprang from humble origins transplanted on a
barren shore, it is of little wonder that he is artistically an
ignoramus.

Pursuing his subject, the benign old gentleman ventured
two statements to the effect that Augustus Saint-Gaudens
became the greatest U.S. sculptor, and that the most noted
living U.S. sculptor is Daniel Chester French, aged 76.

Daniel French did make a statue, at 23, that is as well
known, perhaps, as any in the U.S., "The Minute Man of
Concord." The fact that the Minute Man in question was
famed more by his appearance on thousands of boxes of
Minute Tapioca than by universal acclaim does not alter the
fact that he is a famed minute man and statue. But French's
real successes are the great "Lincoln" in Washington and the
beautiful "Angel of Death." [The latter is in the Forest Hills
Cemetery in Boston.]

FLOWN AWAY: "Soon after we moved here, I took off the JULY 11
dirty old wall paper from the kitchen—several layers of it—
and found, underneath, pictures of all sorts of birds. Some of
the birds I recognized and some I had never seen. They were
right pretty.

"About two years ago I got tired of them and so I got a
can of good lead paint and put a nice coat all over the
walls. A little later I got tired of the paint and put on green
wall paper. Those birds have flown away for good, I guess."

Thus James McGrath, railroad worker, occupant of rooms
in a house on the upper end of Manhattan Island. Experts in
the restoration of paintings ruefully agreed that "those birds
have flown away for good." Ruefully, because the house

Daniel French. His "Minute Man" was on thousands of boxes of tapioca.   *George Bellows. In one picture, a bony oaf is telling a dirty joke. Page 186.*

where James McGrath lived was once inhabited by John James Audubon (1780-1851) famed wanderer of the trackless American wilderness, and painter extraordinary of wild life. Beyond a doubt the birds on Mr. McGrath's kitchen walls were the work of John James Audubon.

Prints of some of Audubon's bird engravings now command many thousands of dollars. Audubon murals would have been a priceless haul.

NOV. 7 **BELLOWS BOOK:** In 1882 George Bellows was born in Columbus, Ohio. In 1903 he was a lanky, nervous boy who played right forward on the basketball five and shortstop on the baseball nine at Ohio State University. Even after he came to Manhattan to be a painter, he often paid for dinner or theatre seats by playing professional ball over the week-ends. He was interested in looking at people and at things so that he could make pictures of them. For 20 years he made pictures, mostly of people doing things very intently. Then, in 1925, he died.

By that time he had achieved an enormous reputation among critics & connoisseurs. His lithographs, especially those of prizefighters and evangelists, had been greatly praised when hung in galleries or reproduced in magazines. Now 195 of them have been collected and published in a book —*George Bellows, His Lithographs.*

One of the works in the book is *Sixteen East Gay Street,* a picture of a street in Columbus, Ohio. It is late afternoon; in the golden twilight everything seems very quiet. If you look at the picture long enough, the man sitting on the porch will fold up his paper and go in to have supper.

The Shower Bath is full of a lot of naked businessmen who have just been trying to exercise. A bony oaf on the springboard is telling a dirty joke to a bald-headed codger with a pot belly.

Stag at Sharkey's is one of a prizefight series. Captious critics have called George Bellows an illustrator rather than an artist. This is because the most important qualities in his work are a sense of the dramatic and an ability to make the movement of his figures so intense that it is almost impossible to realize that they are, actually, stationary. Like all other artists, he is an illustrator of life; like no other artist he has found the themes for his illustrations in the strident banalities of U.S. civilization. Perhaps the only important U.S. artist who never crossed the geographical boundary of his country, he advanced its esthetic frontiers by producing art, which, as well as being indigenous, is both comprehensive and comprehensible, original without being evasive, and humble without ever for a moment becoming humdrum.

MILESTONES

DIED: Jiggs, 7, English bulldog mascot of the U.S. Marine Corps; in Washington; of gastronomical disorder from over-eating. In the service five years, he was buried with full military honors at Quantico, Va.

DIED: Amy Catherine Robbins Wells, wife of Herbert George Wells, famed British novelist; at Dunmow, England; of cancer. Dying a few hours before the marriage of her youngest son Richard, she requested that the ceremony be performed and that no one wear mourning at her funeral.

MISCELLANY

JIMMIED, BOBBIE: In Clearfield, Pa., Mr. and Mrs. Arthur Lewis, childless, were wakened by the cries of a baby. Under a window, deftly jimmied, lay a basket with a baby and a note in it.

"Mr. and Mrs. Arthur Lewis:
My name is Bobbie. I was born in Detroit, Mich., on Aug. 31, 1926. My parents are dead. Please keep me and love me."

The couple kept the baby.

SUBTITLES: In Manhattan, one Henry Fisher, traveling man, writhed in his seat at Keith's hippodrome. Behind him sat someone mumbling the cinema subtitles aloud. Mr. Fisher remonstrated. The mumbler behind struck Mr. Fisher on the head, jabbed him with a knife. Mr. Fisher sued the theatre for $25,000.

SCIENCE

JAN. 10 **LEMMINGS:** Last week, mice were reported in the Waldorf-Astoria. But these mice were dead. They were also, as mice go, famed. They had arrived in the luggage of Explorer-Engineer Grant Carveth Wells of England, who was going to take them to the American Museum of Natural History, where they would be mounted against a background of bleak tundra and labeled *Lemmus norvegicus,* the lemming.

Stubby of tail, tawny of fur, blunt of snout, five inches long, lemmings have histories dating back to Norse mythology and further; back to Miocene days when lemmings periodically migrated from the Scandinavian peninsula to another continent, perhaps lost Atlantis, by land routes which no longer exist.

The lemmings have not yet learned that their oldtime highways are gone. At uncertain intervals (sometimes after five years, sometimes after 20) they mass on an edge of the Scandinavian plateau and start a beeline migration.

They move by the million, having families more plentifully than ever on the march; destroying crops and herbage; preyed on by throngs of bigger beasts. They never hesitate, moving on over every obstacle, lake, river, mountain, until they reach the sea. Here their blind instinct persists and out they swim, still in the line of the migration, until the last one is drowned. Only a few will have stayed behind, hibernating or lacking true lemming instinct, or perhaps so hardy that they have not felt the need for a more congenial home. These will be progenitors of new millions. [Thus did TIME do its bit to perpetuate one of the most persistent pieces of folklore known to natural science. Lemmings do periodically migrate, and occasionally drown in large numbers, but only when driven to it by overpopulation.]

APRIL 18 **TELEVISION:** For centuries men have dreamed of the eye that would penetrate stone walls and miles of space. Last week sight at a distance (television) came true. In Manhattan, in the auditorium of the Bell Telephone Laboratories, Walter S. Gifford, President of the American Telephone & Telegraph Co., talked to his Vice President, General J. J. Carty, in Washington, D.C. Said President Gifford, dapper, cheery: "Hello, General, you're looking fine. I see you have your glasses on." Out of the loudspeaker, General Carty's bass voice boomed: "Does it—ah—does it flatter me?" President Gifford carefully viewed the changing smiling features of the General on the glass in the yellow frame before him. "Yes," he said, "I think it's an improvement."

In Washington, Secretary of Commerce Hoover talked next. Over the telephone wires his voice, his face, the minutest movements of his lips and head were brought to the watchers and listeners in Manhattan. As he spoke into the transmitter, small circles of light moved across his face so rapidly that they seemed to bathe it in a uniform bluish light.

The variations in light and shade, changed into electrical impulses, traveled to Manhattan over the wires. There the moving picture was re-assembled. On a small screen (2 x 2¹⁄₂ in.) the speaker's face and movements appeared distinct and clear; on a large one they were distorted badly.

Television, requiring bulky and expensive apparatus, does not yet loom as a standard addition to the home telephone. But theatre audiences, in the not too distant future, may see super newsreels of prize-fights, launchings, inaugurations, broadcast directly from the scene of the event.

DEATH OF MAXIM: As it must to all men, Death came last MAY 16 week to Hudson Maxim, 74, inventor of deadly explosives. It came slowly, quietly—preceded by 24 hours' coma. It found him at his home at Maxim Park, Lake Hopatcong, N.J. It had tried unsuccessfully, many times before, to find him in his laboratory. Although several of his assistants had been blown to bits, he emerged from all his dangerous experiments with only his left hand missing.

He knew so much about high explosives that he was often playful with them. One afternoon, while entertaining some friends at tea, he poured a few drops of liquid from the burner of the teapot into a vial, said: "Come out on the back porch and I will show you an experiment." Far out into the yard, he flung the vial. A terrific explosion ensued. In that vial, he explained to his friends, there was some nitroglycerine.

His first important discovery was smokeless powder, which he sold to the DuPonts in 1897. Then he produced "Maxim-ite," an explosive that can be shot through armorplate and exploded on the other side. His nephew, Hiram Percy Maxim, invented the Maxim silencer. His older brother, the late Sir Hiram Stevens Maxim, produced the Maxim machine gun which was standard equipment for most of the armies of the world before the War.

Hudson Maxim lost several aides, one arm, but died in bed.   *Dr. Charles G. Abbot. With flies' wings, he studies the heat of the stars.*

JULY 18 **STAR HEAT:** There being no more comets or eclipses sched-uled for this summer, Dr. Charles G. Abbot, assistant secre-tary of the Smithsonian Institution, left Washington last week for Mount Wilson, Calif., to pursue what has been his special study for many years, the heat of stars. Dr. Abbot has climbed the world's most arid mountains to study the sun's heat. Subordinates of his are at present sitting in an extinct South African crater continuing this work, an imme-diate purpose of which is to facilitate long-range weather pre-diction. But far more difficult to measure than the sun's heat, and of more abstruse scientific value, is the heat of stars many light years away. (One light year equals approximately

5,765,696,000,000 miles—the distance light can travel in one year.)

From star heat may be calculated star ages, star diameters, star compositions. Star heat is undiminished by billions of miles of passage through universal vacancy, but when the radiations enter Earth's heavy atmosphere they are dispersed, feebled and as difficult to detect and measure as a whisper in a hurricane. Star heat is best studied at altitudes where Earth's atmosphere is rare. To rare-aired Mount Wilson, therefore, went Dr. Abbot, where he can introduce starlight reflected from the 100-inch Carnegie Institute sky-reflector into his newest and finest radiometer—an instrument so delicate that a part of it is constructed of flies' wings; an instrument ten times as sensitive as Dr. Abbot's last radiometer, with which, "if the Earth were flat and the atmosphere perfectly transparent, it would have been possible to have measured in California the heat of a match struck on the Mississippi River."

"POWER BY WIRELESS": Manhattan newsgatherers went last JULY 25 week, as they have gone annually for many a year, to interview Nikola Tesla on his birthday. This year it was his 71st birthday but Nikola Tesla said nothing that he had not said on his 61st birthday—or his 41st for that matter.

Nikola Tesla, genius extraordinary of electricity, has been predicting since 1895 or so that enormous stores of power will some day be broadcast by radio, that airplanes will need no fuel. They will fly indefinite lengths of time on current flashed to them from any distance.

In 1893—four years before Guglielmo Marconi took out patents in Britain—Nikola Tesla patented in the U.S. a system of wireless transmission. A scarehead newspaper heard his prophecy that soon ships at sea would call electrically for help, to other ships or shore stations, without having any wired connection. The scarehead editor, well aware of his sheet's reputation, said: "We could not afford to print such a piece of inventive lunacy."

Thomas Edison's European agent was the man who brought the young Tesla to the U.S. from his native Croatia. After his first job for Mr. Edison—an all-night job putting a steamer's lighting plant in commission—Mr. Edison ejaculated to an associate: "This is a damn good man!"

Nikola Tesla, the genius of electricity, sits calmly under 25-ft. sparks.

Thomas A. Edison sponsored Tesla, "a damn good man!"

He still works early and late at his laboratory in West 40th St., Manhattan, dining alone at the same hour, at the same table in the Waldorf. Sometimes he visits his experimental plants in Colorado and on Long Island. Six years ago he said: "The matter of transmitting power by wireless is now so well in hand that I can say I am ready now to transmit 100,000 horsepower by wireless without a loss of more than 5% in transmission."

How soon such a Tesla plant will be built is problematical. When it is built automobiles, locomotives, ocean vessels, airplanes, dirigibles—all will have their power receiving apparatus and all draw power from a globe-blanket of high-frequency induction currents. That such a blanket of current would not be detrimental to health can be believed by friends of Mr. Tesla's who have seen a most appropriate photograph of him sitting in a zone of 25-foot electric sparks in his laboratory; calmly reading. [Tesla, as touchy as he was gifted, had broken with Edison in 1885. In 1912 the two were slated to share the Nobel Prize in physics, but Tesla refused to be associated with his former sponsor and the prize went to a lesser Swedish inventor instead.]

NOV. 21 **HOLLAND TUNNEL:** President Coolidge stretched forth his arm to touch the golden lever of the presidential telegraphic instrument. He pressed, and a current of electricity flowed to Manhattan and directly across the Hudson River to Jersey City. At each place, in sight of thousands of crowing spectators, the current caused a pair of great U.S. flags slowly to separate. The Holland Vehicular Tunnel officially became open.

The Holland Tunnel's greatest problem was not its construction, but its ventilation—how to avoid the poisonous carbon monoxide gas exhausted from motor trucks and cars. Ventilation experiments showed that more than four parts of the gas in 10,000 of air was dangerous. To prevent disaster, Chief Engineer Holland installed 84 ventilating fans in four 10 story buildings, two on each side of the Hudson. Part of them blow fresh air into the tunnel floor through vents, others suck vitiated air through ducts in the tunnel ceiling. Thus they change the tunnel air completely 42 times an hour. Fire hazard is prevented by watchmen stationed every few score feet; and there are tunnel fire engines at each entrance.

When Clifford Milburn Holland left Harvard in 1906 he went to Manhattan, saying: "I am going into tunnel work and I am going to put a lot more into it than I'll ever be paid for."

His wife last week told how he worked: "Evening after evening he remained at work. Our dinner hour was always uncertain. If we induced him to attend the theatre, he always went back to the tunnel afterward, spending hours in the field offices and personally supervising the work." It exhausted him and he died in 1924 of heart failure. The states made his tunnel a horizontal shaft to his memory.

MISCELLANY

SPINACH: "My husband likes spinach served at all meals," said a Chicago woman.

"So does mine. Isn't that a funny coincidence?" replied her friend.

It was neither funny nor a coincidence, as these two women soon found—for they were both married to the same man, one Peter Trapani, bigamist.

MIXER: In Stroudsburg, Pa., one William Lacey, road laborer, saw the big concrete-mixer at his job stop functioning. Peering in over the muddy mixture, he saw that a stone had lodged in the machinery. Practical, he crawled inside to remove the stone. Alert, a fellow-laborer noticed the machine was idle. Dutiful, he started it working. After three minutes, Laborer Lacey, his mouth and nose bubbling cement, his clothes torn completely off, his body cut and bruised, made his shrieks heard, was rescued.

RELIGION

FEB. 28 **"ALL CHARGED UP":** "A church without the Holy Ghost is like an automobile without gasoline. Oh, Lord, let there be an outpouring of the Holy Ghost. When I come into a meeting sometimes I feel just like a sponge, dripping with honey and milk. I just give everything I've got. I'm weak when I come out. But I go and pray to Jesus and get all charged up like a battery."

Thus spoke alluring Aimee Semple McPherson in Manhattan last week when she began her conquest of sin there. Said an oldtimer: "I've heard 'em all. She's the only one of the lot can touch Henry Ward Beecher." [Beecher was an eloquent preacher of the late 19th Century, who was famed for his support of women's suffrage, evolution and the abolition of slavery.]

The same week a rival revivalist, the kindly Billy Sunday, arrived in Atlanta, Ga., with a few practical interpretations of the Scriptures. He commented that Dr. Harry Emerson Fosdick and his "pack of pretentious, pliable, mental perverts (Modernists) are dedicated to the destruction of religion and one and all are liars, so labeled by the authority of Almighty God." He called for the expulsion of President Nicholas Murray Butler of Columbia University.

"NEW YORK FOR JESUS": Last week a 14-year-old handmaiden of the Lord stood beside a ripe ecclesiastic, her head upraised and look intent, locks flung back, red lips apart.

The ecclesiast spoke. "I hope," he said, "that this girl will grow into womanhood, ripe and rich, to spread her teachings and faith as beautifully as the flower promises." The churchman was Rev. Dr. S. Parkes Cadman, President of the Federal Council of Churches of Christ in America, and the maiden who paused on his words was Uldine Utley.

Three years before Uldine had entered the Tabernacle of Aimee Semple McPherson in Fresno, Calif. Uldine had entered the tabernacle with her blind grandfather, against her will. The pair had started for the girl's dancing school (she was thinking of going into the movies) but when it was found to be closed that afternoon, grandpappy—hearing choral voices across the street—suggested attending Aimee's revival meeting. They attended, Uldine impatiently.

Eleven-year-old Uldine sat within the enchanting tent. She fidgeted, became still, swayed in her seat and slid from underneath grandpappy's hand, started forth toward the coaxing smiles and silvery sounding voice of the revivalist, out into the aisle, straight to the altar and down on her knees before Aimee, wanting to know how to be a Christian.

Dr. S. Parkes Cadman. He praises Uldine Utley. Page 193.

Uldine Utley: "God wants us to win souls. God wants all of you."

Last week, her conversion, her guileless movements among the circusy proponents of God recurred to the handmaiden in New York. She remembered how papa and mamma then had become religious, converted. Meetings were arranged, hundreds of meetings. Uldine liked to talk about God. The girl grew loquacious, talked all over the country. It is said she has converted 10,000 men.

Once in a little southern town she made rough workmen passing by the railroad yard hold their breath while she spoke to them from atop a pile of tar-smeared ties. An enraptured foreman forgot to blow his whistle.

Last year, many a Fundamentalist reproached Dr. John Roach Straton, Fundamentalist thunderer, when he invited Uldine to his Manhattan temple to speak. The Bible, they said, forbids women's appearance in the pulpit. Fearless Preacher Straton permitted her to proceed, and she gave a sermon based so fundamentally upon the Ark of the Covenant that it soothed the hearts of the reproachful ones. But later in Madison Square Garden she was charged by atheists with violating the child labor laws by preaching for money.

Upper berths, speeches, meals ordered on the dining car with the confidence of a vaudeville trouper, oratory, ecstasies of religious passion, testimonials, quick little dancing steps, trips to foreign lands, cinema show, school, tutor, lollypops, God, salvations, Dr. Cadman.

The pale handmaiden found herself facing the embattled visages of churchmen, curiosity seekers, smart reporters, cynics, all agreed secretly to themselves to be as tolerant as possible. Uldine began to talk.

There were words and phrases and sentences. There was nothing profound about them. They were the glorious old, old story.

"Like a mighty army we are assembled here today.

"We are in one hope and doctrine.

"God wants us to win souls.

"God wants all of you.

"We look forward with one thought and that is to save New York for Jesus Christ."

And then the maiden paused, as if to catch a distant strain. Like an alabaster monument of Joan of Arc she seemed to stand the guardian vestal of the light that dwells in the Hallelujah-and-Amen type of evangelism. And as she spoke her thin childish voice quavered:

"There must be scores of different beliefs in this audience, but we are not divided."

Later Preachers Cadman, Morgan (Fifth Avenue Presbyterian), Keeler (Crawford Memorial Methodist Church), Megaw (Fort Washington Presbyterian), as well as other committee members of the Evangelistic Committee of New York City, decided to sponsor a series of revivals to be held this summer by Miss Utley, in Manhattan.

CARDINAL'S WIT: Rome dispatches, carefully censored, told APRIL 4 no names. But last week in Rome a clever hostess gave a dinner. She invited a witty Cardinal and, for him, a charming lady. But as the Cardinal drew up his chair to the table, he saw too many of the charms of the charming lady beside him; she was fashionably undressed above the waist. On her he bestowed one enfolding glance; then through every course but the last he courteously ignored her to her distress. For his dessert, he judiciously chose a ripe red apple, peeled it and halved it with care. On the charming lady's plate he set one half. "Why?" she smiled innocently back at him. "You must eat it," he admonished her, "for when Eve ate the apple she knew she was naked and felt ashamed."

MORMON UNDERWEAR: "God is unchanging and could not OCT. 24 have permitted this deviation from the established custom," explained one Paul Feil, Mormon, arraigned in Salt Lake City municipal court last week for disturbing the peace.

His appearance in court was the result of his roaring into a meeting of 10,000 members of the Church of Jesus Christ, Latter Day Saints (Mormons), waving banners & flags, and shouting: "A message for Israel!"

The purport of that message was that all Mormons should return to the underwear prescribed by first Mormon Joseph Smith (1805-1844) which left exposed only the head, hands and feet of pious Mormons and was fastened with strings. Winter & summer for three-quarters of a century, Mormons have worn such underclothes.

Two years ago, however, the Church elders decided that modern, advertised "athletic" underwear, short and buttoned, violated no tenet. But their decision vexed many an old-time believer, among them Mr. Feil, aged 50.

The judge suspended sentence against Mr. Feil's disturbance.

SHALT NOT: In Sioux City, Ia., one Alex Kazoz, pious, put in DEC. 26 front of his new house a sign:

This House for Rent—Tenants Must Keep The Ten
Commandments

Last week the sign had been in place for 37 days; the house was unrented.

(**MEDICINE**)

JAN. 24   **INFLUENZA:** Since late November influenza has been increasing throughout western Europe at so alarming a rate that public health officials have come to fear a pandemic, a worldwide occurrence of this disease, such as happened in 1918-19. Already Switzerland, Germany, England and France have been severely hit. At Nantes, France, the undertakers reported last week that they were four days behind with their burials. Their *croquemorts* (professional mourners who accompany the hearse) complained of sore feet and demanded subsidy for new shoes.

In the U.S. last week only 1,863 cases were reported by the U.S. Public Health Service. Said Assistant Surgeon General Claude Connor Pierce: "We have the influenza scare every year, and we find that it is present again in a mild form. We admit we are powerless to act against it, because the actual cause of influenza has never been determined. The advice we give anyone suffering from a cold or the grip at this time of the year is either to stay in bed, or at home, and not to circulate the germ."

FEB. 21   **SEED:** At Winchester, Ky., Dentist E. E. Curry scraped at the decay in a mountaineer's teeth. Probing the large cavity of a molar he prized out a tomato seed that had germinated there and had already thrown out a sprout one-eighth of an inch long.

APRIL 4   **SLEEPING SICKNESS:** No one knew how to cure *encephalitis lethargica* (sleeping sickness) two years ago when Mrs. Jane Norton Grew Morgan, wife of John Pierpont Morgan, contracted the disease. She drowsed for eight weeks, then died. Nor do doctors yet know how to cure *encephalitis lethargica,* which is an acute communicable disease, characterized by drowsiness, apathy and general lethargy.

It is one of the small number of diseases, including cancer

and rheumatic fever, of which the cause is still obscure, and because the cause remains hidden the proper mode of treatment must of necessity remain haphazard and the cure a matter more of chance than of science.

Last week J. P. Morgan became a personal giver. He gave $200,000 for the study and treatment of the sleeping sickness of which Mrs. Morgan died. The money will equip and support an entire floor of the $1,400,000, 12-story hospital building which the Neurological Institute will build in Manhattan in conjunction with Manhattan's growing Medical Centre at 165th Street and Broadway. [*Encephalitis lethargica* has continued to resist efforts to find a cure. But medical experts now agree that the disease is carried by mosquitoes and can best be fought by insecticides.]

ENERGY CALORIES: At the University of Helsingfors, Finland, inquisitive physiologists calculated the amount of energy, as measured by calories (heat units), necessary for humans to do various things. Their findings: AUG. 1

ACTIVITY CALORIES

Activity	Calories	Activity	Calories
Lying still	1	Stone masonry	5.53
Walking slowly	2.6	Heavy gymnastics	6.7
Light gymnastics	2.9	Sawing wood	6.8
House painting	3.3	Polkaing	7.56
Housekeeping	3.31	Charlestoning	7.56
Walking rapidly	3.8	Foil fencing	8.25
Waltzing	3.99	Sabre fencing	8.69
Shimmying	4.02	Running	9.7
Black Bottoming	4.68	Mazourkaing	10.87
Fox trotting	4.78	Wrestling	12.32

MISCELLANY

FREY: In Newark, one August Frey saw a large automobile bearing down on him. He had just enough time to get across the street—no, he didn't have time—yes, he did have time . . . ! As he stupidly hesitated, the car, moving slowly, knocked him flat.

Then August Frey jumped up and dusted off his clothes. In a cheery voice, a little ashamed, a little flustered, he cried: "It's all right, driver! I'm not hurt!"

The driver jumped down, ran over to Frey, shouted: "Oh, it's all *right* is it? Well I don't think it is!" punched August Frey's nose so hard that August Frey fell flat again.

"Maybe that will teach you to keep out of the way of automobiles!", cried the motorist as he drove away.

BUSINESS & FINANCE

Much attention was centered on the automobile industry in 1927. This was the year when General Motors passed U.S. Steel in gross revenue to become the nation's largest corporation. Half the cars on the road were still Fords—but, for the first time, the competition was gaining.

JAN. 3 **MANY AUTOS:** Last week, with the year's motor vehicle registrations completed, the magazine *Motor* gloated: 22,342,457 machines in the U.S., 11% more than in 1925, one for every five people in the country. Seven states registered more than a million cars each—New York (1,818,765), California, Ohio, Pennsylvania, Illinois, Michigan and Texas. Nevada has fewest: 23,933.

JAN. 24 **AUTO SHOW:** To the Grand Central Palace, Manhattan, each day last week flocked hundreds of businessmen, clerks, sports, idlers, professional men, taxi drivers and sailors, some with their ladies, some in groups, all of them peering, prying, pushing and querying, and some of them buying.

Automobiles had attracted them. The following makes were exhibited [dates indicate the year in which most models on this list were phased out of production]:

Auburn [1936]	Elcar [1931]
Buick	Erskine [1930]
Cadillac	Essex [1932]
Chandler [1928]	Flint [1927]
Chevrolet	Franklin [1934]
Chrysler	Gardner [1931]
Davis [1928]	Hudson [1957]
Diana [1928]	Hupmobile [1941]
Dodge	Jordan [1932]
Duesenberg [1937]	Kissel [1931]
Du Pont [1932]	Lincoln

Locomobile [1930]	Pontiac
McFarland [1928]	Reo [1936]
Marmon [1933]	Rickenbacker [1927]
Moon [1931]	Star [1931]
Nash [1957]	Stearns-Knight [1930]
Oakland [1931]	Studebaker
Oldsmobile	Stutz [1934]
Packard [1958]	Velie [1929]
Paige [1928]	Whippet [1931]
Peerless [1932]	Wills-Ste. Claire [1927]
Pierce-Arrow [1938]	Willys-Knight [1933]

People who came to see Fords or Cunninghams were disappointed. For reasons peculiar to their manufacturers these two were not displayed.

PRECEDENT BROKEN: *"Lucky Strikes! A flood of reminis-* MARCH 14 *cences sweeps across my mind. I heard first of this fine cigaret many years ago in San Francisco where my sons and thousands of soldiers were confined in an Army Hospital. I recall the American Tobacco Company's generosity in giving thousands of cigarets to the wounded boys and how delighted they were in smoking them. I recommend Lucky Strikes because they are kind to my throat."*

ERNESTINE SCHUMANN-HEINK

By printing this testimonial beside a picture of famed Singer Schumann-Heink and stating unequivocally: "When smoking, she prefers *Lucky Strikes* because they give the greatest enjoyment and throat protection," the American Tobacco Co. broke an advertising precedent. Theretofore no cigaret manufacturer dared state baldly that women smoke.

Last week another precedent was broken. Singer Schumann-Heink, in Atlanta, Ga., refuted the testimonial: "I never smoked a cigaret in my life, and, although I don't condemn women who do, neither do I approve of it in them. Why, even my sons are not permitted to smoke in my presence on the days I sing." Rarely had so gross an error crept into the advertising of an honest firm.

The explanation was simple. A whippersnapper told his chiefs that he could get an endorsement of *Lucky Strikes* from Singer Schumann-Heink; she had long been a friend of his

Madame Schumann-Heink: "I never smoked a cigaret in my life."

Christian K. Nelson sells 2,000,000 Eskimo Pies daily.

family. To her he said that she could help him earn some money, and she, benign woman, signed a note saying that she knew many American soldiers smoked *Lucky Strikes* in France. Later, too few questions were asked about this windfall testimonial. However, Singer Schumann-Heink's reputation is too solid, she is too revered, to be injured by this boy's hoax.

MARCH 28 **ESKIMO PIE:** The admission of Eskimo Pie Corp. securities to trading on the New York Curb Market last week marked another incident in the life of a Scandinavian immigrant. The trivial business that Christian K. Nelson and Russell Stover began at Omaha, Neb., half a dozen years ago was now a $25,000,000 corporation.

When Christian K. Nelson was graduated from Nevada University just before the War, he went back to Onawa, Iowa, to work in his father's candy store and ice cream parlor. The family had come from Denmark in the '90s. Christian dished out bulk ice cream with chocolate flavor; sold packages of brick ice cream and bars of chocolate. Thus came the idea of a stick of brick ice cream coated with chocolate. Russell Stover, Omaha ice cream maker, said that he could make the confection. He invented the name Eskimo Pie.

Bold advertising of this pert name made their Eskimo Pie

popular immediately. The U.S. licked at cold chocolate bars, and ice cream makers throughout the U.S. sought license to manufacture Eskimo Pie. For every dozen of these pies they made—and at the height of Eskimo Pie popularity 2,000,000 were sold daily—they paid Russell Stover and Christian K. Nelson a nickel. These men grew rich—income $1,000,000 yearly. Said Christian K. Nelson: "I'm going to buy the biggest and best looking motor car that money will buy and drive it at whatever speed I choose right through the main street of Onawa."

SHOES, VEGETABLES: The man who walks into a restaurant SEPT. 5 and orders a vegetable dinner was pointed out accusingly by the National Shoe Retailers' Association in Manhattan last week, called the real culprit in high shoe prices the association declared are coming. The less beef eaten, the less cattle killed, the higher the price of leather, the shoe men explained deftly. A 15% to 20% price increase was predicted because of the growth of vegetarianism.

"PURE, GREEN GREED": Men of wealth were startled last SEPT. 19 week by a newspaper interview issued by Charles R. Flint, 77-year-old, white-whiskered Manhattan multi-millionaire, honeymooning in London with the second Mrs. Flint.

Mr. Flint, who as the "Father of Trusts" made his money in shipping, electric lighting, rubber, chewing gum, munitions, etc., was asked why a man like himself, "after he has amassed millions, goes on increasing his collection instead of retiring and enjoying life." Mr. Flint replied: "There is only one reason. Greed!"

The interviewer protested: "Is it not because of ambition, a craving for power?"

Mr. Flint repeated: "No! It is pure, green greed. Greed, and greed alone, is the reason for a man's wanting to swell his wad million after million!"

Chicagoans recalled that last month their townsman, Julius Rosenwald, chairman of Sears, Roebuck & Co., 115-million-aire, issued a statement on the occasion of his 65th birthday. Mr. Rosenwald said: "I was lucky, not a genius. With rare exceptions, the man who accumulates wealth displays no more genius than the prize-winner in any lottery. It is by luck

Charles Flint, "Father of Trusts," has swelled his wad by greed.

Alfred P. Sloan says G.M. cars are more luxurious than Fords. Page 204.

that a man gets hold of a good thing at the right time and more by luck that he holds on to it."

OCT. 3 **RADIO FAIR:** At Madison Square Garden, Manhattan, was held a Radio World's Fair. Three hundred and one exhibits of receiving sets, binding posts, crystals, coils, batteries were spread over three floors. Experts noted with enthusiasm the predominance of sets featuring the single control lever and operating without batteries from an electric light socket. In their opinion such simplification of radio apparatus will do much to bring instruments into the 21,000,000 U.S. homes that out of a total of 27,000,000 are now without them.

The National Association of Broadcasters, assembled at the Fair, heard themselves flayed by Commissioner H. A. Bellows of the Federal Radio Commission. Said he: "If anything could kill radio, it is the nature of the programs that have been broadcast."

OCT. 10 **FORD v. G.M.C.:** If the approaching automobile war between Henry Ford and General Motors Corp. were symbolized in armaments, Mr. Ford would be a cannon and General Motors a machine gun. When a Ford product strikes the market squarely, as did Model T when first shot into a world of pedestrians, the battle is over. But when the Ford product misses, as Model T has been missing ever since economic prosperity in the U.S. caused the public to shift from mere transportation to touring with style, it misses by a mile.

Though Henry Ford has added to his weapon such potent arms as the Lincoln and an airplane manufacturing unit, his big gun has always been Model T Ford. General Motors Corp., on the other hand, spreads its shots. It sends out a car to strike every purse—Chevrolet, Oldsmobile, Pontiac, Oakland, Buick, LaSalle, Cadillac. It carefully picks up its dead shells and turns them into electric refrigerators, an effective barrage to cover a retreat. It trains its bullets on markets far afield, on Europe, on Australia, scattering its products all over the globe.

Last week lean, suave President Alfred Pritchard Sloan Jr. of G.M.C. and Henry Ford declared that there was no war contemplated between them, that they were shooting at different targets.

Said Mr. Sloan: "If the past is any indication of the future, the new Ford car will be a car that will appeal to a great mass of people. General Motors is in quite a different position. General Motors' idea is to make a car of greater luxury than the Ford, a car that properly belongs to the next higher price class."

Professor Irving Fisher: "The American people are not yet prosperous."

John D. Rockefeller: "A smile is the sun that dissipates despair." Page 206.

DEC. 5 **"NOT PROSPEROUS":** Sharp pencil in hand, Professor Irving Fisher of Yale figured and figured, and last week announced that "while there is cause for national thanksgiving, the best available statistics show that the American people are not yet prosperous in any absolute sense." Four-fifths of them, or about 93,000,000, are earning little more than their barest living expenses.

His reasoning: Total U.S. income last year was nearly 90 billion dollars. Of this, 80% of the population, or about 93,000,000 (the poorest and the "lower middle classes") received 52.8%, or 47.5 billion dollars, or $510 each. That approximates $2,550 for the average family of five persons. It costs a minimum of $2,432.39 for such a family to live in the cities where most of them do live.

DEC. 12 **MODEL A:** How many million people saw the first appearance of the new Ford car last week it is impossible to estimate. In Detroit Henry Ford, his son Edsel and grandsons Henry II and Benson examined the public display before the great Convention Hall's doors were opened to let 100,000 people in. Manhattan crowds were greater. Police were obliged to regulate the queues in other "key cities."

In England the railroads ran excursion trains to the London exhibition. Englishmen paid one shilling & sixpence (36¢) to look at the models and ordered 64,000 cars. In Manhattan a rascal took advantage of the local gullibility. He passed through the showroom throngs with an "order book" in his hand, promising delivery in three weeks upon a deposit of $25. When detectives approached him he ran away with many a $25 stuffed in his coat pockets.

The Ford carries as standard equipment a starter, five steel-spoke wheels, windshield wiper, speedometer, gasoline gauge, ammeter, dash light, mirror, rear & stop light, oil gauge, ignition lock, complete tool set. The gasoline tank is in front of the dash board. Gear shift is standard.

The semi-elliptic transverse springs are the only parts exactly the same as in the old Ford. Otherwise not a single part of the old can be used in the new.

ROCKEFELLER PHILOSOPHY: John D. Rockefeller Sr., aged 88, was enroute to his winter home in Florida last week. At

Savannah, Ga., his train stopped for 15 minutes and deferential reporters sidled into his car. They asked the beaming old man for a statement. He smiled and read to them a tract in his modulated voice. Next he handed them the tract entitled *Sunlit Days*. It read:

"A smile, resting on a foundation of sincerity, is one of the most valuable things in the world. It cheers when nothing else would make an impression. It gives a thrill of which no human agency is capable. A smile has changed the whole course of a human life. A smile serves as a guidepost at a turning point for a man who is hesitating at the intersection of two paths. A smile is the sun that dissipates the clouds of despair. It is just the ray of light that many a soul needs to make life seem preferable to death. It is the cheapest and most valuable gift we can make. When smiles can do so much, why are we not more liberal with them?

"And this," said he finally, "is a copy of my daily prayer which I read at least once daily."

Reporters read: "Heavenly Father, we thank Thee for the glad and wholesome contagion of cheerfulness. If frowns and distempers are contagious, we thank Thee that smiles are not less so. The smile goes forth from face to face. By the strange law of increase, gladness begets gladness. Remembering then that no frown ever made a heart glad, help us go forth to meet the day with high hope and smiling face; and even though it has not been easy to smile, let us rejoice if so we have been able to add to the sun of human happiness and make burdens lighter."

MILESTONES

DIED: William Vanderbilt, 70, dynamite expert, suddenly, at Peabody, Mass. He arranged 75 sticks of dynamite in a circle, stood in the centre, set them off.

MISCELLANY

PICKER: In Buffalo, N.Y., one George Malloy, 19, walking to church, spied and picked up a small disc that bulged in the middle. During a Methodist-Episcopal service he amused himself by picking and stabbing at his curious treasure with his pen knife. His inattention bothered no one until *Blam!* off blew Picker Malloy's thumb and forefinger. His find had been a dynamite cap.

NEWS: In Brooklyn, the Society for the Prevention of Cruelty to Animals demanded the arrest of Louis Riccio, 52, for biting dogs. Mr. Riccio admitted his malefaction. He had bitten the tails off his six puppies to improve them.

CINEMA

JAN. 17 **"THE LADY IN ERMINE"**—If cinema has done nothing else, it has emphasized for two decades that war is hard on ladies. Herein, for instance, an Italian *grande dame* (Corinne Griffith) finds her villa invaded by roaring Austrians. To save her good husband's life, she must surrender to the Austrian general her -----. But she does not. Director and scenarist have contrived an honorable solution, a terrible picture.

FEB. 7 **"THE KID BROTHER"**—Great dark houses crashed and rocked with laughter last week. Funnyman Harold Lloyd is loose again. This time he is Harold Hickory, rabbitty member of a bearish backwoods sheriff's family. He outwits his lumbering brothers and a traveling band of medicine fakers; outflirts the faker's delicious dancer.

MARCH 21 **NEW CATHEDRAL**—Samuel L. ("Roxy") Rothafel invited Manhattan celebrities to the opening of his new "cathedral of motion picture," world's largest theatre, the Roxy. They beheld a vast, bronzed, Spanish Renaissance structure imposing its Moorish splendor upon the corner of Seventh Ave. and 50th St., otherwise a-sprawl with garages, nightclubs, hot-dog stands, pawn-jewelers. Inside it was golden-brown, well ventilated, pagan-like in its florid adornment. Three organists played in grand concert on a Kimball organ, which is said to have the properties of a symphony orchestra. Then came an invocation: "Ye Portals bright, unite us all to worship at beauty's throne." Then a dedication. All was solemn. The audience was awed. The "cathedral" looked every cent of its $10,000,000 advertised cost. The Roxy Symphony Orchestra burst into the "Star-Spangled Banner." The Mayor sprang to his feet. The audience sprang as promptly as possible considering its lap cluttered with hats, coats, canes.

After hours of preliminary tableaux, solo singing, orchestral music, ballet, the cathedral gave over to Gloria

"Roxy" Rothafel. His new "cathedral" cost $10,000,000. Page 207.   *Harry Langdon. In "Long Pants," he woos a Rolls-Royce lady by bicycle.*

Swanson-on-screen who endured through an interminable legend in which a girl, knowing not whether to devote herself to a career as opera singer, to her lover or to a wealthy villain, discovers (in a crystal) the horrible effect of conducting herself for the sake of the career or the loveless wifehood, and thereupon marries the lover.

"LONG PANTS"—The Boy (Harry Langdon) consumes such APRIL 11 inflaming literature as "Don Juan," "Great Lovers of History," "When His Love Grew Cold." Therefore, when his father provides him his first pair of long trousers, the adolescent breaks out in a romantic rash. He mounts his trusty, high-spirited bicycle, dashes out to the park, there meets with a *grande dame* reposing in a Rolls-Royce while her chauffeur mends a flat tire. The Boy, sore smitten, circles the auto, displaying a repertoire of bicyclical virtuosity rivaled only by his vaulting hopes. Amused, the lady kisses her seraph-faced admirer, whose innocence is droll to behold.

Thus compromised, the trousered one needs must slay his contemporaneous sweetheart to be free to follow the grand passion inspired by the lady of the Rolls-Royce. In plenty of time and after many an antic he discovers that the Rolls-Royce lady is unworthy and returns to the girl next door. Harry Langdon's lonely innocence is most excellently done.

Cecil B. DeMille's "King of Kings" shows Christ as a kindly Being.

H. B. Warner in "The King of Kings." As Jesus he looks like a worried actor.

MAY 2 **"THE KING OF KINGS"**—The film, ostensibly sacred, presents Christ in terms most commonly understood, most easily loved: a kindly Being Who performed miracles for others yet suffered physical agonies most heart-rending sooner than save Himself. Producer Cecil B. DeMille's emphasis throughout is upon the pictured Christ's ability to straighten crooked feet, restore sight, raise the dead. To Actor Henry Byron Warner, player of crook roles (*Alias Jimmy Valentine,* etc.), was entrusted the role of Jesus. He acts with commendable dignity, yet, because the director insisted upon "close-ups," he looked like what he might well have been—a worried actor.

JUNE 6 **"ROUGH HOUSE ROSIE"** is moderately diverting nonsense about a hoyden from Tenth Avenue who wants to be a lady (Clara Bow). She makes a hit in a cabaret, appears in society under the patronage of a handsome gentleman friend, distresses her amiable prize-fighting boy friend. But the drinking, love-making, gambling of the upper crust disgust her tender soul so much that she returns just in time to cheer her prizefighter on to a championship. A luridly punning sub-titler adds to the fun. Thus the Czechoslovakian princess is said to have "married twice but her Czechs were no good."

"THE CIRCUS ACE"—Tom Mix and his horse, Tony, do their JULY 18 stuff once again, this time for the reluctant heart of a circus queen. All in all, a good Tom Mixture.

"THE JAZZ SINGER"—Two seasons ago Manhattan and OCT. 17 other cities witnessed approvingly the theatrical tale of a Jewish boy who wanted to go on the stage instead of into his church. His orthodox old father fumed gently, having trained him for a cantor. But circumstance and the boy's yearning for the footlights made him in the end a singer of jazz for the world that lives at night. George Jessel, a jazz singer from revue and vaudeville, played the part and made his name as a straight actor. But in making the picture Mr. Jessel was passed over in favor of the man whom so many worship as their greatest entertainer, Al Jolson.

It is Mr. Jolson's first picture and as such of great import to the history of the current theatre. The Vitaphone permits him to talk and sing his way through the sentimental mazes of the movie adaptation. He is a very great singer of popular songs. In cities where the Vitaphone can be installed and reproduce his voice this picture will eminently repay attendance. [*The Jazz Singer* was the first real "talkie."] It is doubtful if the straight picture version without sound will carry much interest down the byways where they crave Bebe Daniels.

"LOVE" is certainly a poor translation of the title of *Anna* DEC. 12 *Karenina*. It would be natural to suppose that the rest of famed Leo Tolstoi's novel would suffer similarly; that it does not is due in largest part to the acting of Greta Garbo.

The story definitely follows the outlines of what has been called "greatest novel in the world." Anna Karenina meets Count Vronsky one snowy day, has an affair with him that reaches its conclusion when she accepts defeat by stepping in front of a fast train. That any film producer should begin by calling his picture *Love* and end it with this cinematically unconventional tragedy is only one of the many contradictions which make this one of the most striking adaptations yet effected. The memorable moments belong mostly to Swedish Greta Garbo whose beauty infuses the picture with a cold white glow; John Gilbert as Vronsky is too willing to act only with his teeth or his hair.

EDUCATION

JAN. 3 **CHIVALRY:** As reported last week by the Boston *Transcript,* Professor George H. Knight of Ohio State University can find nothing chivalrous in the vocabularies of his students of English. To prove his contention, Professor Knight had catalogued undergraduate terms applied to an unpopular girl: pill, pickle, lemon, dead one, priss, tomato, chunk of lead, drag, gloom, rag, oil-can, crumb, nutcracker-face, flat tire, mess. Ohio State terms for a popular girl: peach, bird, belle, live one, baby vamp, whiz, pippin, star, sweet patootie, choice bit of calico, sweetums, snappy piece of work, pretty Genevieve, thrill, flesh-and-blood angel. Terms which Professor Knight might have discovered had his researches extended beyond the campus at Columbus, Ohio: for an unpopular girl—wreck, piece of bad news, wet smack, foul ball, prune, pig's coat-tail, washout, sad Sadie, hard-boiled virgin, dizzy egg, teaser, gripe, bug-eyed Betty; for a popular—tidy unit, warm baby, knockout, panic, riot, red-hot witch, cat's meow.

JAN. 17 **"COPEY":** When the young gentlemen of Harvard University returned to Cambridge last week, weary of vacation and longing to resume their studies, one of the first things many of them did was to visit the bookshop, and buy a volume (*The Copeland Reader, Chosen and edited by Charles Townsend Copeland*) that had been published during the holidays. It was rather an expensive book. Nevertheless it was a peculiarly desirable book. It was part of a legend. For "Copey" had at last published his anthology.

The home of the legend that is "Copey"—and no disrespect is meant by Harvard men when they thus nickname their Boylston Professor of Rhetoric and Oratory—is up a high but never arduous flight of steps, on the top floor of antique Hollis Hall. Thither, every Monday night of college for some 33 years, have swarmed scores of undergraduates from the passing classes. A hush falls. Some one takes his last cough. "Copey" waits for another last cough and, if none comes, begins to read.

Freshmen inevitably hear of "Copey" within their first week at Harvard, if not long before, but they may pass him many times in the street before knowing him by sight. But on a Monday evening, as soon as the reading begins, a newcomer understands what it is that has made "Copey" the William Lyon Phelps (Yale) of Harvard. The amazingly flexible voice, its sympathies and humor, its clarity, expression and power of creating reality out of written words, bespeaks "Copey" as not only a most popular and learned professor but a great master as well of that most difficult of arts, reading aloud.

The reading may start off with something from the Bible— nothing dull like all those "begatters" but something with action like the Israelites' conquest of Canaan or something portentous out of Revelation. Or it may begin with so different a thing as Lewis Carroll's

> "You are old, Father William," the young man said,
> "And your hair has become very white;
> "And yet you incessantly stand on your head—
> "Do you think, at your age, it is right?"

Of classical selections in "Copey's" anthology there is, of course, a great plenitude. The death of Socrates; "Hark! Hark! the Lark"; "Lycidas"; Gulliver and the Lilliputians; "The Rime of the Ancient Mariner" and "Kubla Khan"; Edward John Trelawny on how they burned Shelley's body; a great deal of Keats; more Tennyson; still more Thackeray and Browning and more Dickens than anyone.

"Copey" is the last of a vanished style in Harvard professors, in professors anywhere, for that matter. He himself is Dickensian, with his piercing glance to identify a caller, with his two bachelor rooms in the garret of old Hollis, with his quick replies which from a less amiable nature might be crabbed but from his seem wry and sprightly.

Every year for 21 years the Harvard Club of New York has had a "Copey" evening, a dinner to which a fortunate company (by invitation only) sit down, followed by a reading. Here Theodore Roosevelt used to come. Here now come

J. P. Morgan and his partner, Thomas W. Lamont. These and many a plain John Smith and Tom Jones whose only claims to fame, perhaps, were their selection of one of "Copey's" courses and their attendance upon his Monday nights at Harvard, gather around, shake hands and exchange greetings with the small man who seems to look fondly down on them all from below. [Charles Townsend Copeland became Professor Emeritus at Harvard in 1928, died in 1952.]

"Copey" of Harvard. He is the last of a vanished style of professors.

Pierre duPont. Tired of supporting schools, he wants the state to do it.

JAN. 31 **FEUDAL DELAWARE:** The State of Delaware did more thinking about public education last week than it had done for eight years. For eight years, whenever a question of public education arose, Delaware had said: "Let Pierre duPont do it." But last fortnight, Pierre duPont was tired of "doing it." Pierre duPont, having personally contributed some $5,000,000 to build public schools and support public instruction in Delaware, now beheld an apathetic legislature about to let public instruction languish for lack of state funds. Pierre duPont made statements:

"I believe the state should appropriate at least $2,000,000 annually to improve the school buildings throughout the state. If the request for this amount is pared it will be a mistake. The next Legislature may make me change my mind, but my present attitude is that I'm through."

In naming a figure he thought his state should spend on public education, Mr. duPont did not speak as an inert and dogmatic philanthropist. The duPonts, almost dynastic, are always dynamic. Pierre Samuel duPont, Wartime President of E. I. duPont de Nemours & Co., now Chairman of its board, recently President of the General Motors Corp., now Chairman of its board, is a financial magnate who is as active as he is important. He is tall and heavy domed, with calm eyes and unagitable lips—a massive, impassive, impressive man. He can make money perhaps more easily than anyone in the U.S. but lets many a chance pass. Instead, he tries to make citizens.

Some years ago Pierre duPont conceived that his native state might be made into an ideal commonwealth. Pierre took education as his domain. He is the one U.S. multi-millionaire who has made the public schools his hobby. This one experi- .nent has cost him $5,000,000. In order to free the state of the expense of a dual system, Mr. duPont undertook to build all of the Negro schools. Thus far he has erected 86 schools for Negroes. Also he has built and given to the state 20 schools for white pupils, and has pooled his money with local districts in erecting 12 schools. Guided by the best experts available, Mr. duPont has provided model accommodations for 17,300 of Delaware's 40,000 school children. Up to the present the state has hardly lifted a finger toward new public school construction and hence the crisis. For how could Delaware do anything with an empty treasury?

The treasury was empty because the tax office was not adequately organized and the taxes were not collected strictly.

Here is where Pierre duPont crossed the tracks of the politicians. Delaware has a $3-per-capita filing fee or tax. If this tax were abolished 100,000 people would cheer for the politicians. It would also leave the bulk of the income tax to be paid by about 680 well-to-do people in Wilmington and environs (many of them duPonts). As a vote-pulling measure it might be tremendously popular. Pierre duPont could go on putting millions of dollars into the school system while most of the beneficiaries would never feel a burden.

So Mr. duPont called a halt. He felt his commonwealth was becoming a feudal state. Generosity had begun to eat into the self-respect of citizenship. [DuPont's chief complaint was that the state was not collecting enough taxes to support public education. The governor appointed him State Tax Commissioner. Tax collections increased—and so did the literacy rate.]

MAY 2 **CUNNING GAUSS:** At the dean's desk in Nassau Hall, Princeton University, sits a slightly bald, slightly stooped slow-spoken gentleman whose grey eye twinkles at a witticism in the French literature he knows so thoroughly, quite as often as his firm lip stiffens to pronounce upon matters of policy and discipline—Dean Christian Gauss.

Lately, authorized by the Princeton trustees, he forbade the young men of Princeton to keep automobiles at college. Dean Gauss became at once unpopular. The motor-loving young men of Princeton baited him by all means—by roller-skating noisily, by driving horse-and-buggies, by wearing placards. ("My Gauss is cooked," and "Mother said I could.")

Then a senior, George Lambert, sporting scion of Listerine (mouth wash, etc.), inspired university admiration by bringing to town an airplane and droning over the campus in it. Airplanes were not mentioned in the Gaussian edict against motor vehicles.

More airplanes came to Princeton and droned above the elms. Dean Gauss said nothing. Students paid $3 apiece for five-minute rides in commercial craft, just to fly over Nassau Hall and snap their fingers. Dean Gauss said nothing—until last week, when he unexpectedly proclaimed an interpretation of his anti-motor vehicle edict which the laziest of campus sag-spines had to admit partook of Solomonic cunning. "We have so many machines on the ground," Dean Gauss began blandly, "that we do not bother particularly about those up in the air, as a fleet of pursuit planes would be needed for effective control. Anyone may fly *over* Princeton—but if he lands here, and runs along the ground, we shall class his plane as a motor vehicle and return him and it to his parents."

OCT. 10 **MERRY MCANDREW:** Most potent of the puffs that blew corpulent William Hale Thompson into the mayoralty of Chicago last April was his loud cry: "Americanism!" Once in office, the Mayor announced a crusade against School Super-intendent William McAndrew, imported three years before from New York City because his recognized ability was need-ed to improve Chicago's educational system.

Mr. McAndrew had vexed the Mayor. He had interfered with the easy-going manner of awarding contracts for school buildings. He had taught that the U.S. Army retreated before the advance of the British on Washington, D.C., in the War of 1812. Roared Mayor Thompson: "I will run that whis-kered pro-British stool pigeon of King George out of town!" To do that His Honor replaced the members of the Board of Education with citizens upon whom he could rely. Soon the Board suspended Mr. McAndrew.

Mayor Thompson. "Run that stool pigeon of King George out of town!"   *Superintendent McAndrew. He insists that U.S. soldiers retreated in 1812.*

Eleven members constitute the Board. Six of them, a ma-jority, could vote the superintendent out of office. Last week it appeared as though six of them, hearty henchmen of Wil-liam Hale Thompson, *would* vote Mr. McAndrew out. The trial seemed but a protracted formality. But it was of inter-est, because this was the first time a superintendent of schools had ever been tried in Chicago. The charges were insubordi-nation and unpatriotism. Evidence adduced to prove the lat-ter charge: "He refused to recommend to the School Board that the school children be permitted to donate small amounts of money for the purpose of reconditioning the famous American battleship *Old Ironsides*. He recommended history text books which contained pro-British propaganda and which omitted the name and exploits of many foreign and native-born heroes of the American Revolutionary War."

Through a long afternoon filled with soporific technicalities, the "stool pigeon of King George" tilted far back in his swivel chair, read the Chicago *Tribune* comic strip about Andrew Gump, Minerva Gump, etc. Superintendent McAndrew might avoid dull afternoons in court by simply resigning. This he refused to do. Said he: "They'll fire me all right. But they'll have to stage a burlesque show to do it!"

NOV. 14 **IN CHICAGO:** The Chicago Board of Education entered their high-ceilinged meeting room. In their impassiveness they resembled Indians at a pow-wow with white men. Superintendent Wm. McAndrew, on trial for insubordination, looked at them with contempt. Another of his many intermittent hearings was about to commence.

But no testimony pertinent to the legal charge of Superintendent McAndrew's "insubordination" was offered. A group of 29 civic organizations published a resolution: "Four or five sessions of this trial, occupying as many weeks, have now been held; but charges on which the Superintendent was suspended have not been argued. Instead the time has been taken up by trivial and irrelevant matters, with the evident intention of prolonging the trial until the Superintendent's term expires in February. In the meantime Chicago has no Superintendent of Schools. The President of the Board has usurped the Superintendent's powers, and the schools are being run without the professional direction which the law requires."

Shrewd, they added a paragraph which their rambunctious Mayor William Hale Thompson would understand: "We have become convinced that the present situation is a real crisis. It concerns a million parents—all voters—with enough power to enforce any demands they decide must be made to safeguard their children's interests." [McAndrew's contract expired in 1928. He was found guilty of insubordination and lack of patriotism. He sued for libel but withdrew the suit in 1930 after the charges against him were dropped.]

THE PRESS

The tabloids, small-format newspapers that could be more easily read than the standard-sized papers during the rush hour in New York subways, made their appearance in the 1920s. They quickly established a reputation for sensational journalism with their inflammatory and sometimes wholly fictitious reporting of sex and crime. The now-defunct New York Graphic was the worst of these, and TIME *devoted a good part of its 1927 press section to describing the way the Graphic and other tabloids dragged out the scandalous divorce proceedings between a 51-year-old real-estate millionaire named Edward "Daddy" Browning and his teen-aged wife, "Peaches." In 1927 the tabloids also made much of a particularly sordid crime, the Snyder-Gray "sashweight murder," and found ways to feature the antics of an eccentric millionaire, Harry K. Thaw, who had been released from an insane asylum after having murdered the architect Stanford White 20 years before.*

ORGY: With the frank grin of a degenerate, the most abnor- FEB. 7 mal sheet in U.S. journalism, Publisher Bernarr ("Body Love") Macfadden's New York *Evening Graphic,* last week embraced the divorce hearings of a pawky lecher and his fleshy girl-wife. There are thousands of Edward West Brownings in the U.S., but never before had one sprawled forth whose pathological condition included lust for publicity. The porno-*Graphic,* closely followed by its loose-lipped fellow-tabloids, the Hearst *Mirror* and the Patterson-McCormick *Daily News,* and abetted by an accommodating judge, proceeded with an exploitation to which previous obscenities seemed a prelude almost refined.

Pressing its usual policy, the *Graphic* had a paunchy man in pajamas and a plump girl in a film of silk underwear re-enact for *Graphic* cameras the more revolting moments described by Mrs. Browning. Faces of the real characters, pasted in these photographs and the *Graphic*'s front pages were spread with the admittedly faked results.

The Hearst *Mirror* covered its front page with close-up portraits of the Brownings and shaking letters were used to print "FLAMING YOUTH." Subtitle: "His Mania Causes Peculiar Love for Young Girls." Text: "A famous (anonymous) alienist diagnoses his case as 'pathological pedophilia,' a symptom of a disease of the brain classified as a sexual aberration." The Patterson-McCormick *Daily News* delivered such headlines as "PEACHES'S BRIDAL SECRETS," "HUNT PEACHES'S 50 SHEIKS."

FEB. 14 **MACFADDEN:** Recently, at the height of the Browning-Peaches orgy of pornography, conscience-stricken editors tried hypocritically to explain that in probing into the sex life of a babbitt-lecher they were acting as "surgeons to the public mind." The hypocrisy of this excuse appeared, last week:

"THAW BREAKS LOOSE!" screamed the Bernarr Macfadden porno-*Graphic* tabloid last week, even as the Browning-Peaches story guttered. For this there was not even the excuse that the public does not know all there is to know about Harry K. Thaw. The *Graphic* pretended that its story would be a "warning" to "young girls" not to go out with Mr. Thaw. What maid, wife or widow needs further warning against Harry Thaw?

Yet the *Graphic* splashed a composite photograph, representing Harry Thaw trying to strangle a young woman, across its cover; and printed a picture of an apartment house with the caption: "Where Harry Got Rough."

Other headlines scattered through a single issue of the porno-*Graphic*: "THAW ATTACKS PRETTY GIRL IN HIS LUXURIOUS ROOMS" (the "pretty girl" was a dance hall hostess, one Marcia Estardus); "LURED TO HIS HIDDEN HOME AND CLUBBED" (the "hidden home" was an ordinary apartment. Miss Estardus knew who Mr. Thaw was and went to his apartment voluntarily. She was not "clubbed," but said that Mr. Thaw had beaten her with a hair brush which she wrenched from him.)

Last week Publisher Bernarr Macfadden was haled to court. Superintendent John S. Sumner of the New York Society for the Suppression of Vice represented that he had re-

ceived complaints against the *Graphic*'s front pages from
people with children who could not help seeing newsstands.
The Tombs Court issued a summons charging Publisher Macfadden and some underlings with violation of that clause of
the penal code prohibiting literature "principally made up
of criminal news, police reports, or pictures or stories of deeds
of bloodshed, lust or crime."

It was the first time Mr. Macfadden had been haled to
court in years. His first arrest was in 1901, when Federal
authorities got after the posters for one of his early beauty
shows (a modest affair in tights but warm for its day). His
second arrest was brought about by that primate of prudence,
Anthony Comstock, only succeeded in causing the Macfadden beauty show of 1905 to attract mobs that nearly burst
Madison Square Garden.

The full extent of the Macfadden press needs the official
Macfadden figures to set it off in its true magnificence:

	Readers
Physical Culture (monthly)	400,000
True Stories (weekly)	2,111,000
Movie Weekly	440,000
True Romances (monthly)	650,000
Dream World (monthly)	200,000
True Detective Mysteries	150,000
Modern Marriage ("the be happy magazine")	150,000
Muscle Builder	80,000

DELIRIUM: The bipeds who buy Bernarr Macfadden's N.Y.   MARCH 28
porno-*Graphic* were treated last week to something new in
sensations. The *Graphic*'s clever mental-opium makers prolonged their new delirium for days and days. They had paid
the late Mr. Rudolph Valentino's closest friends, enemies
and parasites to help them compose kaleidoscopic fake photographs and spirit messages in which the dead man described the tearing of his soul from his body, the uprush into
the Hereafter, the ghostly hosts, his mother, memories,
women friends, earthly emotions remembered, heavenly sensations. He met Enrico Caruso, who posed with him for the
Graphic camera beside a massive pillar, both draped in
sheets, smiling clearly, fresh-shaven, pomaded, watching a

throng of people or spirits rush up wide steps to a warlike stage setting. And on the Saturday special edition in sepia, "Rudy's spirit," nakedly muscular from the navel up in a blazing cauldron, posed against a brazen shield, profile turned to heavenly radiance.

The *Graphic* folk no longer pretend their work is journalism. They simply call it "tabloids." Assistant Managing Editor Martin Weyrauch of the porno-*Graphic* said: "Tabloids are just as inevitable as jazz. They are as truly expressive of modern America as World's Series baseball, skyscrapers, radio, the movies, Billy Sunday, and beauty contests. They are not so far above the common herd as to have no concern in the interests of everyday life."

APRIL 25 **CARNIVAL:** It was carnival week again in Manhattan. This time a muscular corset-salesman had murdered a middle-aged art editor assisted by the editor's adulterous wife. The details, unusually gruesome, included poisoned whiskey, picture wire, binding, gagging, taking turns at skull-smashing with a window-weight, and $104,000 in life insurance.

The murderers had confessed separately and were reviling each other from their prison cells. Judd Gray, the corset-salesman, was pleading insanity and saying he had been led astray, debauched. Ruth Snyder, the wife, was professing horror and penitence, calling her paramour a low "jackal." Also there was even a child, Lorraine Snyder, aged 9, to heighten the emotionalism of the trial. Lorraine still believed her father and mother were temporarily away "on a trip."

Bernarr Macfadden's porno-*Graphic,* as usual, made the most striking announcement of all. It anticipated the Snyder murder trial with a public proposal that all Manhattan's newspapers be called to conference by the state crime commission; that they all agree to limit their daily courtroom reports to 500 words.

It was an offer in thorough good faith—which the *Graphic* well knew would never be accepted. Having let off a lot of loud sincerity, and furnished itself with blank ammunition to fire at the crime commission in future, the *Graphic* assembled its most unscrupulous picture fakers and prepared to make its "Peaches" Browning and Valentino exploits look amateurish.

Bernarr Macfadden. His porno-Graphic revives Valentino. Page 218.

W. R. Hearst. Father urged patience with fools; Willie took the advice.

HEARST: "When William Randolph Hearst was very young," AUG. 15 once wrote Hearst columnist Arthur Brisbane, "when he was running the San Francisco *Examiner* after leaving Harvard, he complained to his father, U.S. Senator George Hearst, that so many men were fools. Father Hearst replied: 'That's true, Willie. But let us not be too hard on fools. If there were not so many of them life would be less easy for you, for me and for some others.'"

Presumably William Randolph Hearst has whispered this advice to himself many times. He has followed it faithfully. William Hearst came to Manhattan in 1895 where, with money borrowed from his mother, he acquired the *Morning Journal.* Later Mr. Hearst rechristened it the New York *American.* It was the yellow wrappings of the "funnies" in this newspaper from which grew the household epithet "yellow journalism." Then he brought out a little sister of the evening (the *Evening Journal*). These two papers were the steppingstones in Mr. Hearst's climb to pinnacles of domination in the sensational newspaper field.

Today the *American* is weakening. The terrible tabloids have out-Hearsted Hearst and the morning New York field in screams and scandals is dominated by the *Daily News.* For a time Mr. Hearst fought back by publishing a tabloid insert in the *American,* which did not pay out. Then he resorted to a tabloid of his own (he has several in the U.S. now) and his *Daily Mirror,* picture paper, is on the make with about 412,000 copies sold every morning.

Since that far-off day when "Willie" Hearst came to Manhattan his record has been one of astounding success in the field of publishing. He controls at least 25 newspapers, eight magazines, two press syndicates and film newsreels. His papers sell to over 13,000,000 people daily—or nearly 10% of the nation's total population.

William Randolph Hearst is called an attractive man. His is a great, tall, 220 lb. figure with long arms and big hands. His eyes are bluish grey, and it is said, not very kind. He is quiet, almost bashful, and possesses quantities of that illusive thing called personality. In his Harvard days he played the banjo and sang songs. He still dances, solo, if notably elated. He loves candy. He does not drink or smoke. He collects art wholesale.

SEPT. 5 **GRAPHIC DESCRIPTION:** The day after the Sacco-Vanzetti execution the *Evening Graphic,* gum-chewers' sheetlet published in Manhattan by Bernarr Macfadden, blazed on the newsstands with a huge headline:

SACCO AND VANZETTI
ROASTED ALIVE

Delving within, palpitating readers found the story of the execution by one Jack Grey, *Graphic* reporter.

"Come into this death house with me," began Mr. Grey. Lurid details followed. Among them: "Elliott, the official killer, stood to the right of him with a fiendish grin on his face. He leaped, literally leaped, to the switchboard. The switch went in. Sacco's hands doubled into a knot. The veins in his long, thin, white hands began to rise and kept on rising until I thought they would burst and drench all of us with blood."

A decidedly graphic description. Gullible readers devoured it. Careful readers laughed, for it was a fact, published in newspapers throughout the land, that W. E. Playfair of the Associated Press was the *only* newspaperman permitted in the death house to view the execution.

BOOKS

"PERSONAE: THE COLLECTED POEMS OF EZRA POUND"—In FEB. 14 Paris, after several years in London, lives a thin-bearded, long, supple blade of a man, middle-aging but of feverish vitality, whom "the foremost English novelist" (Ford Madox Ford) calls "the greatest living poet." He is a genuine "original" on that shore of exotic wreckage and treasure, the Left Bank. That he was born in the U.S. is unimportant except that his inability to subsist there argues his febrility. There is about him much of the hothouse plant which, luxuriating in the warmth and humus of countries long inhabited, would perish in the rigors of a "wilderness." His name is Ezra Pound.

When first he appeared in London, a most erratic youth much given to violent tennis and fencing, more violent language and gestures, and to two strong veins of poetry, lyric and satirical, he was adopted by descendants of the Pre-Raphaelite movement—as far as a wildish young man can be adopted. They liked his "splendid invective," fashioned after the Greeks.

Poetry being essentially a personal thing, none may credit nor gainsay Novelist Ford's estimate of Poet Pound. As criticism it is a foolish phrase. But it is certain that Ezra Pound is
> . . . a poet that doth drink life
> As lesser men drink wine.

"ELMER GANTRY"—Author Sinclair Lewis, whose position MARCH 14 as National Champion Castigator is challenged only by his fellow idealist, Critic Henry Louis Mencken, has made another large round-up of grunting, whining, roaring, mewing, driveling, snouting creatures of fiction which, like an infuriated swineherd, he can beat, goad, tweak, tail-twist, eye-jab, belly-thwack, spatter with sty-filth and consign to perdition.

What folk of the 21st Century are going to ask about 20th

Poet Ezra Pound is too much the hot-house plant to live in the U.S.

Edwin Arlington Robinson writes of romance in 4,000 lines. Page 226.

Century cinemas, tabloid newspapers and this book, is: "Did such people really live in the U.S.?" Their hastier historians will say: "Yes," and show convincing clippings from the N.Y. *Times* about Aimee Semple McPherson. But the clerical creatures in *Elmer Gantry* are children of ideas and the ideas seem to have been whipped up out of unhappy memories of the Sauk Centre Sunday School.

The sea, wise men have observed, is the great civilizer; Sinclair Lewis was born in Minnesota. His style has never transcended the monotonous.

MAY 2 **"YOUNG MEN IN LOVE"**—Michael Arlen. Last week a ship set out from England, bearing to the U.S. that suave young cosmopolite, born Dikran Kuyumjian beside the Bulgarian Danube some 35 years ago, whose activities on the banks of the Thames as Michael Arlen, Anglo-Armenian raconteur, spread his fame to the banks of the Hudson.

Michael Arlen's agents last week announced that his novel and play of 1924-25, *The Green Hat,* are to have a third incarnation, as cinema, perhaps with Norma Talmadge. More directly responsible for Mr. Arlen's arrival was the U.S. publication of his new novel.

Second comings are less breathless than firsts. He will not feel whole literary cocktail parties hanging on his lightest utterance, for it is well agreed now what a pleasantly trite clam he is sometimes and how low he once brought bold Edna Ferber.

The conversation (commonest version):

Miss Ferber: "Why, Mr. Arlen, you look almost like a woman!"

Mr. Arlen (softly): "And so do you, Miss Ferber."

Toward his writing, too, he will find a reaction. Here as in England people have decided that his glamor is false; that no one, except in books for maids and butlers, was ever so gallant, arrogant, terse of speech, deep of feeling, precious of wit as Mr. Arlen's high-strung Mayfairians.

"TRISTRAM"—Distinguished ladies and gentlemen met in a MAY 23 Manhattan theatre last fortnight to pay a U.S. poet the almost archaic compliment of hearing his newest work and appraising it. Mrs. August Belmont (stage name: Eleanor Robson) read aloud for all. The poet was Edwin Arlington Robinson.

Judged worthy of the attention of the members of the Literary Guild this month, the poem, 4,000 lines long, begins and ends with small Isolt of Brittany, whose hands are made to seem more fabulously white than ever, set off against the shadowed course of events at a frowning castle across the channel. There Tristram has a name upon his lips that becomes a cry, a despairing exultation: "Isolt, Isolt of Ireland!"

He and that dark lady of love cling together on a parapet above foam-spread rocks. The poet makes a marvel of their love, putting it beyond time and space, above life.

Poet Robinson has written exquisitely of high romance. His lines, flexibly austere, trace out the action sharply and whip passion to its perfect pitch. But then, often, the simple words are tortured and strained to sustain ecstasy. Then the lines ache like tendons not strong enough to keep a soaring hawk aloft, needing a gust of action, a wing-beat of refreshed emotion to lift the poem again.

"THE GLORIOUS ADVENTURE"—The new book by roman- MAY 30 tic, poetic, enthusiastic, sparkling, dauntless, bubbling, impetuous, adventurous, dramatic, enthralling, etc. Playboy Richard Halliburton begins with a *"Crash!* The lightning in a rage split the writhing firmament from Thessaly to the Cyclades in one blazing, blinding glare. Streaks of fire burst into the inky darkness, inflaming the abyss about me and lashing at the clouds that hurtled past."

It is Jove, Author Halliburton explains, angrily tossing thunderbolts because a whimsical, gay, incorrigible, dramatic, inspired, etc. young American is at the beetling, rugged, sacrosanct, fierce, rugged, granite pinnacle of Mt. Olympus and proposes to spend the night.

There follow in rapid succession the summit of Parnassus, scaling the Acropolis at midnight, swimming the Hellespont, playing Ulysses ("handsome, heaven-sent Greek") and reading "The Return of Ulysses" at Ithaca, having completed what was begun, a trip in the wandering wake of Ulysses doing all he did and several things besides.

As hundreds of thousands of U.S. clubwomen already know, Playboy Halliburton *did* swim the Hellespont, to catch up with Byron and Leander. And the dourest male skepticism will be disarmed by our hero's frank confessions that he took a taxi over the last seven miles of his race from Marathon to Athens in the very tracks of Pheidippides; that diving for sponges in the Gulf of Gabes gave him an earache. Also, knowing his public, Author Halliburton carefully explains that whenever the companion happened to be a female they stayed at separate hotels.

Richard Halliburton. His female companions stay at separate hotels.

Virginia Woolf. She spies from thickets on the human soul. Page 228.

"TO THE LIGHTHOUSE"—Virginia Woolf. The stream-of-consciousness technique is present as before in author Woolf's previous novel, *Mrs. Dalloway*. Now, in her brilliant offensive on the human soul, she does not perpetrate an open advance. Weaving, stalking, spying from thickets, she discovers the nature of her prey. The actual capture she leaves to those who, reading her book, are her companions in the chase.

"THE EARLY WORM"—Robert Benchley (Illustrated by Gluyas Williams). Funnyman Benchley's creek of comedy has by no means yet run dry. He babbles gently on in parody of Sherwood Anderson, H. G. Wells, Calvin Coolidge. His method of *reductio ad imbecillum* is to expound a subject in its simplest terms, putting caricaturist's emphasis on one or two superficial details. Example: "According to Dr. Max Hartmann there is no such thing as absolute sex. If 60% of your cells are masculine, you rate as a male. If 60% of your cells are feminine, you sit with the girls. All combinations are possible up to 99 and 1, but the 100 percenter is a myth. Dr. Hartmann says so. This is going to be a big surprise to a lot of people."

"THE MAGIC MOUNTAIN"—Thomas Mann. "An unassuming JUNE 13 young man was traveling, in midsummer, from his native city of Hamburg to Davos-Platz in the Canton of the Grisons, on a three weeks' visit." Soon after his arrival, he perceives that his cigars have a flat taste. Before his three weeks are over, he has a bad cold. Before his return to Hamburg, to a world at war, he has spent seven years in a mortal fairyland.

As Hans Castorp eats, sleeps, falls in love with Madame Chauchat, talks to his cousin Joachim, he reproduces in miniature man living in a community of death. Author Mann shows how men can adapt themselves to an environment of mortality by forgetting its existence. So countries squabble and chatter in the presence of catastrophe; so men, in the shadow of an enormous horror, pursue their silly and incongruous intrigues.

"DUNT ESK"—Milt Gross. "Oohoo, nize baby—oohoooo JULY 25 —Hm—Look from henimals a book! So geeve in de book a

look so tell poppa wot it stends dere de henimal—ah—ah—
"Baby—Squshlzzrrlx!!!

"Yi yi yi!! A HAPE he spuck! A Hape!! Yi yi look de peecture!! Is a hape, no?? So I say, 'Baby, dollink, wot's dees??' So he saz me, 'A hape!' Look it stends:

> 'Haye stends for hape
> Wot he leeves in de trizz;
> Whan a nidds a gless meelk
> He'll a cuccanot squizze!!' "

All Milt Gross's humor is like this. There is no satire, no attempt at subtlety, beyond the infinite subtlety of the extraordinary dialect in which his characters cavort. They—Mr. & Mrs. Feitlebaum, Looy, Isidore, Nize Baby, Mrs. Noftolis —are continuously excited. Author Gross has been called a "great stylist." He is best understood when read aloud.

SEPT. 12 **"MISS BROWN OF X.Y.O."**—E. Phillips Oppenheim. When Henry Ford marketed his ten millionth flivver, a musician composed a symphonic poem to celebrate the event. Edward Phillips Oppenheim has now published his 100th novel, and though not one of his creations has been a flivver, somebody should salute Mr. Oppenheim with at least a small trumpet. Never was the Oppenheim genius more clearly displayed. Observe the manner in which he has aimed to please extra specially with Novel No. 100.

What type of feminine English fiction reader may be calculated to suffer most from "an unprobed spirit of romance?" Why, who but a typist? Very well, then, such shall be Mr. Oppenheim's heroine; her name, just plain Edith Brown.

And what type of man would most attract such a young woman (remember, she is earnest, honest)? Well, how about a mature, reticent, adventure-scarred world traveler. His name could be Dessiter—Colonel Dessiter. It might be a good plan to conceal his first name till the very end.

And finally, what idea, what theme for Novel No. 100 would best please light fiction-readers right now? Why, the menace of Communism, to be sure. The newspapers are full of it. Typist, world-traveler, Communism—the very thing. Hurrah, we're off!

Without professing to be a prophet, author Oppenheim notes that he foretold the Boer War in one novel, the World War in 14 novels. When the World War ended, Mr. Oppenheim's friends sympathized. He would have nothing further to write about, they feared. But now, a guileless reader of handwriting on walls, a firm insister on plausibility, he finds that "the stage is set for even more tragic happenings."

"DEATH COMES FOR THE ARCHBISHOP"—A large part of SEPT. 26 Miss Willa Cather's pre-eminence as a novelist is due to her ability as a scholar. Her offering for this season is more scholarly than creative—a reconstruction of the episcopal works of the first Roman Catholic bishop of her beloved New Mexico. She draws him with esthetic reverence, an immaculate conception of a missionary in buckskins who, lost and athirst in the desert, still retained elegance, distinction and "a kind of courtesy toward himself, toward his beasts, toward the juniper tree before which he knelt and the God whom he was addressing."

The book is filled with colorful people, rainbow scenery, amazing weather. The lean, kind, sandy figure of Kit Carson welcomes the Bishop at Taos. Navajos, Zunis, Acomas, remnants of the cleanly pueblo tribes, move quietly about in smaller villages, vivid as their blankets and pottery, drawn

Willa Cather. She is a good novelist because she is a good scholar.

Ernest Hemingway. "Manuel was facing the bull; he felt the horn go in."

with the patient accuracy of an archeologist. Everywhere history is made to move in a living atmosphere, for that is the highest excellence of Miss Cather's writing, her mastery of intangibles. When she paints a mesa, she remembers the cloud mesa above it. Two bronzed runners passing over some sand dunes remind her of "the shadows that eagles cast in their strong, unhurried flight."

OCT. 24 **"MEN WITHOUT WOMEN"**—Ernest Hemingway. One story in this collection, *The Undefeated,* is about an old bull fighter, fighting in a dark arena. "Manuel was facing the bull again, the muleta held low and to the left. The bull's head was down as he watched the muleta. . . . He felt the sword buckle as he shoved it in, leaning his weight on it, and then it shot high in the air, end-over-ending into the crowd. Manuel had jumped clear as the sword jumped. The first cushions thrown out of the dark missed him. Then one hit him in the face, his bloody face looking toward the crowd. . . . 'Thank you,' he said. 'Thank you.' Oh, the dirty bastards. . . . As he tripped on a cushion he felt the horn go into him."

The Killers is about two men who go into a restaurant to shoot Ole Anderson. First they put the cook and the waiter in the kitchen. Then they talk to the proprietor and wait for Ole Anderson to come in. At five minutes to seven they decide he is not coming in. Nick—the cook said, 'I can't stand to think about him waiting in the room and knowing he's going to get it. It's too damned awful.' "

Fifty Grand is about a prizefighter. *Today Is Friday* is about Christ. A *Pursuit Race* is about a snowbird. There are nine other stories in the book.

The Sun Also Rises, published last winter, made critics realize that at least one of the Americans who live in Paris can do something more important than sit about in restaurants. Its little hard sentences were like round stones polished by rain and wind. The book had the sharp determined rhythm of a person walking upstairs; there was no literary gesticulation, no wasted energy, no flourishing.

The stories in *Men Without Women* have the same qualities. Totally objective, they are as clear and crisp and perfectly shaped as icicles, as sharp as splinters of glass. It is impossible to read them without realizing that seldom if ever before has a writer been able to cut so deeply into life with the 26 curved tools of the English alphabet.

"PREJUDICES"—H. L. Mencken. This, like the first five vol- OCT. 31 umes of its series, lives up to its title. Author Mencken's style is that of a capable blacksmith. His hammer is large and noisy but it usually descends squarely on his anvil. So gritty are the workman's hands, so sweaty is his face that it is easy not to realize that for the most part he is engaged upon no more important a task than flattening pennies.

"THE BRIDGE OF SAN LUIS REY"—Thornton Wilder. "On Friday noon, July the 20th, 1714, the finest bridge in all Peru broke and precipitated five travellers into the gulf below." Now why had a bridge upon whose miraculous high path everyone in Peru had stepped at one time or another postponed its decay to include these particular people in its destruction? Was it an accident or an intention?

Author Wilder explores the lives of the five; each one had achieved in life, just before the falling of the Bridge of San Luis Rey, a kind of completion. So at the end, "There is a land of the living and a land of the dead and the bridge is love, the only survival, the only meaning." The delicacies of Author Wilder's prose cannot be intimated in so rude a summary of his book, which will be acceptable mainly to those who are sophisticates in both life and letters.

MILESTONES

MARRIED: Pola Negri, cinemactress; to Prince Serge Mdivani of Georgia (now a state in the Russian Union); at Seraincourt, France.

DIVORCED: Ernest Hemingway, author of *The Sun Also Rises;* by Mrs. Hadley Richardson Hemingway; in Paris.

DIED: Mrs. Nancy Baker, 101, able gingersnap-maker, at Galena, Ill. Her snaps were sampled and praised by Presidents Grant, McKinley, Roosevelt.

MISCELLANY

PLASTERS: In Chicago, one William Glauber and one Frederick Knauff, friends for years, gave each other black eyes. Reason: Mr. Knauff had a cold. Mr. Glauber, promising a cure, stuck large porous plasters on Mr. Knauff's chest, back, abdomen. Mr. Knauff got well. Then Mr. Glauber peeled off the plasters, peeling off also Mr. Knauff's means of livelihood in a circus, to wit, a tattooed portrait of Abraham Lincoln (chest); tattooed landscapes, ships, anchors, Uncle Sams (abdomen); nude females, palms, boats (back).

INDEX

Numerals in italics indicate a picture of subject mentioned.

A

Abbot, Dr. Charles G., *189, 190*
Acosta, Bert, 177, 180
Addams, Jane, 51
Advertising: cigaret, 200-201; Eskimo Pie, 202
Airlines, passenger, 181-182
Akihito (Crown Prince of Japan), 124
Albert (King of Belgium), 37, 101
Alfonso (King of Spain), 157
Alvarez, Lilli de, 159-160, *163*
Amaro, Joaquin, 127, 128
America (airplane), 178, 180, 181
American (newspaper), 222
American Civil Liberties Union, 44
American Girl (airplane), 182, 183
American Legion (airplane), 178
Anderson, Judge Albert B., 71
Antheil, George, *173*-174
Arlen, Michael, 225-226
Army, U.S., 37; food rations of, 68
Army Air Service, 69, 70
Art, in U.S., 184, 186
Astaire, Adele, 169
Astaire, Fred, 169
Astrid (Crown Princess of Belgium), 102
Ataturk, Kemal, 154, *155*
Athletics (Philadelphia), 158
Audubon, John James, 185
Automobile: sales of, 199-200, 203-204; show in New York, 199-200
Averescu, Gen. Fofoza Alexander, 143

B

Balchen, Lieut. Bernt, 24, 180
Baldwin, Stanley, 82, *83,* 86, 87; requests Commons to break diplomatic relations with U.S.S.R., 89-90
Baldwin, Mrs. Stanley, *86,* 87
Ballet Mécanique, Antheil, 173
Banking, bills on in Congress, 29
Banks, 29
Barendrecht, (ship), 182-183
Barrie, James Matthew, 88
Barron, Clarence W., 14-15
Barry, David S., 30
Baseball, 157-159, 164-165
Baudouin (Prince of Belgium), 102
Bellanca, Giuseppi M., 177
Belgium, 101-102
Bell Telephone Laboratories, 188
Bellows, George, *185*-186
Bellows, H. A., 203
Benchley, Robert C., 51, *52,* 228
Bennett, Arnold, 57
Bennett, Floyd, 178
Bey, Tewfik Rushdi, *155,* 156
Birger, Charles, 62-63
Birth control, 75-76
Blanton, Representative Thomas L., 28
Bloom, Representative Sol, 28
Bloom, Vera, 44
Borah, Senator William E., 22, *23, 74,* 115, 135
Boulder Dam project, 24-31

Bow, Clara, 209
Boxing, 161-164
Brandeis, Justice Louis Dembitz, 59
Brandeis, Mrs. Louis Dembitz, 50
Bratiano, Jon, 143, 145-146
Briand, Aristide, 96-97, 100
Bridge of San Luis Rey, The, Wilder, 232
Britain: breaks off diplomatic relations with U.S.S.R., 90; and Chinese nationalist movement, 103-105; influenza epidemic in, 197; and naval armament, 11-12, 97-99; and World Court, 29
British Commonwealth, 82-95
Broun, Heywood, 57
Browning, Edward West ("Daddy"), 218, 219
Browning, Mrs. Edward West ("Peaches"), 218, 219, 221
Bucharin, Nikolai, 151
Budget Bureau, U.S., 68
Bulgaria, 102-103
Burke, Billie, 24
Burlesque, 166-*167*
Butler, Nicholas Murray, 193
Byrd, Commander Richard Evelyn, 24, 177-178, 180-181

C

Cabinet, British, 82
Cabot, Elliot, 169
Cadman, Rev. Dr. S. Parkes, 193, *194, 195*
Calles, Ernestine, 126
Calles, Natalia, 126
Calles, Plutarco Elias, 41-43, *126;* reconciled with U.S., 128; support of Alvaro Obregon, 129, 130-131
Calories, needed for energy, 198
Canada, 12-13
Cancer, 197
Cantor, Eddie, 166
Capone, Alphonse ("Scarface Al"), 67, 71
Carol (Crown Prince of Rumania), 141-142, 146
Carpenter, Judge George A., 45
Carty, General J. J., 188
Cather, Willa, *230,* 231
Cavalry, U.S., maneuvers of, 70
Chamberlain, Sir Austen, 153
Chamberlain, Clarence D., 24, 177
Chiang Kai-shek, 103, 106-108, 109, 110; marriage of, 110-111
Chiang Kai-shek, Mme., 111
Chiappe, Jean, 111, 112
Chicago: gang war in, 71
China: nationalist movement in, 103-104, 107, 109, 149. *See also* Nanking
Churchill, Winston Spencer, *83,* 84-85, 89, 105; publishes book on World War I, 91
Circus Ace, The, 210
Colbert, Claudette, *168*
Coli, Capt. François, 177, 179
Colombia, 25
Columbia Aircraft Corp., 177
Columbia Phonograph Co.: prize for end to Schubert's "Unfinished Symphony," 175
Comintern, Soviet, 149-150

G

H

I

J

K

L

PICTURE CREDITS

x

PRODUCTION STAFF FOR TIME INCORPORATED
John L. Hallenbeck (Vice President and Director of Production),
Robert E. Foy, Caroline Ferri and Don Sheldon
Text photocomposed under the direction of Albert J. Dunn and Arthur J. Dunn

QUOTES OF THE YEAR

President Coolidge *(making a surprise announcement—p. 20):* "I do not choose to run for President in 1928."

Mrs. Evangeline Lodge Lindbergh *(on hearing that her son has taken off for Paris—p. 35):* "I am proud to be the mother of such a boy."

Bartolomeo Vanzetti *(shortly before he and Nicola Sacco were executed—p. 56):* "We die for anarchy. Long life to anarchy!"

Al Capone *(on leaving Chicago for a Florida vacation —p. 67):* "Let the worthy citizens of Chicago get their liquor the best they can. I hope I don't spoil anybody's Christmas by not sticking around."

Senator James A. Reed of Missouri *(on hearing that President Coolidge fished for trout with angleworms—p. 74):* "Any trout that would bite on a worm is degenerate."

Dictator Benito Mussolini *(on women—p. 118):* "Women are trusting, confiding little animals. Women cannot create. They are to men what men desire them to be."

A Scotsman *(to golfing genius Bobby Jones—p. 160):* "Ye're nae a gowfer at a'—ye're juist a machine."

ANSWERS TO PICTURE QUIZ—1: Mustafa Kemal, dictator of Turkey; 2: Queen Mary and King George V of England; 3: King Michael of Rumania; 4: Novelist Michael Arlen; 5: Generalissimo Chiang Kai-shek; 6: French Foreign Minister Aristide Briand; 7: Composer Richard Strauss; 8: Baseball's Connie Mack; 9: Novelist Sinclair Lewis; 10: Notre Dame Coach Knute Rockne; 11: Publisher William Randolph Hearst; 12: Mystery writer E. Phillips Oppenheim; 13: British Prime Minister Stanley Baldwin; 14: The U.S.S.R.'s Leon Trotsky; 15: Radio Announcer Graham McNamee; 16: Soprano Geraldine Farrar.